Social Work with Looked After Children

Second edition

CHRISTINE COCKER

LUCILLE ALLAIN

Series Editors: Jonathan Parker and Greta Bradley

Los Angeles | London | New Delhi
Singapore | Washington DC

Learning Matters
An imprint of SAGE Publications Ltd
1 Oliver's Yard
55 City Road
London EC1Y 1SP

SAGE Publications Inc.
2455 Teller Road
Thousand Oaks, California 91320

SAGE Publications India Pvt Ltd
B 1/I 1 Mohan Cooperative Industrial Area
Mathura Road
New Delhi 110 044

SAGE Publications Asia-Pacific Pte Ltd
3 Chuch Street
#10–04 Samsung Hub
Singapore 049483

Editor: Luke Block
Production Controller: Chris Marke
Project Management: Deer Park Productions
Marketing Manager: Tamara Navaratnam
Cover Design: Code 5 Design Associates
Typeset by: Pantek Media, Maidstone, Kent
Printed by: MPG Books Group, Bodmin, Cornwall

First published in 2008 by Learning Matters Ltd
Reprinted in 2008
Reprinted in 2010
Second edition published in 2013
Reprinted 2013

British Library Cataloguing in Publication Data

A catalogue record for this book is available from the
British Library.

ISBN: 978 0 85725 919 6 (pbk)
ISBN: 978 1 44625 708 1

Contents

Acknowledgements

Thanks to the people who have helped us in so many ways, particularly Fiona Alderman, Jane Anderson, Nikki Bradley, Helen Cosis Brown, Adi Cooper, Frania Cooper, Elaine Creith, Paul Dugmore, Sarah Gosling, Lucia Grun, Helen Hingley-Jones, Marion Ingram, Ravi Kohli, Rebecca Scott and Nicky Torrance. Thanks also to the Staff in the Social Work Curriculum Group at Middlesex University and to all the students we have taught on the Middlesex programmes for their enthusiasm and energy. Finally, thanks to Kate Lodge, Di Page and Jonathan Parker for their patience and support over the time it has taken us to write this book.

Second edition

Thanks to those who have helped with this second edition: Fiona Alderman, Jane Anderson, Adi Cooper, Helen Hingley-Jones, colleagues from Middlesex University and the University of East London. Thanks also to Luke Block and Helen Fairlie from the Learning Matters team.

Introduction

This book is written primarily for social work students and newly qualified social workers who are beginning to develop their skills and knowledge about looked after children. It is also likely to be of interest to more experienced social workers who are supervising students on work placements, for professionals in health and education who are involved in work with looked after children, for foster carers and for those who are interested in developing a career in social work. The focus of the book is twofold in that it details the organisational systems and structures that are part of the assessment and planning processes for looked after children. This is then closely interwoven with what the emotional development, educational, health and cultural needs of looked after children are and how they can be met through social work and a range of other services.

The book aims to highlight the views of looked after children through the use of case studies and from research findings involving young people. The aim is to help you understand what skills and knowledge you need in order to accompany looked after children through the key events they may experience, including change, loss and the development of new relationships. Being a looked after child usually means that a child does not live with their birth family but in foster care, residential care or with a new family who are going to adopt them. Sometimes looked after children live with family members, and this is called kinship care or family and friends placements. All looked after children have a social worker who is responsible for a number of functions in relation to their care and support needs.

The book critically reviews the emotional development, educational, health and cultural needs of children and young people living away from home and identifies strategies for supporting and addressing them. The participation of children and young people is examined both as a group process and through individual life story work. A range of key skills that are required for direct work with young people are presented with a focus on communicating with children and young people of different ages, with different cultural and linguistic needs, including the needs of disabled children who may have specific communication requirements.

Social work education and links to practice

Since the first edition of this book in 2008 there have been significant changes within the social work profession, including social work education. The professional body is now The College of Social Work (TCSW) and the regulatory body is the Health and Care Professions

Council (HCPC). There is a new Professional Capabilities Framework developed by TCSW, which is linked to the Standards of Proficiency developed by the HCPC. In addition to this, all social work education programmes need to be reapproved, taking into account these new frameworks and the curriculum guides published by TCSW.

This book has been carefully mapped to the new Professional Capabilities Framework for Social Workers in England, as well as the Quality Assurance Agency (QAA) social work subject benchmark statements, and will help you to develop the appropriate standards at the right level. These standards are:

- **Professionalism**

  Identify and behave as a professional social worker committed to professional development.

- **Values and ethics**

  Apply social work ethical principles and values to guide professional practice.

- **Diversity**

  Recognise diversity and apply anti-discriminatory and anti-oppressive principles in practice.

- **Justice**

  Advance human rights and promote social justice and economic wellbeing.

- **Knowledge**

  Apply knowledge of social sciences, law and social work practice theory.

- **Judgement**

  Use judgement and authority to intervene with individuals, families and communities to promote independence, provide support and prevent harm, neglect and abuse.

- **Critical reflection and analysis**

  Apply critical reflection and analysis to inform and provide a rationale for professional decision-making.

- **Contexts and organisations**

  Engage with, inform, and adapt to changing contexts that shape practice. Operate effectively within your own organisational frameworks and contribute to the development of services and organisations. Operate effectively within multi-agency and inter-professional settings.

- **Professional leadership**

  Take responsibility for the professional learning and development of others through supervision, mentoring, assessing, research, teaching, leadership and management.

References to these standards will be made throughout the text and you will find a diagram of the Professional Capabilities Framework in Appendix 1 (see page 209). Each chapter also relates to specific parts of the social work subject benchmark statements – you will find extracts from the statement in Appendix 2.

Each chapter of this book identifies the relevant Professional Capabilities Framework and links them to case studies and practice examples.

The case studies can be used to highlight key areas of practice enabling you to think through options, critique decision-making and evaluate ethical dilemmas. You can undertake the case studies alone or in small groups; hopefully they will help you to review your own assumptions about what children need and how best these needs can be met.

Book structure

All chapters have been revised and updated, reflecting the plethora of new guidance and practice initiatives that have been a feature of social work over the past four years. A number of volumes of The Children Act 1989 Guidance have been reissued and the coalition government look set to introduce new legislation on adoption in the next year via the Children and Families Bill 2013, announced in the Queen's speech in May 2012. The chapter content is as follows:

Chapter 1 introduces previous and current key policy developments that are central to understanding the position of looked after children and how practice has been shaped by significant events, including the development of the children's rights agenda. There is an examination of the role of the 'corporate parent' and the state in relation to looked after children, which is followed by the presentation of statistical data identifying demographic trends, helping to show who looked after children are.

Chapter 2 presents the legislative framework that governs social work practice with looked after children throughout the UK. The chapter explores the relevant sections of the Children Act 1989 and makes links to specific duties and powers that social workers have when working with looked after children. The chapter discusses five key pieces of legislation, which are:

- Children Act 1989;

- Children (Leaving Care) Act 2000;

- Adoption and Children Act 2002;

- Children Act 2004;

- Children and Young Persons Act 2008.

Chapter 3 outlines pathways into becoming a looked after child and discusses different routes in and out of care and the various placements children might be in while being looked after, including fostering, residential care, kinship care and leaving care services. We provide a national overview of data collected on looked after children, and discuss the structures and processes integral to the requirements of caring for looked after children. Information is presented about why different types of care are used for looked after children, accompanied by explanations relating to placement choice.

Chapter 4 discusses the centrality of assessment in relation to working with looked after children and introduces different approaches to assessment, which will help you in undertaking this work. The chapter also explores care planning and contact and the importance of good record keeping, with links made to the legal processes around care proceedings.

Chapter 5 discusses communication skills, participation, children's rights and life story work. This chapter introduces good practice in relation to communicating with children at different ages and at different stages of development. This is linked to participatory approaches and the development of children's rights. Life story work is explored as an essential tool to help children understand their past and plans for their future.

Chapter 6 explores key issues for practice when working with children from diverse communities. We discuss the position of black and minority ethnic children and unaccompanied asylum-seeking children who are looked after and the contemporary debates and tensions about asylum and refugee status. Models of good practice for direct work are discussed with an exploration of cultural competence models.

Chapter 7 discusses the key issues in relation to disabled children who are looked after. The special features of respite care and longer-term care are explored and how the needs of children with complex needs can be met. The importance of inter-professional collaboration in this area of practice is presented.

Chapter 8 focuses on what life is like for a looked after child and starts by introducing the concepts of attachment, adversity and resilience. We discuss why it is important that you understand these concepts and the theories that underpin them.

Chapter 9 discusses in more detail the emotional and psychological support that looked after children may require, the importance of understanding the role of child and adolescent mental health services and how professionals can work together to support the mental health needs of children who are looked after.

Chapter 10 outlines current debates and presents good practice models in relation to the educational needs and attainment levels of looked after children. This is linked to 'corporate parenting', leaving care and debates about social inclusion. The chapter also presents information about the health needs of looked after children, what research tells us about this and presents good practice models.

Chapter 11 discusses what adoption and permanence mean, and the ways in which these occur within the looked after system. The essential legal and procedural issues related to this area of practice are presented along with current statistical data about the numbers of children adopted from care.

Chapter 12 focuses on leaving care, describing what this means and identifying key policies, processes and services that are available. We also discuss research findings about the position and needs of young people who use these services.

Dedications

CC: for Adi, Frania, Rivka and Shane

LA: for Howard, Hannah and Phoebe

Chapter 1
Policy and statistics

ACHIEVING A SOCIAL WORK DEGREE

This chapter will help you to develop the following capabilities from the **Professional Capabilities Framework**:

- Knowledge
  Apply knowledge of social sciences, law and social work practice theory.
- Contexts and organisations
  Engage with, inform, and adapt to changing contexts that shape practice. Operate effectively within your own organisational frameworks and contribute to the development of services and organisations. Operate effectively within multi-agency and inter-professional settings.

It will also introduce you to the following standards as set out in the 2008 social work subject benchmark statement
5.1.1 Social work services, service users and carers
5.1.2 The service delivery context
5.5.3 Analysis and synthesis

Introduction

This chapter focuses on the development of government policy in relation to looked after children and will help you to understand how policy and legislation in this area of practice has been informed by the children's rights agenda plus findings from research about the experiences and circumstances of looked after children. Invariably, children's experiences of the care system have been shaped by and have shaped the policy and legislative landscape. The chapter will advance your knowledge of how social policy in this area of practice has evolved; how this is influenced by society's views about childhood, adolescence and the family; about the protection and vulnerability of children; and views about parents' and children's rights. Berridge (2012) discusses the relationship between research, policy development and the use of pilot projects to introduce new initiatives. He argues that although governments have stated their commitment to policy-making based on research evidence, *that promise has been largely unfulfilled* (p28). He refers to Weiss (1999, in Berridge, 2012) who *argues that social scientists are naive if they believe that policy making is mainly influenced by research rather than a broader range of competing interests, ideologies, other information and institutional constraints* (p29). Policy-making is therefore most likely to be influenced by an amalgam of priorities and findings, one of which is research and lessons from front-line practice. Public policy-making with regard to looked after children often arouses strong feelings, and differing political views influence policy directions and social work practice. For example, the coalition government's focus on changes to adoption (see Chapter 11) and their commitment to cutting bureaucracy and streamlining processes so that front-line social workers are more supported to make professional judgements which are based on a sound knowledge base and informed by research evidence. This also links with the Munro Review of Child Protection (Munro, 2011).

The previous Labour government showed their commitment to improving the lives of looked after children through a number of reforms including the 'Care Matters' agenda. These reforms have been acknowledged as a *major landmark in social policy as it relates to children and young people in care* (Frost and Parton, 2009, p95) and shows a sustained commitment to improving the experiences of and outcomes for looked after children and care leavers (Berridge, 2012). The Coalition government has also pledged their commitment to improving services for looked after children. As part of the Education Select Committee process (House of Commons, 2011) the improvements made by the previous government were noted but it was stated that more needed to be done. This has included changes and revisions to the care planning and care leavers guidance Department for Children, Schools and Families (DCSF), 2010b; Department for Education (DfE), 2010 and revised systems to reduce the delays in the length of time of care proceedings, thus facilitating faster decision-making about the future plans for looked after children, which links to the Family Justice Review (Ministry of Justice, DfE and Welsh Government, 2011). Links are made to Chapter 2 and the underpinning legislative framework as well as contemporary policy and legislative developments, including the Children Act 2004; *Care matters* (DfES, 2006f) and *Care matters* (DfES, 2007) which resulted in the Children and Young Persons Act 2008. Since April 2011 there has been a revised legislative framework for looked after children which includes Care Planning, Placement and Case Review Regulations (2010), Children Leaving Care Regulations (2010), Fostering Services Regulations (2011) and Children's Homes Regulations (2011). Detailed information about these changes and how the child should remain at the centre of all process can be accessed at www.education.gov.uk. The chapter starts by outlining statistical data about who looked after children are, and then goes on to chart the main policy milestones in relation to looked after children, showing how they have influenced practice and the development of 'corporate parenting'.

Who is a looked after child?

A looked after child can be voluntarily accommodated by the local authority through parental request, or can be looked after and subject to a care order. Local authority duties towards looked after children are detailed in specialist law text books including Brayne and Carr (2010) and Johns (2011). When children are voluntarily looked after, those with parental responsibility can remove the child/ren from the accommodation at any time, without prior notice being required. Although no notice of removal is required, if there are concerns about the child's welfare, applying for an emergency protection order should be considered (Brayne and Carr, 2010, p275). Local authorities will, whenever possible, work in partnership with parents and it is important that you as the social work build respectful and professional relationships with key family members remembering to keep the child at the centre of your work.

Definitions and terminology

'Looked after children' or children 'in care'? As stated by Johns (2011, p50), using the term 'in care' is not legally correct, although many looked after children use this term and it is used by the government in the White Paper, *Care matters: Time for change* (DfES, 2007). However, in this book we primarily use the term 'looked after children'. Various terminology is used interchangeably in the literature, including 'children in care' and 'looked after children'. The term 'looked after child' was introduced with the Children Act 1989 and is defined in section 22(1) of the Act, making it clear that the term 'looking after' applies to children who are the subject of care orders and those children who are accommodated.

Terminology and meanings in relation to looked after children in Scotland are different. The legislation governing practice with looked after children in Scotland is the Children (S) Act 1995, and although there are similarities between the Children Act 1989 which underpins practice in England and Wales and the Children (S) Act 1995, there are also some significant differences. These are especially in relation to a distinctive system used only in Scotland, which is called the children's hearing system (Hothersall, 2008). Thus in Scotland, a child who is referred to the children's hearing system may become the subject of a formal supervision requirement and will be referred to *as looked after by the local authority even through they may continue to live at home with their own family* (Hothersall, 2008, p90). Details of the terms used within the Scottish legal system pertaining to looked after children are detailed in Hothersall (2008).

Who are looked after children? Statistical data

In the Green Paper, *Care matters: Transforming the lives of children and young people in care* (DfES, 2006f), the fluidity and diversity of the looked after population is highlighted. There is a discussion about how there has been an increase in the numbers of looked after children, due to children spending, on average, longer periods being looked after, despite fewer numbers of children starting to be looked after.

> *... there are around 60,000 children in care at any one time, ... 0.5% of all children. ...85,000 children will spend some time in care over the course of a year with many entering and leaving care rapidly.*
>
> (DfES, 2006f, p14)

Statistical data about the profile of looked after children is collected and produced annually by the DfE and is available from www.education.gov.uk/rsgateway/DB/SFR/s001026/index.shtml. The following statistical data relates to the period ending 31 March 2011. It shows that:

- in 2011 there were 90,920 children who were looked after at any time during the year ending March 2011;

- a total of 65,520 children were looked after at 31 March 2011, an increase of 2% from 2010 and an increase of 9% since 2007;

- 27,310 children started to be looked after during the year ending 31 March 2011. This is a decrease of 3% from the previous year, but an increase of 14% from 2007;

- 26,830 children ceased to be looked after during the year ending 31 March 2011, an increase of 6% from 2010 and an increase of 7% from 2007;

- 74% of children who were looked after at 31 March 2011 were in a foster placement;

- 3,050 looked after children were adopted during the year ending 31 March 2011, a decrease of 5% from 2010 and a decrease of 8% since 2007 (www.education.gov.uk/rsgateway/DB/SFR/s001026/index.shtml);

- for 62% of looked after children, the main reason social services first became involved was due to abuse and neglect, and this figure has remained largely consistent over the past five years;

- more boys (56%) than girls (44%) are looked after;

- the greatest numbers of looked after children are in the 10–15 year old age group, 37%;

- most looked after children are of white British origin, 74%;

- most children are looked after under a Care Order, 60%.

These statistics will help you to gain an overview of who looked after children are and give you a framework, which will aid your understanding of the range of issues discussed in the following chapters. Some of the statistics directly report on the numbers of looked after children in specific groups, whereas other data directly links to government priorities: for example, placement stability, which research has also identified as central to the emotional and psychological well-being of looked after children (see Chapters 8 and 9).

ACTIVITY **1.1**

The highest numbers of looked after children are in the 10–15 year old age group. What implications do you think this might have for social work practice and why do you think there are higher numbers of looked after children in this group?

COMMENT

This could mean that more intensive parenting and family support are needed at particular points for some families, particularly where there are complex and multiple long-standing problems. This issue is discussed in Care matters: Time for change (DfES, 2007, Chapter 2) where it was identified that older young people, on the edge of care, might be supported to stay at home or be successfully reunited with their family if the right sort of home-based, intensive family support intervention was available. To address these issues pilot projects were developed and delivered using the following intervention models: Multi Systemic Therapy (MST), for children on the edge of care or custody, Multi-dimensional Treatment Foster Care (MTFC) and KEEP (parenting skills for foster carers) and Functional Family Therapy (FFT) (DfE, 2011e, p3). The intention is to continue to develop these interventions from April 2011 to March 2015 and evaluate the outcomes. These are very promising developments and it is helpful that the government

---

is committing to funding longer-term interventions linked with evaluative research into outcomes. This also links to the coalition government's agenda to support families living in the community through the Families with Multiple Problems project. However, this project has been more contentious due to questions about inaccurate data identifying that there are 120,000 troubled families in England. This is discussed by Ramesh (2012) who states that the government has let propaganda triumph over fact *as the data regarding poverty does not necessarily mean that poor families are committing crimes, are in engaged in anti-social behaviour or that their children are truanting from school.*

You might have started to think about how difficult early childhood experiences can impact on adolescents' emotional well-being. For example, it can *often be during adolescence that attachment problems become most pronounced* (Daniel, et al., 2010, p208). Alongside the physical and psychological upheaval that all adolescents experience, additional family problems can make adolescence for some young people a frightening and bewildering time. See Chapter 8 for information about attachment theory and resilience.

Policy development: How did we get to where we are today?

Historically, substitute care has been provided for children going back hundreds of years. During the nineteenth and early twentieth centuries children who could not be looked after by their families or were orphaned or abandoned were mainly cared for in large residential institutions (Colton, et al., 2001). These institutions were set up by philanthropists like Dr Barnardo as an alternative to the bleak and inhumane workhouses. During the Second World War, many children were evacuated and sent to live with substitute carers; for some children their experiences were positive but for others they were not. Following the Second World War legislation was passed (the Children Act 1948) with the aim of strengthening the legal and procedural framework surrounding the needs of children placed in substitute care.

Subsequent legislation has sought to further improve the well-being of children and their families: these include the Children and Young Persons Act 1963; the Children and Young Persons Act 1969; the Children Act 1989; the Children Act 2004; and the Children and Young Persons Act 2008. There have been a number of different trends and models in the provision of substitute care for looked after children. These are identified by Colton, et al. (2001, p171) as ranging from a focus on foster families prior to the 1970s, followed by a focus on permanency and adoption in the 1970s, a prioritisation of biological families in the 1980s and then in the 1990s the extended family and kinship networks became more central. These different trends are also linked with a range of different underling philosophies about family life and what is best for children.

RESEARCH SUMMARY

Stein (2006c, p11) refers to a period of 20 years between the mid-1960s and mid-1980s as the missing years from our history of child welfare. He describes how there were no central government statistics or management information data about looked after children and neither was there a child-centred approach to meeting their needs. Issues of sexual abuse had not been fully recognised by social workers and other professions, and during this period children were a marginalised group (Parton, 2006). Evidence has revealed that there were fundamental breaches in levels of care and protection offered to looked after children and many children were sexually and physically abused by the carers who were supposed to be looking after them (Utting, 1991, 1997; Waterhouse, 2000).

Children were often powerless, with very few opportunities to express their fears. There were no children's rights services, no telephone helplines and few avenues of communication available to children. Their voices were not heard, so some took action by running away from residential care as a way of trying to escape the abuse. Rather than running away being seen as a cry for help, it was often seen as difficult and disobedient conduct and led to further punishment. Stein (1983) describes how societal attitudes towards children in this period were ambivalent and dismissive. These attitudes were intensified for children in care who were often from poor and marginalised families and were seen by some as orphans or criminals.

ACTIVITY *1.2*

The social construction of childhood

We have said that societal attitudes in the past were often dismissive towards children, and children were not seen to have 'rights' in the same way as they do now. Childhood is defined in law as a specific period up to when a young person is 18 years old, although in different societies and at different points in history, childhood may have been seen differently. Authors, including Aries (1962) and Hendrick (1994), explore the different constructions of childhood over the centuries, and this shows how we might have different ideas about what childhood means and how children should be treated at different stages of their development and that this is dependent on when we were born and what our own experiences have been.

Can you think about some of the differences a looked after child in the early 1960s, who is 10 years old, might experience, compared to a looked after child in 2013? Think about where the child might be placed, the contact arrangements, partnership work with parents, statutory reviews, visits by social work staff, involvement in plans, participation in looked after children forums and access to leisure activities.

COMMENT

You may have come to the conclusion that a looked after child in the early 1960s had far fewer opportunities to participate in decisions about their care, less certain contact arrangements and may have been placed in a large residential institution with uncertain arrangements for future plans.

Your answers probably reflect the changing perspectives of society about looked after children and children in general. Views about children's rights and needs have differed over time and are dependent on the historical, societal and environmental context of any given period. In addition, your answers will also be influenced by your own experiences of childhood.

Institutional abuse of looked after children

Abuse of children in residential care became a *dominant preoccupation in the 1990s* (Parton, 2006, p42). Parton goes on to refer to research undertaken by Corby, et al., (2001), which *identified eighteen public inquiry reports into abuse of children in residential care between 1967 and 2000* (p42). In response to the huge number of concerns about the abuse of children in care and extensive media coverage, the government undertook an independent review led by Sir William Utting, who was Chief Inspector of the Social Services Inspectorate (Utting, 1991). In his report he made a number of key recommendations: that looked after children should have the opportunity to participate in decisions; that staff should have more training and higher qualifications; as well as ensuring that there was greater management scrutiny of establishments and the individuals working in them, who were caring for looked after children (Utting, 1991). The latter recommendation was made as it was felt there had been widespread failure in the management of services and protection for looked after children.

Further concerns about the sexual abuse of looked after children led to more inquiries and the setting up of a national review, also led by Sir William Utting. This review, *People like us: The report of the review of the safeguards for children living away from home* (Utting, 1997), had at its main task the assessment and review of safeguarding arrangements for looked after children in foster care and residential care. It is described by Parton (2006, p44) as fundamental in shaping future policy and practice with looked after children. In *Working together* (1999) emphasis is given to the importance of safeguarding looked after children. The key points are:

- valuing and respecting children and promoting their self-esteem;

- external scrutiny of institutions and openness within them;

- well-trained and knowledgeable staff;

- independent advocacy for children and ensuring they have access to a trusted adult outside the institution;

- open, clear and child-friendly complaints procedures;

- rigorous recruitment and selection procedures;

- staff supervision and support;

- 'whistle-blowing' policies, ensuring staff can speak out if they have concerns;

- respect for diversity;

- vigilance from staff about the risk of people external to the residential unit who may abuse or exploit the young person.

    (Adapted from Department of Health (DoH), Home Office, Department for Education and Employment (DfEE), 1999, pp63–4)

One of the consequences of the abuse of looked after children in residential care was a decline in the numbers of children placed in residential establishments. Currently, most looked after children (71%) are placed in foster care, with a focus on trying to ensure children are placed within their own local authorities (DCSF, 2007a).

Quality protects

The concerns about child welfare services and the sheer number of inquiries led to the government developing the *Looked after children* materials (DoH, 1995). Another key turning point in policy terms was the launch of the *Quality protects* (QP) initiative in 1998, which was a five-year programme. This government strategy focused on supporting local authorities to improve outcomes for all children in need, including looked after children. Funding of £375 million accompanied the programme for the first three years and local authorities were required to meet key targets and priorities. Developing and providing local foster placements for looked after children was a key aspect of the *Quality protects* programme (DoH, 1998d) and local authorities received ongoing additional investment to support them in developing better placement choice. The initiative *Choice protects* has the overarching objective of improving placement options and stability linked to improved outcomes. This issue is also a major priority in the Green Paper *Care matters: Transforming the lives of children and young people in care* (DfES, 2006f) and in the White Paper *Care matters: Time for change* (DfES, 2007).

Current policy

Current policy for looked after children focuses on a range of issues including the health and education needs of looked after children; (see Chapter 10), their emotional needs (see Chapter 9), as well as the importance of quality social work practice in terms of assessment and care planning (see Chapter 4). The White Paper (DfES, 2007) identifies a range of key priorities for looked after children services, which are informed by concerns from the past, by the sharing of good practice initiatives, through findings from research and by the views of looked after children themselves and their families. From this you can see that social policy is influenced by a multiplicity of factors and that there are connections between policies. This can be seen in the links between *Care matters: Time for change* (DfES, 2007) and the underpinning approach central to *Every child matters* and the Children Act 2004, where there is a focus on collaborative working and shared responsibilities across all agencies for vulnerable children and families (see also Quinney, 2006). The key priorities specified in *Care matters: Time for change* (DfES 2007) are:

- improving opportunities in terms of educational attainment;

- prioritising looked after children in school admissions;

- helping children access leisure activities and hobbies;

- improving health outcomes;

- improving the role of corporate parents;

- improving family and parenting support;

- more local, stable placements;

- improving standards of foster care;

- arrangements for leaving care.

  (DfES, 2007, pp 5–11)

Corporate parenting

In the *Care matters* Green Paper (DfES, 2006f) the positives in policy and practice develop-ments since the 1980s are outlined, as well as statistics which highlight the disadvantages looked after children experience, even when compared to children who are similar to them in many ways but not looked after. Therefore one of the central themes in the Children and Young Persons Act (2008) is corporate parenting. 'Corporate parenting' is a term used to refer to the collective responsibility local councils have to provide quality care and achieve good outcomes for looked after children and young people leaving care. This approach focuses on supporting and delivering better care and parenting to the most vul-nerable children. It was developed partly in response to the child abuse scandals (referred to earlier in the chapter) in the 1970s and 1980s and a realisation that looked after chil-dren were especially vulnerable, as they often do not have a consistent adult advocating for them. The policy also links with the requirements of the Children Act 1989 and the duty councils have to safeguard and promote the welfare and education of all the children it looks after.

Local authorities are thus required to do all that a good parent would do. The educa-tional attainment aspect of corporate parenting is given further focus and direction in the Children Act 2004. The policy essentially means that local authorities are required to have in place effective systems for safely parenting and caring for looked after children. You are probably asking how the state can be a parent. In Johns (2011) the differences between parenthood, parenting and parental responsibility are outlined. 'Parenting' is referred to as upbringing and everyday care. Therefore, if you are the social worker for a looked after child, you will be partly responsible for ensuring that child is treated as a unique individual and ensuring that their needs are met by carers and other professionals who are responsi-ble for them.

The Children and Young Persons Act (2008) reinforces the collective responsibility local authorities have in relation to corporate parenting. There is recognition that corporate parenting of looked after children is very complex, due to the numbers of people involved so services must be co-ordinated to ensure children do not miss out. One of the key areas children and young people have expressed concern about is in relation to having frequent changes of social worker. The children who were consulted repeatedly said they wanted stability, both in terms of their day-to-day carers and their social worker. In response to concerns about corporate parenting a number of key elements were identified by the government for introduction by local authorities. They include:

- senior management responsibility for corporate parenting arrangements;
- children's participation in each local authority and the development of a Children in Care Council;
- direct contact between senior managers and looked after children through the Children in Care Council;
- effective management information including quantitative and qualitative data;
- a pledge in every local authority for looked after children;
- details of the arrangements should be in the Children and Young People's Plan.

(DfES, 2007, p21)

Creating more consistency for looked after children has been a concern for a number of years. Munro (2001) outlines some criticisms and concerns expressed by looked after children about changes in their social worker. They are as follows: distress at frequent changes of social worker; lack of an effective voice at reviews; lack of confidentiality and feeling that they did not have a confidante. In this study, young people talked about the importance of their social worker in their lives, as they acted as a strong and powerful ally. Do you recognise any of the issues raised by the young people in the study?

CASE STUDY

Joshua who is 12 years old and his sister Maria, who is eight years old, live with foster carers and the carers' birth children. Joshua is a keen footballer and part of his school team. He plays football after school but also has a match once every month, early on Saturday mornings with other school teams. His foster carer says that she cannot take him on Saturday mornings as she has other commitments with her birth children and also has to look after Maria. The foster carer's husband is at work and so cannot help. How would you approach this issue?

COMMENT

One of the issues that looked after children complained about in the Department for Education and Skills (2006f) consultation was feeling singled out as different. If Joshua could not be supported to go to his sports activities he might feel excluded and different to other children. One of the priorities identified in Care matters (DfES, 2007) is that looked after children should be supported to engage in hobbies and sporting activities. These sorts of activities help children's self-esteem and support their friendship networks. To resolve matters you might ask the foster carer to discuss transport options with the teacher, talk to Joshua about what he wants to do and establish whether it is feasible he travels with another family. You may have to arrange additional travel arrangements and pay for transport. If you are acting as a corporate parent you would make every effort to ensure that Joshua and his sister have the same advantages and opportunities as all other children.

Details of policy developments for young people leaving care and for other children with a range of needs are outlined in the following chapters. You will see from the discussion that it has taken many decades for policies focused on looked after children to fit together in a coherent way. The current policy and legislative direction aims to bring together a comprehensive range of safeguards, policies and procedures which will hopefully address the social exclusion and disadvantage that many looked after children experience. The aim is to create nurturing and supportive care experiences, so that looked after children have the opportunity to achieve their full potential and therefore increase their future life chances.

CHAPTER SUMMARY

In this chapter we looked at policy developments and government statistics and explored the historical development of policies relating to looked after children. We examined the links between policies, how ideas about childhood and the family have changed over time and how they have influenced the development of social work practice and policy generally. We showed how lessons from the past have been integrated into the key priorities enshrined in *Care matters: Time for change* (DfES, 2007) and in the Children Act 2004. We discussed the concept of corporate parenting and how it is seen as central to improving the lives of looked after children.

FURTHER READING

Berridge, D and Brodie, I (1998) *Children's homes revisited*. London: Jessica Kingsley.

The book analyses changes in residential child-care practice over a ten-year period, and shows how policy shifts and changes in society's attitudes towards children influence policy and practice for looked after children.

Department of Health (1998) *Caring for children away from home: Messages from Research*. Chichester: Wiley.

This book contains summaries of a number of research studies commissioned by the Department of Health in response to the serious concerns about residential care. The book gives a helpful overview regarding residential care and makes recommendations for improving practice with looked after children.

Frost, N and Parton, N (2009) *Understanding children's social care: Politics, policy and practice*. London: Sage.

This book gives an excellent policy overview and analysis of child and family social work linked to key issues for practice.

James, A and James, A (2004) *Constructing childhood – theory, policy and social practice*. Basingstoke: Palgrave.

This book will help you to understand the meaning of 'childhood', the diversity of children's experiences of childhood and how prevailing societal attitudes and beliefs about childhood and children are reflected in policy and legislation.

Chapter 2
The legal framework

Introduction

There are a number of different sources of legal influence on social work practice and it is important that these are identified and understood by social work students and practitioners in terms of grasping the significance of the law for day-to-day work. For example, you should be able to distinguish between primary and secondary legislation; know the difference between a duty and a power; know the difference between Green and White Papers, Bills and Acts; understand the processes associated with each in creating new legislation; understand the role of case law in determining precedent and the influence that this then has over decision-making; be able to identify government policy and statutory guidance as appropriate to looked after children and understand its status within the wider legal framework; and keep up to date with changes and developments in this area. This is not an easy task. Although you may appear daunted at the prospect of working within legal structures, and keeping abreast of developments that affect your practice, this is essential. While it is not possible to provide an in-depth analysis of the above-mentioned sources of law (please refer to Brammer (2010) or Brayne and Carr (2010) for a comprehensive overview), this chapter will provide you with a broad outline of the critical aspects of law that will underpin your practice with looked after children. See Johns (2011) in this

Learning Matters series for a more detailed discussion of the law in social work practice more generally.

The legislation which is key to your work in this area includes:

- Children Act 1989;

- Children (Leaving Care) Act 2000;

- Adoption and Children Act 2002;

- Children Act 2004;

- Children and Young Persons Act 2008.

This legislation will be summarised below. The Adoption and Children Act 2002 and the Children (Leaving Care) Act 2000 are further explored in the relevant chapters: Chapter 11, 'Adoption and permanence'; Chapter 12, 'Leaving care'. Additionally, Chapter 3, which explores pathways into care, expands on relevant legal aspects.

The areas of the Children Acts 1989 and 2004 that will be covered in this chapter include: an introduction to the basic principles of the Children Act 1989; local authority accommodation; emergency orders, care orders and supervision orders; care proceedings and care plans; the roles of the Official Solicitor and Children's Guardian; independent visiting; the importance of contact for looked after children; the local authority's responsibilities toward looked after children; and education and looked after children (Children Act 2004). The Children and Young Persons Act 2008 will be summarised and discussed.

In addition to this primary legislation, additional statutory guidance and other significant documents exist that are important for practice. These include:

- Children Act 1989 Guidance and Regulations Volume 1: Court Orders;

- Children Act 1989 Guidance and Regulations Volume 2: Care Planning, Placement and Case Review;

- Children Act 1989 Guidance and Regulations Volume 3: Planning Transition to Adulthood for Care Leavers;

- Children Act 1989 Guidance and Regulations Volume 4: Fostering Services;

- Children Act 1989 Guidance and Regulations Volume 5: Children's Homes;

- Adoption and Children Act 2002: Adoption Statutory Guidance;

- Adoption National Minimum Standards;

- Fostering National Minimum Standards;

- The Green Paper *Care Matters: Transforming the lives of children and young people in care*;

- The White Paper *Care Matters: Time for change*.

Definitions of key terms

There are a number of terms and phrases that you will come across when working in this area. These include: looked after children and children in care (please see definitions in Chapter 1); parental responsibility; working in partnership; significant harm; in the best interest of the child; the welfare checklist; the 'no order' and 'no delay' principles. The following definitions will provide you with some clarity about these terms.

Parental responsibility

The Children Act 1989 moved away from referring to 'parental rights' to acknowledging 'parental responsibilities'. These are outlined in section 3 as: *all the rights, duties, powers, responsibility and authority which by law a parent of a child has in relation to the child and his property* (section 3(1) Children Act 1989). Parental responsibility can be conferred through a number of routes.

If married at the time of a child's birth, both parents will have parental responsibility, and an unmarried mother will also have parental responsibility. Should unmarried parents subsequently marry then the birth father will also acquire parental responsibility. If in a civil partnership, then the non-biological parent has the ability to acquire parental responsibility via court application. From December 2003, if an unmarried father is present when the baby's birth is registered and his name is on the birth certificate, then he will have parental responsibility. For fathers not registering their children's birth, and for fathers who are not married to the mother of their child, if their child was born before December 2003, they have to acquire parental responsibility by way of a recorded agreement with the mother or by application to the court. For a female partner who is not in a civil partnership with the birth mother, parental responsibility can be acquired via application to the Court for a Residence Order (section 8 Children Act 1989). The Adoption and Children Act 2002 also introduced new ways for step-parents who are married or in civil partnerships to acquire parental responsibility with the agreement of both birth parents (where this applies) provided they both had parental responsibility, without the other birth parent losing parental responsibility.

Parental responsibility is also acquired by anyone holding a Residence Order (which determines where a child should live), a Special Guardianship Order (section 14a Children Act 1989 and section 115 of the Adoption and Children Act 2002), the adoption agency and the adoptive parents upon the making of a Placement Order (section 21 of the Adoption and Children Act 2002), and an Adoption Order (section 46) and by the local authority when a child is the subject of an Emergency Protection Order, Care Order or Interim Care Order, or when someone is appointed guardian under a will. If parental responsibility is given by way of a Residence Order or to a local authority via a Care Order, it can be removed by courts via the cessation of the order which gave parental responsibility to the applicant. A parental responsibility order to a father can also be revoked. Upon adoption via the Adoption and Children Act 2002, the parental responsibility of everyone else (including the local authority, anyone with a Residence Order or other order which gives parental responsibility, and birth parents) ceases.

Working in partnership

Regarding the care of looked after children, for those children who are subject to interim care or care orders, local authorities can determine the extent to which a person with parental responsibility can meet their parenting obligations while the child remains in local authority care. This is referred to as the '49%/51% partnership balance,' with the local authority having at least 51% of the decision-making authority in the partnership. However, the local authority is required to work in partnership with those people who have parental responsibility for the child. The court does limit the local authority's power in that a local authority *cannot change the child's name or religion, appoint a guardian or consent to an adoption order (s33(6))* (Brammer 2010, p206).

Significant harm

The term 'significant harm' is the threshold for state involvement in private family matters and is referred to in the Children Act 1989, but it is not defined as such. Under s. 31 of the Children Act 1989, 'harm' is defined as *ill treatment or impairment of health or development*; 'development' is described as *physical, intellectual, emotional, social and behavioural*; 'health' can be *physical or mental health*; 'ill treatment' includes *forms of ill-treatment that are non-physical* (Children Act 1989).

In the best interest of the child

This is one of the most over-used phrases in child and family social work. While there are important principles inherent within the phrase concerning the paramountcy of the child in decision-making, unfortunately what is construed as being in the 'best interest' of the child is often debatable and contentious. The Children Act 1989 and the Adoption and Children Act 2002 are consistent in their use of the word 'paramount' to denote the centrality of the child in decision-making within the court arena.

When a court determines any question with respect to

(a) the upbringing of a child; or

(b) the administration of a child's property or the application of income arising from it, the child's welfare shall be the court's paramount consideration.

(Section 1, Children Act 1989)

This is known as the 'welfare principle' or the 'paramountcy principle'.

While this section of the Act sets out the court's priorities in decision-making for individual children, the emphasis on paramountcy for local authorities differs in terms of finite resources that local authorities have to support a significant number of children in need or looked after living within their area. This does not mean that plans and decisions cannot be made which are geared towards the individual needs of children. Effective decision-making and planning are a part of everyday social work and weighing up the different needs of children in terms of the resources, services, time and energy of the social worker and the social work agency is the bread and butter of social work practice. Understanding and navigating through the inherent contradictions and complexities within these different professional roles and responsibilities is crucial. See the Green Paper *Care matters* (DfES, 2006f, p32) for an illustration of the different people and agencies involved in a looked after child's life, compared to a child living at home.

Welfare checklist

The welfare checklist is also contained within section 1 of the Children Act 1989. There is a similar list within the Adoption and Children Act 2002. These checklists contain a list of areas which the court should consider in making decisions about children involved in public law proceedings, and in the Adoption and Children Act 2002, agencies are also required to consider this list as well as the court. The list is not in any order of priority, nor is it complete (see Table 2.1).

The 'no order' principle

Another main principle inherent within the Children Act 1989, and replicated in section 1(6) of the Adoption and Children Act 2002, is the 'no order' principle. This states that an order should not be made unless it is really needed, specifically:

> ... it [the court] shall not make the order unless it considers that doing so would be better for the child than making no order at all.

> (Section 1(5) Children Act 1989)

This might sound rather obvious, and it is. However, it underlines the need for orders to have positive benefits for children and avoid courts and court processes creating complicated and unwarranted interventions into children's lives.

The 'no delay' principle

The last principle that will be covered in this summary is that of 'no delay'. This is also repeated in section 1(2) of the Adoption and Children Act 2002.

> In any proceedings in which any question with respect to the upbringing of a child arises, the court shall have regard to the general principle that any delay in determining the question is likely to prejudice the welfare of the child.

> (Section 1(2) Children Act 1989)

Again, this is stating something that is self-explanatory. Both Acts recognise the harmful effects of delay on children. Underpinning this is the understanding that the effect of delay is different for children than for parents and that ultimately children's needs must come first.

Table 2.1 The welfare or paramountcy principle, principles of 'no delay' and 'no order' and the welfare checklist

Children Act 1989		Adoption and Children Act 2002	
Section 1 Welfare or Paramountcy Principle	When a court determines any question with respect to (a) the upbringing of a child; or (b) the administration of a child's property or the application of income arising from it, the child's welfare shall be the court's paramount consideration	Section 1 Paramountcy Principle	(1) This section applies whenever a court or adoption agency is coming to a decision relating to the adoption of a child (2) the paramount consideration of the court or adoption agency must be the child's welfare, throughout his life
Section 1(3) Welfare Checklist	The court must have regard to	Section 1(4) Welfare Checklist	The court or adoption agency must have regard to the following matters (among others)
a	The ascertainable wishes and feelings of the child concerned (considered in the light of his age and understanding)	a	The child's ascertainable wishes and feelings regarding the decision (considered in the light of the child's age and understanding)
b	His physical, emotional and educational needs	b	The child's particular needs
c	The likely effect on him of any change in his circumstances	c	The likely effect on the child (throughout his life) of having ceased to be a member of the original family and become an adopted person
d	His age, sex, background and any characteristics of his which the court considers relevant	d	The child's age, sex, background and any of the child's characteristics which the court or agency considers relevant
e	Any harm he has suffered or is at risk of suffering	e	Any harm (within the meaning of the Children Act 1989) which the child has suffered or is at risk of suffering
f	How capable each of his parents, and any other person in relation to whom the court considers the question to be relevant, of meeting his needs	f	The relationship which the child has with relatives, and with any other person in relation to whom the court or agency considers the relationship to be relevant, including: (1) the likelihood of any such relationship continuing and the value to the child of its doing so (2) the ability and willingness of any of the child's relatives, or of any such person, to provide the child with a secure environment in which the child can develop, and otherwise to meet the child's needs the wishes and feelings of any of the child's relatives, or of any such person, regarding the child
g	The range of powers available to the court under this Act in the proceedings in question		
		Section 1(5)	States that in placing a child for adoption the adoption agency must give due consideration to the child's religious persuasion, racial origin and linguistic background

Continued

Section 1(5) The 'no order' principle	Where a court is considering whether or not to make an order under this Act with respect to a child, it shall not make the order unless it considers that doing so would be better for the child than making no order at all	Section 1(6) The 'no order' principle	The court or adoption agency must always consider the whole range of powers available to it in the child's case (whether under this Act or the Children Act 1989); and the court must not make any order under this Act unless it considers that making the order would be better for the child than not doing so
Section 1(2) the 'no delay' principle	In any proceedings in which any question with respect to the upbringing of a child arises, the court shall have regard to the general principle that any delay in determining the question is likely to prejudice the welfare of the child.	Section 1(3) the 'no delay' principle	The court or adoption agency must at all times bear in mind that, in general, any delay in coming to the decision is likely to prejudice the child's welfare

ACTIVITY 2.1

Compare the wording of the paramountcy principle, principles of 'no order' and 'no delay' and the welfare checklist in the Children Act 1989 (CA 1989) with the ones in the Adoption and Children Act 2002 (ACA 2002). What are the differences? What are the similarities?

COMMENT

A number of observations can be made in comparing these checklists.

- *The same language is used in both pieces of legislation in that the ACA 2002 checklist is heavily influenced by the CA 1989 one, which means that the ACA 2002 falls in line with the principles established in the CA 1989.*

- *Although the CA 1989 applies directly to courts only, it is very influential for local authorities and it is common practice for them to use these subsections as a basis for their report-writing and evidence to the court. It also highlights any other significant factors that need to be taken into consideration in their recommendations and associated decision-making. The ACA 2002 also applies to agencies.*

- *The ACA 2002 is explicitly concerned with professionals thinking through the long-term impact of a decision such as adoption for the child.*

- *The role of birth parents, extended family and other significant people in terms of discharging ongoing parental responsibilities in meeting the needs of the child is significant (CA 1989). The ACA 2002 explicitly requires agencies and courts to consider how children will maintain contact with birth family members (and other significant people) but there is no presumption of contact, whereas there is under the Children Act 1989. The ACA 2002 also requires local authorities to examine other possible permanent caring arrangements for the child within their wider community.*

- *Look specifically at the wording contained within these sections of legislation: 'shall', 'must', 'have regard to', 'is likely to', and think about how this could be interpreted by the courts or agencies. Which are they obliged to do and which are discretionary?*

The Children Act 1989

We are now going to describe the variety of routes into care that children take and the different responsibilities that social workers have in respect of looked after children.

As we outlined in Chapter 1, of the approximately 65,000 children who are looked after in England in any one day (some 90,000 children will pass through the care system in any year), a variety of legal obligations will exist for social workers who have the responsibility for overseeing the planning for these children. It is important to understand that these children do not comprise a static group as just under half will return home within six months. Although the majority of these children will be in foster care, some will be in residential care, some with relatives and some with parents. Nearly two-thirds of children looked after have care orders (section 31 of the CA 1989), while the other children are 'accommodated' (section 20 of the CA 1989).

There are two main routes for children into care. The first is via accommodation, under section 20 of the CA 1989. This provision is intended as a service to support parents – thus section 20 is contained under Part III of the Children Act 1989 'Local Authority Support to Children and their Families' (Brayne and Carr, 2010). The provision of accommodation occurs on a voluntary basis. The parent(s) retain parental responsibility for their child and the local authority does not obtain parental responsibility under this section. The child should be returned to the parents upon their request.

The second route into care is via court involvement and care proceedings, made under Part 4 of the Children Act 1989. The child in question could become subject to either an Emergency Protection Order (section 44 CA 1989); Interim Care Order (section 38 CA 1989); or a full Care Order (section 31 CA 1989). In all of these options the local authority obtains parental responsibility for the child as long as the order is in force. This is shared with the parent. If a child enters care through this route the 'threshold criteria' must be met. However, the criteria are different in relation to Emergency Protection Orders or Interim Care Orders. The degree of certainty that is required is different. This criteria is outlined in section 31(2) CA 1989; a court is only able to make a care order if a child is suffering or is likely to suffer significant harm. See Brammer (2010, pp254–59) for detailed explanations of these terms.

A court can only make a care or supervision order if it is satisfied –

(a) that the child concerned is suffering, or is likely to suffer, significant harm; and

(b) that the harm or likelihood of harm, is attributable to –

(i) the care given to the child, or likely to be given to him if the order were not made, not being what it would be reasonable to expect a parent to give to him; or

(ii) the child's being beyond parental control;

AND; It is better for the child for an order to be made than no order at all.

(Section 31(2) CA 1989)

The court has a little-used power to make a care order where a child safety order is in force but there has been failure to comply with the requirements. In this case the court does not have to be satisfied that the threshold has been met.

A further explanation of pathways into care is given in Chapter 3.

Procedure to apply for a care order (or supervision order)

In order to apply for a care order or supervision order the local authority (or 'authorised person' – NSPCC) issues an application and serves it on each person with parental responsibility at least three days before the date of the first court hearing; hence these orders are not appropriate for emergencies. The local authority should also submit a statement at this time, which sets out: the facts of the case, including family details; the action the local authority has taken hitherto; and why an order is necessary. If you have prepared this evidence you will have to be available to be questioned upon it. The Protocol for Judicial Case Management currently sets out the procedure for public law applications and this was replaced in April 2008 by the Public Law Outline (PLO). Volume 1 of the Children Act 1989 guidance was reissued in 2008. The PLO was updated again in 2010 (HM Courts and Tribunal Services, 2010).

At the first court hearing the court will give directions. This sets out the timetable for the appointment of a children's guardian, when the parents should file their evidence together with follow-up evidence from the local authority, whether any experts (such as paediatricians, psychiatrists, clinical psychologists and so on) will be instructed, who by, and dates will be identified for the submission of reports, the next court hearing/final hearing as appropriate and any interim applications. Care proceedings must always start in the family proceedings court but can be transferred to higher courts depending on the level of complexity of the individual case.

The court has the power to make interim orders if an order is required before the date of the final hearing. Often many interim orders are given by the court before the date of the final hearing while further information and evidence are collected and submitted and plans are drawn up. Any interim order can only last for 28 days, though orders are often renewed with the consent of all the parties after negotiation.

Separate care plans are required for each child and must be drawn up before a final order is made by the court. There is now a statutory requirement to this effect introduced by the Children Act 2004 – contained in s31(3A). The LA Circular LAC(99)29: 'Care Plans and Care Proceedings' sets out the criteria, which contains five key elements (see Table 2.2): the overall aim; the child's specific needs, including contact; views of others; placement details and timetable for permanency; and management/support to be provided by the local authority. Care plans should not be based on general policy considerations and should also consider arrangements for leaving care (where teenagers are involved). The court needs to consider the care plan and say whether it is in the best interests of the child. The court can not alter the content of the plan but it can refuse to make an order on the basis of the content of the plan (see Volume 2 of the Children Act 1989 guidance, reissued in 2010 (DCSF, 2010b)).

Table 2.2 Care plans: Five key elements (Brammer 2010, pp261–2)

1	Overall aim	Includes summary of the case and timetables that social workers are working to
2	Child's needs	Includes a number of different elements: contact with family and significant others; needs arising from race, culture and religion or language; special education; health or disability. Also how have the wishes and views of the child been obtained and how have they been taken into consideration in the plan?
3	Views of others	Similarly, how have the wishes and views of the child's parents and others with a sufficient interest in the child been obtained and how have they been taken into consideration in the plan?
4	Placement details and timetable	This should include details about proposed placements and timescales, including plans for reunification if applicable; specific arrangements for health care, education and other services to be provided; contact arrangements and details of how the parents will be involved in day to day arrangements. When adoption is a possibility, a twin track approach should be discussed and outlined
5	Management and support by the local authority	Includes identifying specific individuals responsible for implementing the overall plan, including allocating specific tasks to named individuals (including parents and children); and outlining contingency plans. Children and parents must also be aware of the processes for making representations or complaints

Case law has been influential in determining how care plans are implemented. The Court of Appeal case *re W and B* required local authorities and/or guardians to return to court when care plans were not discharged appropriately. This was then rejected by the House of Lords on the grounds that it would amount to courts effectively supervising the local authority in its undertaking of its parental responsibility. However, the House of Lords said:

I cannot stress too strongly that the rejection of this innovation on legal grounds must not obscure the pressing need for the Government to attend to the serious practical and legal problems identified in the Court of Appeal…one of the questions needing urgent consideration is whether some degree of court supervision of local authorities' discharge of their parental responsibilities would bring about an overall improvement in the quality of child care provided by local authorities.

(Brammer, 2010, p262)

A parent who is dissatisfied with the care plan can apply to discharge the care order after six months or bring an application under the Human Rights Act 1998. In addition, the Independent Reviewing Officer can refer a case to an officer of the Children and Family Court Advisory and Support Service (Cafcass) if appropriate; see s26(2A) CA 89 and reg2A of the Review of Children's Cases Regulations 1991.

Duration and discharge of a care order (or supervision order)

Care orders last until a child is 18 unless it is discharged earlier by the court. New applications cannot be made once a child has reached 17. If the child is in care (or being accommodated) they are entitled to aftercare support under section 24 of the Children Act 1989. This is further expanded upon in Chapter 12 'Leaving Care'.

A care order can be discharged by an application to the court that made the original order by any person with parental responsibility, the child, or by the local authority. In order to get the order discharged, evidence should be supplied by the applicant to show that there is no longer any need for the order. The court would take into account the factors in the welfare checklist.

A supervision order only lasts for a year on the first application. If it is not renewed before then it automatically expires. However, a supervision order can be extended. This allows the local authority to dispense with the requirement to prove the threshold criteria a second time. They now only need to show that an order is still needed to safeguard the welfare of the child. However, this can only be extended for a maximum of three years, which includes the period of time in the original order. If you miss the deadline for extending the order, the local authority will have to start all over again.

The effects of a care order are considerable. The local authority obtains parental responsibility and can overrule anybody else with parental responsibility (though they must consult them before making any decisions about the child's welfare if it is reasonably practicable to do so). Under a care order a child is being looked after by the local authority so it must provide accommodation and maintenance and hold regular looked after reviews. It is interesting to note that although one has to show the same threshold for supervision orders the effect of a supervision order is very different. The local authority does not obtain parental responsibility and so is reliant on exerting influence via befriending and negotiation.

A local authority's duties to all looked after children

Sections 22 and 23 of the Children Act 1989 outline a number of duties that local authorities have which apply to all looked after children, regardless of whether children are accommodated or subject to a care order. See Table 2.3 for a summary of these duties.

Any placement has to comply with extensive guidance and regulations described in Volume 2 of the Children Act 1989 guidance reissued in 2010 (DCSF, 2010b).

Table 2.3 Local authority duties to looked after children in Children Act 1989

Section	Legislative text from Act (only parts of each subsection are listed)	Summary
s22	Duties of local authorities in relation to children looked after by them	
s22(3)	It shall be the duty of a local authority looking after any child – (a) to safeguard and promote the child's welfare; and (b) make use of services available for children cared for by their own parents as appears to the authority reasonable. S22(3a) The duty of a local authority under subsection (3) (a) to safeguard and promote the welfare of a child looked after by them includes in particular a duty to promote the child's educational achievement. This is also mentioned in s22C(8)b).	This sets out the overarching requirements to keep the child safe and support the child's development whilst in care. The other duties covered in s22 include: • requirements for placements; • providing accommodation near to a child's home so far as is reasonably practical and consistent with the child's needs (see s22C); • provide accommodation of siblings together where this is practicable and consistent with their welfare (see s22C(8)c); • provide suitable accommodation for disabled children, given any particular needs a child may have (see s22C(8)d); • make arrangements for the child to live with his/her parents; person with PR; the holder of a residence order, SGO etc, or other person connected to the child, unless to do so would not be reasonably practical or consistent with the child's welfare etc; • not to place a child in accommodation that would restrict his/her liberty unless the conditions to do so are satisfied; consult with the relevant local authority; • keep the required statutory records; • consider representations; • carry out reviews within required timescales.
s22(4)	Before making any decision with respect to a child whom they are looking after, or proposing to look after, a local authority shall, so far as is reasonably practicable, ascertain the wishes and feelings of – (a) the child; (b) his parents; (c) any person who is not a parent of his but who has parental responsibility for him; and (d) any other person whose wishes and feelings the authority consider to be relevant, regarding the matter to be decided.	There is a requirement to ascertain the wishes of feelings of relevant people when making decisions about a child, including the child, and to then think about how these wishes can be incorporated into plans for the child.
S22(5)	In making any such decision a local authority shall give due consideration – (a) having regard to his age and understanding, to such wishes and feelings of the child as they have been able to ascertain; (b) to such wishes and feelings of any person mentioned in subsection (4)(b) to (d) as they have been able to ascertain; and (c) to the child's religious persuasion, racial origin and cultural and linguistic background.	Look at the particular needs of the child (race, language, culture and religion) amongst other things.

The CYPA 2008 added a number of new subsections (B-G) to S22 CA 1989. These are expanded below:		
s22B	It is the duty of a local authority to maintain a child they are looking after in other respects apart from the provision of accommodation.	s22B is concerned with the maintenance of looked after children.
s22C	(7) In determining the most appropriate placement for C, the local authority must, subject to the other provisions of this Part (in particular, to their duties under section 22) – (a) give preference to a placement falling within paragraph (a) of subsection (6) over placements falling within the other paragraphs of that subsection; (b) comply, so far as is reasonably practicable in all the circumstances of C's case, with the requirements of subsection (8); and (c) comply with subsection (9) unless that is not reasonably practicable. (8) The local authority must ensure that the placement is such that (a) it allows C to live near C's home; (b) it does not disrupt C's education or training; (c) if C has a sibling for whom the local authority are also providing accommodation, it enables C and the sibling to live together; (d) if C is disabled, the accommodation provided is suitable to C's particular needs. (9) The placement must be such that C is provided with accommodation within the local authority's area.	This deals with the ways in which looked after children are to be accommodated and maintained. There are new requirements here in terms of location of placement, and there is a continued emphasis on not disrupting a child's education.
s22D	1. Where a local authority are providing accommodation for a child ('C') other than by arrangements under section 22C(6)(d), they must not make such arrangements for C unless they have decided to do so in consequence of a review of C's case carried out in accordance with regulations made under section 26. 2. But subsection (1) does not prevent a local authority making arrangements for C under section 22C(6)(d) if they are satisfied that in order to safeguard C's welfare it is necessary – (a) to make such arrangements; and (b) to do so as a matter of urgency.	There should be a review of child's case before making alternative arrangements for accommodation.
s22E		This deals with an aspects of placements in children's homes provided, equipped and maintained by an appropriate national authority.
s22F		This covers the Regulations that apply regarding children looked after by local authorities: Part 2 of Schedule 2 of the Act applies here.
s22G	1. It is the general duty of a local authority to take steps that secure, so far as reasonably practicable, the outcome in subsection (2). 2. The outcome is that the local authority are able to provide the children mentioned in subsection (3) with accommodation that – (a) is within the authority's area; and (b) meets the needs of those children. 3. The children referred to in subsection (2) are those – (a) that the local authority are looking after, (b) in respect of whom the authority are unable to make arrangements under section 22C(2), and (c) whose circumstances are such that it would be consistent with their welfare for them to be provided with accommodation that is in the authority's area. 4. In taking steps to secure the outcome in subsection (2), the local authority must have regard to the benefit of having – (a) a number of accommodation providers in their area that is, in their opinion, sufficient to secure that outcome; and (b) a range of accommodation in their area capable of meeting different needs that is, in their opinion, sufficient to secure that outcome. 5. In this section 'accommodation providers' means – (a) local authority foster parents; and (b) children's homes in respect of which a person is registered under Part 2 of the Care Standards Act 2000.	This covers a general duty of a local authority to secure sufficient accommodation for looked after children.

The CYPA 2008 also introduced a number of new subsections under S23 of CA 1989. These are listed below:

s23	Provision of accommodation and maintenance by a local authority for children whom they are looking after.	Sections A and B: There is a duty on the LA to provide accommodation and to maintain looked after children. One of the most important decisions made about a child is where they will live. There are a number of options including: a relative, foster parent, children's home, or at home with their parent. The LA can pay carers a boarding out allowance but can't pay parents. The child's placement should be as near to home as possible. This section also covers duties for young people who have left care concerning pathway plans and personal advisors. This will be covered in Chapter 12.
s23ZA	1. This section applies to – (a) a child looked after by a local authority; (b) a child who was looked after by a local authority but who has ceased to be looked after by them as a result of prescribed circumstances. 2. It is the duty of the local authority – (a) to ensure that a person to whom this section applies is visited by a representative of the authority ('a representative'); (b) to arrange for appropriate advice, support and assistance to be available to a person to whom this section applies who seeks it from them. 4. Regulations under this section for the purposes of subsection (3)(a) may make provision about – (a) the frequency of visits; (b) circumstances in which a person to whom this section applies must be visited by a representative; and (c) the functions of a representative. 5. In choosing a representative a local authority must satisfy themselves that the person chosen has the necessary skills and experience to perform the functions of a representative.	This section deals with issues of contact between the child and a representative from the local authority, most often the child's social worker.
s23ZB	1. A local authority looking after a child must appoint an independent person to be the child's visitor if – (a) the child falls within a description prescribed in regulations made by the appropriate national authority; or (b) in any other case, it appears to them that it would be in the child's interests to do so. 2. A person appointed under this section must visit, befriend and advise the child.	This section covers Independent visitors. If the child objects to the appointment of an independent visitor either before or after one is appointed, then the local authority shall terminate the arrangement.
s34	The LA must apply to the court if it wishes to terminate contact, unless under s34(6) it is necessary to refuse contact in order to safeguard and promote the child's welfare. This power or refusal is for use in urgent situations and lasts 7 days, after which approval of the court is required.	It is important to consider appropriate contact arrangements with relevant people. There is a presumption of contact and research evidence shows better outcomes for children if contact is maintained. if a child has had infrequent communication, the LA should appoint an independent visitor whose role is to advise, assist and befriend. See s23ZB.

Looked after children reviews

Each placement must have regular looked after reviews. The purpose of the review is to check on the child's progress as a looked after child, progress in the placement and the progress of the plan that has been drawn up for the child, including contact arrangements. The review will identify changes that are necessary to meet the child's needs. The first review must be held four weeks after a child becomes looked after, the second after a further three months, and the third and each subsequent review after six months. A social worker must consult with the child, parents and other significant people in the child's life (teachers, health professionals, therapists) when making decisions about the child, and these people should also be involved in the looked after review process. The child should attend the review, as should the parent unless there is any reason why the parent should be not invited (e.g. fear of violence, or parent is in prison). An independent reviewing officer (IRO) should chair the review. A permanency plan should be drawn up at the second looked after review and evaluated regularly. This is also the opportunity to check on educational and health progress for the child (please refer to Chapter 10 for further information). This would include the Personal Education Plan (PEP) drawn up by the school and any special educational needs (SEN) provision put in place for the child. The school will have its own review process and timetable associated with the PEP and SEN plan (The Review of Children's Cases (Amendment) (England) Regulations, 2004). The review will also examine other looked after children documentation (the Action and Assessment Records) in order that the IRO can be assured that the necessary documentation is being completed and that any recommendations arising from these records are being appropriately actioned and reviewed. The responsibility for completion of the Action and Assessment Records rests with the social worker although other professionals (including the foster carer, child and adolescent mental health services (CAMHS) worker, teacher, for example) may well complete various sections of the records, as might the child (depending on their age and level of understanding). Please also see Chapter 4, which discusses looked after children's reviews, for further information.

Children Act 1989 regulations and guidance

There are nine volumes of regulations and guidance which are important to read as they contain supplementary material. Volume 4 is on Fostering Services (DfE, 2011d). It contains details concerning:

- Arrangements for Placement of Children Regulations 1991.

- Fostering Services (England) Regulations 2011.

- Placement of Children with Parents Regulations 1991.

- Contact with Children Regulations 1991.

- Definition of Independent Visitors Regulations 1991.

- Review Children's Cases (Amendment) (England) Regulations 2004.

- Representations Procedure Regulations 2006.

- National Minimum Standards for Fostering Services 2011 (DfE, 2011f).

This has been updated and is essential reading for social workers working in this area.

Secure accommodation

Secure accommodation is covered under section 25 of the CA 1989. There are a small number of children under 18 who will need to be placed in secure accommodation. As this type of accommodation restricts their liberty, there are a number of criteria that must be met before this course of action can occur:

...a child who is being looked after by a local authority may not be placed, and, if placed, may not be kept, in accommodation provided for the purpose of restricting liberty ('secure accommodation') unless it appears –

(a) that –

(i) he has history of absconding; and is likely to abscond from any other description of accommodation; and

(ii) if he absconds, he is likely to suffer significant harm; or

(b) that if he is kept in any other description of accommodation he is likely to injure himself or other persons.

(Section 25(1) CA 1989)

These criteria must be satisfied to a high standard and it is generally necessary to show that the local authority has tried various other types of accommodation and the child has either put themselves at risk by repeatedly absconding or they have caused or threatened significant harm to themselves or someone else in various settings (Brayne and Carr, 2010).

The local authority can place a child they are 'looking after' in secure accommodation for up to 72 hours on the authority of the Director of Children's Services but any further detention must be sanctioned by a court order. If the 72 hours expire on a Sunday or a bank holiday it will continue to the next working day, when the local authority must make its application to the court (having given 24 hours' notice to the parents and the child) and this application must contain detailed evidence showing why secure accommodation is the only option open to them. The court will usually ask the reasons why a child cannot be held in other types of accommodation. Secure accommodation is a last resort – when anything else would be too risky for the child and/or other people. The agreement of the parent is important. If the parent does not agree then the local authority would need to make an application to the court (Brayne and Carr, 2010). The welfare checklist does not apply in secure accommodation applications.

A secure order may not be made on a child under 13 unless the local authority has the consent of the Secretary of State for Health. It lasts for three months and may be extended by further applications for six month periods. If it cannot be justified any longer then the local authority must place the child in open accommodation even before the order has lapsed (Brammer, 2010).

Other legal representatives and their roles

As well as the local authority having a range of specific roles and responsibilities, others also have clearly defined roles. These are described below.

Children's guardian

A children's guardian is appointed by the court to safeguard the interests of the child. The historical basis of this can be traced back to the Maria Colwell inquiry in 1974, where the published report commented on the potential usefulness of an independent social worker involved in complex cases. The guardian *ad litem* service was initially established in 1984 (Brammer, 2010). A children's guardian is usually an independent social worker or a probation officer who advises the court on the wishes of the child, depending on the age and understanding of the child. The guardian will review the options available to the child and comment on their suitability. The guardian will also arrange for the child to have separate legal representation where this is necessary.

Official solicitor

The official solicitor looks after the legal interests of children. The official solicitor is usually appointed by the court in complex cases in either public or private proceedings. This role has now been integrated into Cafcass along with the children's guardian and the court welfare officer.

Children and Family Court Advisory Support Service (Cafcass)

Cafcass was launched, on 1 April 2001, bringing together the Family Court Welfare Service, the children's division of the official solicitor's department and the guardian *ad litem* and reporting officers who used to work for local authorities on a self-employed basis. It is responsible for advising the courts on the right arrangements for children who are the subject of family court proceedings (Brayne and Carr, 2010).

Independent visitors

The role of the independent visitor is to advise and befriend looked after children who may have infrequent or no contact with family members, or other significant people from their past. However, if the child objects to an independent visitor being appointed and the local authority is satisfied that the child is of sufficient age and understanding to make an informed decision, then an independent visitor will not visit the child. Independent visiting is not widely used. Only about a third of local authorities in England and Wales were regularly using independent visitors at the end of the 1990s (Knight, 1998). The independent visiting role has been strengthened under CYPA 2008 (see s23ZB of CA 1989 for further details).

CASE STUDY

Independent visiting

William is 13. He has been looked after (accommodated) for six years. His mother has lived in a nursing care home for ten years following a serious car accident where she broke her neck and sustained brain damage. William does not know his father. After his mother was admitted to hospital 11 years ago, William went to live with his maternal grandmother, who died when he was seven. Before she died social services had been involved with William, as there were concerns about the care he was receiving from his grandmother. William has one older sister who is 21 and has also spent periods of her childhood as a looked after child. Since being looked after William has had over 12 placements – ten of which were foster placements (some in-house, some private agencies). Two years ago he was placed in a specialist therapeutic residential placement some 500 miles from his home community and area where he grew up. Despite making some progress in this placement, he has had no visits from any family member since arriving at the placement.

Identify the ways in which William could benefit from having an independent visitor. How would you go about setting this up?

COMMENT

Some of the benefits for William in having an independent visitor involved are:

- *that William's independent visitor could attend his looked after reviews;*

- *to undertake an advocacy role for William;*

- *to visit him more frequently than a social worker, and in a different capacity;*

- *to provide continuity of contact over a long period of time;*

- *to enable William to build a supportive relationship with an adult which can be a model for other appropriate child/adult relationships.*

A number of independent visiting schemes are run through charities such as Action for Children.

Independent Reviewing Officer

The appointment of an independent reviewing officer (IRO) to oversee the effectiveness of care planning processes for each looked after child is a legal requirement under section 118 of the Adoption and Children Act 2002. The statutory duties of the IRO, as listed on the DfE website are to:

- monitor the local authority's performance of their functions in relation to the child's case;

- participate in any review of the child's case;

- ensure that any ascertained wishes and feelings of the child concerning the case are given due consideration by the appropriate authority;

- perform any other function which is prescribed in regulations.

In discharging these duties, the IRO has a number of specific responsibilities which include:

- promoting the voice of the child;

- ensuring that plans for looked after children are based on a detailed and informed assessment, are up-to-date, effective and provide a real and genuine response to each child's needs;

- identifying any gaps in the assessment process or provision of service;

- making sure that the child understands how an advocate could help and his/her entitlement to one;

- offering a safeguard to prevent any 'drift' in care planning for looked after children and the delivery of services to them;

- monitoring the activity of the responsible authority as a corporate parent in ensuring that care plans have given proper consideration and weight to the child's wishes and feelings and that, where appropriate, the child fully understands the implications of any changes made to his/her care plan.

In March 2010 new statutory guidance for local authorities and independent reviewing officers was issued on care planning and reviewing arrangements for looked after children (DCSF, 2010c). The IRO handbook (DCSF, 2010d) is reissued guidance for IROs about how they should discharge their distinct responsibilities to looked after children. It also provides guidance to local authorities on their strategic and managerial responsibilities in establishing an effective IRO service.

The CYPA 2008 further extended and strengthened the IRO's responsibilities from monitoring the performance by the local authority of their functions in relation to a child's review, to monitoring the performance by the local authority of their functions in relation to a child's case, as set out in sections 25A–25C of the CA 1989. The idea behind this change is for the IRO to be viewed as an independent practitioner responsible for the oversight of the child's case, and therefore ensure that the child's interests are protected throughout the care planning process. The amended 1989 Act and the regulations specify:

- the duties of the local authority to appoint an IRO;

- the circumstances in which the local authority must consult with the IRO;

- the functions of the IRO both in relation to the reviewing and monitoring of each child's case; and

- the actions that the IRO must take if the local authority is failing to comply with the regulations or is in breach of its duties to the child in any material way, including making a referral to Cafcass.

    (DCSF, 2010d, pp7–8)

Leaving care

The Children Act 1989 requires local authorities to have mechanisms in place to support looked after children beyond the age of 18 years or who left care after turning 16 when the local authority no longer has parental responsibility for the child. The phrase used in the legislation is 'advise, befriend and assist'. Under the Children Act 1989 this responsibility occurs between the ages of 16 and 21. Generally, looked after children will become independent considerably earlier than children who are not in care. Many looked after children have vulnerabilities, which may well have affected their physical and mental health, as well as their educational achievements at GCSE and A level. The support offered by local authorities in line with the 1989 Act was not enough to ensure that young people were adequately supported through this transitional period to adulthood and independence. The DoH (1999b) publication *Me, survive, out there?* is one of a number of research studies showing the vulnerability of young people leaving the looked after system. Because of this inconsistency of provision across England and Wales, the Children (Leaving Care) Act 2000 introduced a number of changes to improve support to looked after children leaving care, up to the age of 24. Please refer to Chapter 12 for further information.

Children (Leaving Care) Act 2000

Under the Children (Leaving Care) Act 2000 (C(LC)A 2000) a local authority must provide personal and practical support (including accommodation and which can include cash) to their care leavers, and keep in touch with them until the age of 21. Care leavers must meet the criteria to receive leaving care support. They must be either 16 or 17 and have spent 13 weeks in care which started after their 14th birthday and ended after they reached the age of 16. Most care leavers are no longer able to claim welfare benefits – the local authority has to support them. Financial systems are administered by each social services department.

Additionally, a local authority also has duties to prepare eligible children for independence. This includes drawing up a pathway plan when the young person turns 16, which maps out a clear route to independence and covers areas such as education, health, accommodation, employment and any contingency plans. Personal advisers will co-ordinate these plans and work with young people throughout this transitionary period. This may include helping the young person find training, employment or education opportunities and acting as the 'connexions' adviser. The pathway plan must be kept under six-monthly review, and for education and training support, can go beyond the age of 21, to when the young person turns 24.

The local authority that is responsible for the pathway plan and associated support is the one who last looked after the young person. If the young person lives in a different area outside of the originating local authority's geographical boundaries, the new local authority is not responsible for the young person's support (Brammer, 2010; Brayne and Carr, 2010).

Adoption and Children Act 2002

This law reformed the Adoption Act 1976 and brought adoption into line with the principles contained in the Children Act 1989 (see above). The historical context of adoption and many other details of this Act are covered in Chapter 11.

In summary, the Adoption and Children Act 2002 introduces: placement orders (covering placement and consent); special guardianship; a number of other features of adoption, including who can adopt (lesbian and gay couples and unmarried couples can now jointly adopt); step-parent adoption; and provides the legislative underpinning for Adoption Panels, the Adoption Register and post-adoption support. There is more of an emphasis on the openness of adoption, as well as the adoption process, with courts obliged to consider contact arrangements (this falls short of a presumption of contact with adoption) and adopted adults being entitled to see their adoption records.

Statutory guidance for the Adoption and Children Act 2002 was updated in 2011 and this is important supplementary reading (DfE, 2011c).

Children Act 2004

This major piece of legislation emerged from the Green Paper *Every child matters* (DfES, 2003), which was the government's response to the public inquiry report into the death of Victoria Climbié in 2000. *Every child matters* introduced five key outcomes that should direct all work with children. These are:

- staying safe;
- being healthy;
- enjoying and achieving;
- making a positive contribution;
- achieving economic well-being.

These five outcomes are to be found in virtually all government documentation and guidance about children issued since the publication of *Every child matters* in September 2003. However, since the 2010 elections and change in government, little mention has been made about the five key outcomes. They remain current policy, but expect a change in this sometime over this parliamentary term.

The changes introduced by the Children Act 2004 are too numerous to cover in detail in this chapter, as this legislation underpins all work in children's services, across a multi-agency context and some changes are still being implemented at the time of writing. In summary, the main areas include: structural changes to the way in which children's services are organised (each local authority will have a director of children's services including education and social services, and a Lead Member Local Government Councillor for children's services) the appointment of a children's commissioner in England, Wales, Scotland and Northern Ireland; the establishment of Children and Young People's Plans; the inspection of children's services; information databases set up by children's services authorities which contain basic information about all children and young people living in a local authority area in England; statutory underpinning of integrated working across agencies and the Local Safeguarding Children Boards (replacing the Area Child Protection Committees or ACPCs). There is no specific reference to children's trusts in the Act – there is simply a duty to co-operate with relevant partners contained in s10. This can include pooling budgets.

In terms of specific changes for looked after children, the 2004 Act adds emphasis to a local authority's duty under section 22 of the Children Act 1989 to safeguard and promote the welfare of looked after children, to specifically include the duty to promote educational achievement of looked after children (Brammer, 2010). This will be further examined in Chapter 10.

Additional government guidance has also been published following the passing of the Children Act 2004, including the publication of a revised version of 'Working Together' in 2006 and 2010 and the introduction of a common core assessment tool for all agencies to use when assessing families.

The coalition government has published a consultation on statutory guidance to safeguard and promote the welfare of children, including draft guidance (DfE, 2012c). The consultation finishes in September 2012 and the DfE's intention is to produce a revised version of Working Together that is significantly slimmer than its predecessor and takes into account many of the recommendations of the Munro review (Munro, 2010a, 2010b and 2011).

Children and Young Persons Act 2008

The purpose of the Act is to reform the statutory framework for the care system in England and in Wales to ensure that children and young people receive high quality care and to drive improvements in the delivery of services focused on the needs of the child. Two of the main features of this Act are the attempts via legislation to improve the stability of placements and improve the educational experience and attainment of young people in local authority care or those about to leave care. This has implications for local authorities in developing appropriate policies and implementing these at a time where local authority resources are under considerable strain.

Some of the main provisions of the 2008 Act are as follows:

- Local authorities will be empowered to enter into arrangements with other bodies in the voluntary, private and not for profit sector in its discharge of its care functions, to enable regulation of these providers and to require them to be registered under Part 2 of the Care Standards Act 2000; but this does not include delegating such functions to other local authorities. A pilot scheme will be established to monitor how local authorities enter into arrangements with other bodies in respect of their care functions.

- Sufficient and appropriate accommodation for children will be secured in local authority care, which includes an emphasis on local placements.

- There is an amendment to the duties of IROs.

- The Act places a new duty on local authorities to appoint a representative to visit all looked after children, wherever they are living and provides a power to extend the duty to other groups of children who were looked after but have ceased to be so.

- It extends the duty on local authorities to appoint an independent person to visit, befriend and advise any looked after child if doing so is in the child's interests.

- There is an emphasis on education and training for children in care and young people who have recently left care.

- The Act requires local authorities to pay a bursary to a former relevant child who goes on to higher education.

- Individuals who are responsible for caring for disabled children can be assisted by being given breaks from their care duties.

- The rights of relatives who are entitled to apply for a residence order or a special guardianship order without leave of the court are now extended to include those with whom the child has lived for a continuous period of one year.

New Developments: Children and Families Bill 2013

This Bill was announced in the Queen's speech in May 2012. Through this legislation the government is planning to overhaul the SEN system and reduce delays in the family justice and adoption systems. In terms of the major provisions in the Bill that would have a direct effect on looked after children, the government has announced the following:

The Bill would introduce a single, simpler assessment process for children with SEN or disabilities, backed up by new Education, Health and Care Plans – part of the biggest reforms to SEN provision in 30 years.

It would speed up care proceedings in family courts so children do not face long and unnecessary hold ups in finding permanent, loving and stable homes – with the introduction of a new six-month time limit on cases and other reforms. Children currently wait an average of 55 weeks for court decisions.

It would include legislation to stop damaging delays by social workers in matching parents to ethnic minority children – black children already take 50 per cent longer to be adopted than white children or those of other ethnicities.

(www.education.gov.uk/inthenews/inthenews/a00208753/childrens-bill-family-support)

CHAPTER SUMMARY

A comprehensive understanding of the law and how it applies to practice is essential. The legal framework for social workers and others working with looked after children involves a working knowledge of five pieces of legislation: Children Act 1989; Children (Leaving Care) Act 2000; Adoption and Children Act 2002; Children Act 2004; and Children and Young Persons Act 2008; as well as keeping abreast of the latest in policy and guidance publications and case law which influences practice. There are a number of key terms which you should be familiar with, including: parental responsibility; significant harm; in the best interest of the child; welfare checklist; welfare principles; no order principle; and no delay principle. These are consistently found throughout these pieces of legislation.

CHAPTER SUMMARY *continued*

Finally, it is important to understand the respective roles of other legal agencies who may be involved in the lives of looked after children. These include: children's guardian; the official solicitor; and other Cafcass representatives.

FURTHER READING

Brammer, A (2010) *Social work law* (3rd edition) Harlow: Pearson Education Ltd.

This is one of two comprehensive textbooks on law for social workers currently available. This is written in an accessible style and contains a number of case studies to enable application of the law to practice. A companion website has also been developed to support the material in the book.

Brayne, H and Carr, H (2010) *Law for social workers* (10th edition) Oxford: Oxford University Press.

This is the second of the two comprehensive textbooks. This book also has many case studies and a companion website as an aid to learning.

Ministry of Justice, Department for Education and Welsh Government (2011) *Family Justice Review Final Report Nov 2011*. London: Crown Copyright. (Accessed at www.education.gov.uk/ publications/standard/publicationDetail/Page1/FJR-2011)

This publication is also known as the Norgrove Report and is a highly influential report arising from a review undertaken of work undertaken in family Courts.

Please read the Guidance for the Children Act 1989 and the Adoption and Children Act 2002 listed below. It is all available electronically at www.education.gov.uk:

- Children Act 1989 Guidance and Regulations Volume 1: Court Orders
- Children Act 1989 Guidance and Regulations Volume 2: Care Planning, Placements and Case Review
- Children Act 1989 Guidance and Regulations Volume 3: Planning Transition to Adulthood for Care Leavers
- Children Act 1989 Guidance and Regulations Volume 4: Fostering Services
- Children Act 1989 Guidance and Regulations Volume 5: Children's Homes
- Adoption and Children Act 2002: Adoption Statutory Guidance

Legislation

Adoption Act 1976

Adoption and Children Act 2002

Children Act 1989

Children Act 2004

Children and Young Persons Act 2008

Children (Leaving Care) Act 2000

Civil Partnership Act 2004

Local Authority Social Services Act 1970

Chapter 3
Pathways and placement types

Introduction

This chapter will examine the different pathways into care and the different types of placements children might be in while in care. Additionally, the national data set on looked after children will be introduced and discussed to show the national care context, patterns of placements and care pathways.

The Children Act 1989 is a critical piece of legislation, which applies to all children. Howard (2005, p36) comments:

> The Act's philosophy is that the best place for children to be brought up is within their own family and that children in need can be helped most effectively if the local authority, working in partnership with parents, provides an appropriate range and level of services.

Understanding the use of this legislation to balance the (sometimes competing) responsibilities of support and protection is important. The Children Act 1989 deals comprehensively with the protection of vulnerable children. It also enables children in need to receive supportive services from the state, while remaining with their families, with parents maintaining parental responsibility for their child if care is required for a short period of time, due to particular circumstances. However, Howard (2005, p23) comments:

> The new terms 'accommodation' and 'looked after' were created to emphasise the proposed partnership approach. Efforts were made to reframe accommodation in terms of working alongside parents, but it became clear that in effect, this was hard to achieve...it was commonly acknowledged that repeated episodes of accommodation led to a drift into long term care...

A more discerning examination is therefore required to understand the way this philosophy has been translated into practice. Even though technically the support services available under Part 3 of the Children Act are available to support children and their families who are in temporary difficult situations, local authority resources will play a big part in determining how this support is offered to individual families.

Why are children in care?

Provisions exist within the legislation for families to receive preventative support, which can include accommodation under section 20 of the Children Act and includes respite care for children with disabilities. However, the majority of children in care are in care because they and/or their families have serious problems, which cannot be resolved quickly within their families and communities. Many of these children have been vulnerable for a great many years prior to their experiences of care. Their families have often received many support services available in the community, and these services (for whatever reason) have not been able to adequately assist these families and children with the problems many of them face – hence the children's need for state care. We are still learning about the cause, effect and significance of the situations many of these children have experienced, and the long-term nature of the support and assistance required to move children on toward a different future. The evidence supports the analysis that poverty is a major factor in many cases. In this regard the government Green Paper, *Care matters* (DfES, 2006f), placed significant emphasis on preventative services as well as on ways in which outcomes could be improved for children in care. This was an ongoing theme over a number of years for the previous Labour government and policy-makers alike, as well as those undertaking research in this area. The coalition government is continuing this interest, with legislation planned within its first term. We will summarise some of the relevant research findings and policy ideas later in this chapter.

Pathways into care

There are two main pathways into public care. One route is via 'accommodation' under section 20 of the Children Act 1989, which is a voluntary arrangement made under Part 3 of the Children Act 1989 (Family Support and Prevention), between the local authority and a child's parent. Under this arrangement the parent retains parental responsibility for their child and they can ask their child to be returned to them at any time. The local authority does not have parental responsibility for the child and must liaise with the parent and work in partnership with those who have parental responsibility for the child to discuss and agree all matters to do with the child's welfare. This arrangement is also used for those children where there is no person with parental responsibility for the child; the child is lost or abandoned; or the person who has been caring for the child is prevented (for whatever reason and for however long) from providing suitable care or accommodation for the child. For example, unaccompanied children may be accommodated; children whose parent(s) have died and have no surviving relatives may also be accommodated; young people who are struggling whilst living at home during their teenage years for whatever reason and their parent(s) need support as the situation cannot be managed within their immediate family; and a parent may have a serious illness and be hospitalised for significant periods and there might not be family members who can care for the child(ren).

The second route is via court involvement, instigated under Part 4 of the Children Act 1989, where the child becomes subject to either an Emergency Protection Order (section 44 of the Children Act 1989); Interim Care Order (section 38 of the Children Act 1989); or a Care Order (section 31 of the Children Act 1989). In all of these options the local authority shares parental responsibility for the child with the parent as long as the order is in force. If a child enters care through this route the 'threshold criteria' must be met. These criteria are outlined in section 31(2) of the Children Act 1989: a court is only able to make a care order of a child *is suffering or is likely to suffer significant harm*. See Brammer (2010, pp252–9) for detailed explanations of these terms.

There is a third pathway into care, which is via the provision of Secure Accommodation (section 25 of the Children Act 1989). Apart from an overview of secure accommodation provided later in the chapter, this chapter will not explore this route in any significant detail, as knowledge of this area of social work falls within the areas of 'youth justice'. Please see Pickford and Dugmore (2012) for further information on this and many other aspects of social work and youth justice.

An application for a care order or secure accommodation is most often an indicator of extremely serious family problems for those children entering care. The parents of these children entering care are disproportionately more likely to have individual problems such as mental illness, learning difficulties or substance misuse problems. They are almost always also socially disadvantaged in some way, with most living in poverty. A significant proportion of children coming into care are from either one-parent or reconstituted families. By themselves, these factors do not create disadvantage; rather it is a cumulation of a number of different factors, most often including poverty, which tends to be significant. Many of the children entering care tend to have serious problems, including education and physical and mental health issues, and this may be part of the reason that a child enters care. Several of these issues are considered elsewhere in the book (see Chapter 9 for mental health issues and Chapter 10 for education and health issues).

Accommodation

The provision of 'accommodation' for a child on a voluntary basis is intended to be seen as a service to support parents. Section 20 (1) states that:

Every local authority shall provide accommodation for any child in need wit area who appears to them to require accommodation as a result of –

- *there being no person who has parental responsibility for him;*
- *his being lost or having been abandoned; or*
- *the person who has been caring for him being prevented (whether or not permanently and for whatever reason) from providing him with suitable accommodation or care. [The duty only arises if the child has nowhere else s/he can reasonably be looked after; parents cannot just expect the local authority to look after the child automatically.]*

While the main emphasis of section 20 is support and partnership with parent(s), children can also be removed from potentially harmful situations with parental consent. Real examples of this include: where a child protection investigation concerning an adult living at the child's address was in progress, and the social workers investigating the circumstances had concerns about the child's safety while remaining at home; a parent approached a local authority for support, saying her 14-year-old child was beyond her control; a parent with a terminal illness requested help in caring for her six-year-old and seven-year-old children, upon admittance to hospital. Section 20 accommodation only requires the consent of one parent. If the young person is over 16, then they can ask to be accommodated and parental consent is not required. The local authority has power to provide accommodation for children aged between 16 and 21 where this would safeguard and/or promote a child's welfare. For example, if a 16-year-old's family relationships had broken down to the extent that she/he had been 'kicked out' of home and there was little chance of immediate reunification, and there was nowhere within the extended family or friendship network where the young person could stay, then the local authority would need to consider whether the young person was 'in need' and, if so, what support they would require.

If anyone with parental responsibility for the child objects to a local authority providing accommodation, then the local authority may not provide it. The parent may remove the child from the accommodation provided by the local authority at any time (s20(8)). However, a balance should be struck between the benefit to the child in being removed from the placement against the likelihood that the parent will destabilise the placement if the child remains. If necessary, the local authority can consider care proceedings if the grounds exist for this course of action (Brayne and Carr, 2010). There may also be a number of preventative projects or services available within your local authority. Examples include: support care (Brown et al., 2005); and family group conferences (Lupton, 1998; Jackson and Morris, 1999; Brown, 2003).

RESEARCH SUMMARY

The evidence of the use of accommodation under section 20 of the Children Act as a support to families shows a conflicting picture. This service is not as supportive to parents as it might first appear. Donaldson (2006) found that the provision of accommodation was frequently used inappropriately. A substantial number of the children who were accommodated shared similar characteristics to those who were subject to care proceedings. Part of the 'misuse' of accommodation was also due to social workers not involving parents

Continued

appropriately in care planning; not communicating sufficiently with parents concerning long-term plans; and having unrealistic expectations about the level of parental change required. This also led to care proceedings being initiated regarding those children who were accommodated at the point at which parents tried to remove their children from accommodation. Donaldson argues that for many children the provision of accommodation became a precursor for legal involvement and this finding is replicated in other studies (Hunt et al., cited in Donaldson, 2006). Evidence also suggests that those children who are accommodated over a long period of time (more than two years) have poorer care planning processes in place than those children who are subject to care proceedings (Howard, 2005; Donaldson, 2006). Consequently they were more likely to suffer 'drift' within the care system than those children subject to care proceedings.

Work undertaken by Dickens, et al. (2007) and Schofield, et al. (2007) identifies a number of reasons for variance between 24 local authorities in the numbers of children starting to be looked after, and the care experiences of those children looked after for more than four years. These variances include: social deprivation factors within the specific local authorities; the type of departmental culture; local policies and operational processes; availability of preventative services; level of resources and staffing levels; and the style of staff attitudes. Schofield, et al. (2007) track the long-term care experiences of looked after children and young people in these 24 local authorities, through a number of different placements (foster family, residential care, adoption and birth family). The authors question central government-led performance indicators which rely on raw statistics. Instead they comment on the complexity of children's experiences in achieving stability and permanency. They emphasise that these more complex processes in the lived experiences of such children are not clearly reflected in performance management data, and consequently conclusions from the latter do not accurately capture the former (Littlechild, 2007, p594).

Care orders

A local authority can apply for an Emergency Protection Order, Interim Care Order or a Care Order if it believes that a child living in its area is suffering or is likely to suffer significant harm. The local authority has to show that its intervention in terms of gaining parental responsibility for the child, providing the child with a care plan, outlining where a child will live, making other support services available to the child, and providing permanence plans for the child (among other things) will safeguard the welfare of the child. This is known as the 'threshold criteria'.

Section 31 (2) of the Children Act 1989 states that:

(2) A court may only make a care or supervision order if it is satisfied –

(a) that the child concerned is suffering or is likely to suffer significant harm; and

(b) the harm/likelihood is attributable to –

(i) the care given to the child, or likely to be given to him, if the order were not made, not being what would be reasonable to expect a parent to give him; or

(ii) the child's being beyond parental control.

It is also important to note that an order will not be made unless there is a need for one. In other words, do you need an order if the parents are willing to co-operate? Social workers must also consider the no order principle (s(1)5) as well as the welfare checklist (s(1)3).

The Children Act 1989 does not define 'significant harm' even though this is the threshold for state involvement in private family matters. Brammer states:

> The Lord Chancellor described the criteria as the 'minimum circumstances which should always be found to exist before it can be justified for a court to even begin to contemplate whether the state should be enabled to intervene compulsorily in family life'. The phrase was intended to be broad and flexible in order to incorporate a wide range of circumstances; in fact it has caused major interpretational problems and a succession of case law decisions.
>
> (2010, p253)

Under s31 of the Children Act 1989, 'harm' is defined as 'ill treatment or impairment of health or development'; 'development' is described as 'physical, intellectual, emotional, social and behavioural; 'health' can be physical or mental; and 'ill treatment' includes the non-physical.

ACTIVITY 3.1

The use of s 20 Accommodation versus s 31 Care Orders (Children Act 1989)

On the basis of the material discussed above, make a list of the pros and cons for the child, for the parent and for the local authority of using section 20 Accommodation and section 31 Care Orders.

COMMENT

The exercise is designed to make you think about the differences between 'support' and 'protection' in terms of your legal responsibilities toward families and children, and the implications of these for your practice. Here are some of the differences in the use of the two pieces of legislation.

- *The local authority will share parental responsibility with the birth parents (section 31) or the local authority will not have parental responsibility – only the parent(s) will have this (section 20). Foster carers do not have parental responsibility for children under either of these legal options.*

- *Section 20 accommodation is a 'support' to parents and they can ask the local authority to provide accommodation for their child should they be unable to provide this within their existing extended family and community networks. If the local authority agrees to provide this service, the parents can ask for their child to be returned to them at any time.*

Secure accommodation

Occasionally it is necessary to restrict the liberty of children by placing them in secure accommodation. Under s 25(1) of the Children Act 1989 a child's liberty may not be restricted, even under a care order, unless the following criteria have been satisfied:

Either:

- *the child has a history of absconding and is likely to abscond from any other type of accommodation; and*
- *if he absconds, he is likely to suffer significant harm; or*
- *that if he is kept in any other description of accommodation he is likely to injure himself or other persons.*

This is a high standard. It is generally necessary for the social worker to show that the local authority has tried various other types of accommodation, and the child has either put themselves at risk by repeatedly absconding or they have caused or threatened significant harm to themselves or someone else in various settings.

The local authority can place a child they are looking after in secure accommodation for up to 72 hours on the authority of the Director of Children's Services; any further detention must be sanctioned by a court order.

The local authority must put evidence before the court of regular absconding from different types of local authority accommodation and the potential for suffering significant harm during his/her absconding (i.e. a habit of running away by itself is not enough).

A court will usually ask for reasons why a child cannot be held in a particular kind of accommodation. Secure accommodation is a last resort, when anything else would be too risky.

The welfare checklist does not apply in secure accommodation applications. However, the child must be legally represented, and a child's guardian should also be appointed (Brayne and Carr, 2010).

A secure order may not be made on a child under 13 unless the local authority has the consent of the Secretary of State for Health. It lasts for three months and may be extended by further applications for six-month periods – if it cannot be justified any longer then the local authority must place the child in open accommodation even before the order has lapsed (Brammer, 2010).

CASE STUDY

Pathway into care

You are allocated a family of four children: Martha, aged two; Cameron, aged four; Mary, aged seven; and Sean, aged nine. Martha and Mary are placed together in a foster placement and Cameron and Sean are in another foster placement seven miles away. The older two children are attending schools local to where they live, which are different schools to each other and different to the school they attended prior to coming into care. All four children are currently accommodated under section 20 of the Children Act

1989. Their mother is a drug user and six months ago she left the children in the care of their father, who is alcohol dependent. The children's father asked for the four of them to be accommodated after the first week as he could not cope. It is clear he cannot be considered as a carer for the children in the long term because of his alcohol dependency issues. Despite extensive searching for the children's mother, she cannot be located and has not been seen since she left the children with their father. The children's mother and father are both white Irish. The father is adamant he does not want his extended family or his partner's extended family involved in caring for these children. Your job is to put together a permanency plan for these children.

COMMENT

Consider the legal 'looked after' status of these children. In terms of putting together a care plan and a permanency plan for these children, what can you decide and arrange given these children are accommodated under section 20 of the Children Act and as such you do not have parental responsibility?

What are you unable to decide without parental permission? You will also need to understand the difference between a care plan and a permanency plan and the timescales for each – see Chapters 4 and 8 for further information. A permanency plan must be drawn up after the second statutory looked after review (fourth months following accommodation).

In terms of planning for the future for these children, you will need to have different plans – one for each child. You might also consider the options within each plan and associated timescales, depending on whether you manage to find the children's mother and identify her wishes in respect of the children's futures, as well as talking with the children's father. In terms of long(er)-term planning, think about whether all four children need to be placed together (this would be the preferred option, but is not always possible) or whether the sibling group should be separated because of the particular needs of individual children or to enhance the likelihood of obtaining permanency more quickly for the children (see Fahlberg, 1994). This is known as a 'together or apart' assessment. These are tough decisions and there are other professionals who can assist, in terms of assessing sibling relationships (e.g. CAMHS services; National and Specialist Adoption and Fostering Clinic at the Maudsley Hospital, London). You will also need to become familiar with the process of family finding for the children, as other people will also be involved in working with you and the children (e.g. fostering services).

National English Data on 'looked after children'

The National (English) Data is data collected by the DCSF from the 150 local authorities in England on a variety of areas concerned with looked after children. This is based on a return supplied by all local authorities in England called the SSDA903. Similar data are collected in Scotland, Wales and Northern Ireland. Additional data are collected from local authorities via the children in need census and the social services performance indicators. This forms part of the quality monitoring and reporting processes used to determine the star ratings of councils across England.

In examining this data set for 'looked after children', it is clear that these children are not a homogenous group. On 31 March 2011, 65,520 children were in state care. Of this number, 56% were male, 44% were female. This percentage has remained fairly constant since 2002. Of the total number of children in care, 76% were aged ten or older (up from 58% in 2002), 24% were aged four or under; 74% were in foster placements (up from 66% in 2002). Of the 5,680 looked after children eligible to sit GCSEs during 2010/2011, 13.2% achieved 5 A*–C GCSEs including English and Maths, compared to 57.9% of the general population. 31.5% achieved 5 A*–C GCSEs, compared to 78.1% of the general population. However, in order to contextualise these education data, two things need to be taken into account.

First, the length of time children spend in care is important. There is a great deal of movement within the care population over a year, and those children who spend more than two years in care are a small minority of the overall number of children in care at any one time. In any given year, up to 40% of the children who come into care will only do so for a number of weeks or months and will return home within six months. In addition to this, in 2011 4.7% of children were adopted, with a further 3.7% placed for adoption. Finally, 15% of this number left care aged 16 or older.

Of the total number in care at 31 March 2011, 30% (or 20,000 children) had been looked after for at least two and a half years, with 69% of this number, or 13,770 children in the same placement for the preceding two years, or placed for adoption (DfES/ONS, 2011). It is these 20,000 children who Bullock, et al. (2006) regard as *growing up in care*. Many of these children come into care when they are older, having experienced abuse and neglect prior to entering care. Those children who are older have an increased likelihood of having long-standing physical and/or mental health issue(s), including learning disabilities. For these children, it follows that their educational achievements will be disrupted, and/or they will be performing well below the average of their peers. These patterns will already be in place at the point at which a child becomes looked after. Chapter 10 examines education and health issues for looked after children and Chapter 9 examines mental health issues.

Behind these facts and figures which highlight national trends and averages, there is a great deal of variation in the figures and performances of individual councils. Dickens, et al. (2007, p600) believe that *underlying need has been shown to account for some but not all of the variation between authorities*. Dickens, et al. (2007) mention the role of the York index as a *measure of social deprivation in relation to children's social services*. There are five socio-economic variables used to identify deprivation: families receiving income support; families where illness or disability is long-term; families living in flats; single-parent families; and population density. While these are a relatively poor indicator of rates of children becoming looked after, they are a *better guide to the number looked after at 31st March each year* (Dickens, et al., 2007, p600).

Placements

Looked after children are placed in a number of different settings. The majority of children are cared for in foster placements. However, 6% of children are placed at home with parents; a further 9% are in residential children's homes, including secure units; a further 3% are in residential schools, lodgings and other residential settings; while 4% are placed for adoption. The DfE (2011h) state that of the 20,000 children under 16 who have been looked after for two and a half or more years (those in long-term care), 67% had been living in the same placement for the last year. Placements are used differently depending on the age and the issues the child brings with them into the care system. Even though there is evidence emerging about the different outcomes that children in long-term care (over two and a half years) achieve in different placements (Sinclair, 2005), this relationship is complex and it is unreliable to causally link placement choice and outcome for the child.

Types of placement

Section 23 of the Children Act 1989 states that every local authority has a duty to provide accommodation and to maintain looked after children. One of the important decisions social workers will be involved in is identifying the type of placement the child may need, and then, where possible, matching the child with the appropriate placement. The local authority can place children with family members or relatives (kinship care), or any other suitable person (e.g. foster carers or a residential children's home) and can pay them a boarding-out allowance but the local authority cannot pay the child's parent for caring for them. Ideally the placement should be as near to the home of the child as possible.

Any placement is subject to complying with regulations, which are too detailed to list here, and each child is subject to regular reviews using the 'Looked After Children' (LAC) documentation. These two review processes are dictated by two different sources of guidance. The first is the LAC guidance mentioned above, and the looked after children reviews have been covered in detail in another chapter (Chapter 4 has further information). The second is the Fostering Services Regulations (DfE, 2011d) and National Minimum Standards (DfE, 2011f) applicable to fostering services. Together, these regulations and standards form the basis of the regulatory framework under the Care Standards Act 2000 (CSA) for fostering services. The important thing is that reviews need to happen regularly in accordance with the published regulations and guidance and need to involve the child, carers, parents and all other professionals who are involved in working with the child. These looked after children reviews are the basis for care planning for children, and are where many important decisions are made about future plans for children, including permanency planning. The first review for any child looked after (including accommodated children and children who are subject to care proceedings) should take place in the first month of the child being in care; the second should take place after a further three months; and then each review should take place at six-monthly intervals from that point onwards. A permanence plan should be written and agreed at the second review.

Foster care

Foster care has been practised in the UK for many decades. Foster care includes a variety of different kinds of placements.

- **Emergency placements** These are placements to which children or young people are moved with very little or no notice and preparation because of an emergency. Often there is not much knowledge available for the child or family about the foster carers and there is not a lot known about the child in terms of their care, support, health and education needs to pass on to the foster carers. These placements are usually very short term (a matter of days or weeks) while another placement is identified. Most local authorities have a number of specifically identified foster carers who are emergency carers.

- **Short-term placements** These are foster placements which are not long term or permanent. Children can move to a short-term placement in a planned way, and the way in which this is negotiated with the child and parent(s) has an effect on the success of the placement (Sinclair, 2005). The irony is that often short-term placements last many years while permanency plans are enacted.

- **Respite care** A number of children require support whilst remaining living at home with their parents. Respite care involves children staying with another family or at a residential facility on what is often a regular basis (e.g. over a weekend – this might be once a month or three times a year) in order to give the child and adults break time. These are situations where a package has been negotiated to support parents continuing to care for their child. Some respite care arrangements will involve children being accommodated under section 20 of the Children Act 1989. This type of care is often provided to children who have disabilities, but can also be used with parents who require other kinds of support in parenting their children, including foster carers and adopters. The support care initiative (Brown, et al., 2005) shows how a number of local authorities use this kind of care in practice.

- **Long-term placements** Identifying permanency in placements is high on the agenda for children and young people in terms of what matters to them when they cannot return to their birth families (Sinclair, 2005). A number of children will be adopted and will leave the care system at that point. However, the majority of children who are adopted are young (under five), with a number of children aged between five and ten also placed with adoptive families. Other children will be placed with relatives on a permanent basis. However, there are a number of children, mostly older, who do not wish to be adopted and extended family members are not able to help with their care on a permanent basis. This is where placements with foster carers which are identified as long term can be helpful in providing permanency for children and young people. Such placements can involve continued contact with parents and siblings and there is also provision for 'special guardianship'. See Chapter 11 for further information. Fahlberg (1994, p249) comments:

  In assessing the various options for permanent placement, special attention must be paid to commitment and flexibility. Commitment reflects the adults' interest and willingness to be available to meet the child's needs, while flexibility refers to the ability to respond to changes in the situation...these factors need to be assessed in terms of what people say, what they do and what they have said and done in the past.

- **In-house foster care provision** This is another name given to the fostering services provided by individual local authorities, and will often be the first place social workers in that borough will refer to, should they need a family placement for a child. Fostering social workers undertake a variety of work, including: assessment of prospective carers; running campaigns to recruit carers; providing ongoing training, supervision and support; reviewing foster carers as required by national fostering guidance and regulations; organising and overseeing the placement of children in foster care (emergency, short-term and long term).

- **Independent fostering agency provision** There are many independent fostering agencies that are not run by local authorities that recruit, assess, supervise and support foster carers to looked after children. The majority of these agencies are run for profit, and charge fees that are higher than the local authority would pay to use its in-house fostering resources. Local authorities use these agencies because there is a shortage of foster carers nationally and often there are not enough carers within their in-house provision to care for the numbers of children requiring placements. Local authorities might also use independent fostering agencies for children with specific needs that their in-house provision cannot meet. Often the support available to foster carers in independent agencies is more comprehensive (for example, they are provided with 24-hour support; foster children may have access to therapeutic support made available by the independent agency, which is included in the fees paid by the local authority), which means that foster carers working for independent agencies are able to work with children with quite challenging needs.

Other types of foster placements emerging include the following:

- **Remand foster care** Remand fostering provides short-term care for young people awaiting sentencing in youth justice courts. The foster carers involved have received specialist training and work in close partnership with youth offending teams and the courts (NACRO, 2004).

- **Multidimensional treatment foster care** This approach was developed in the USA as an alternative to residential treatment for adolescents with complex needs and challenging behaviour (including offending behaviour). In the UK the previous Labour government piloted this approach for use with adolescents and a second approach, working with young children aged three to six years, focused on prevention.

The foster carers and the biological (or adoptive) parents involved in the programme receive parenting training, which emphasises the use of behaviour management methods in order to provide a structured and a therapeutic living environment. The carers also have access to a single multi-disciplinary team, providing a combination of mental health, education and social support services. Specific treatment approaches are used, including cognitive, behavioural and family therapies. Treatment foster care is viewed as a cost-effective alternative to residential care (Roberts, et al., 2005; DCSF, 2007b; Roberts, 2007; Holmes, et al., 2008).

Residential care

For many years, residential care has been viewed as a last resort for children entering care because of the high-profile inquiries and investigations into abuse and neglect within children's homes throughout the UK. These included: the Waterhouse inquiry, which investigated abuse in Welsh children's homes in the 1970s and 1980s, published in 2000; and the Pindown inquiry published in 1991 (Levy and Kahan, 1991), investigating conditions in a number of Staffordshire children's homes in the 1980s. However, foster care is not appropriate for all children, as some children cannot live within families due to their own experience of dysfunctional family life. There are strengths in identifying residential care as an option for those children who cannot live within families Scottish Institute for Residential Child Care (SIRCC), 2006; Smith, 2009). Clough, et al. (2006) believe that effective residential child care can be achieved with good knowledge, appropriate processes and best practice. They emphasise the importance of correctly assessing the needs of young people and matching these to placements.

The Waterhouse Report comments that all *residential placements should be designed to be developmental and therapeutic rather than merely custodial* (2000, p856). In England there are a number of well-established therapeutic communities such as Childhood First and the Caldecott Foundation that have psychosocial or psychotherapeutic approaches to caring for vulnerable children in residential settings. Please see the websites of these two organisations listed at the end of this chapter for further information. Residential care often deals with young people who are in crisis, have a variety of complex needs and have often experienced several placement moves. While suggesting that the outcomes for these children are often perceived as negative, these 'challenges' to good quality residential care – *high levels of behavioral problems, further placement instability, and the poor education and health outcomes that have been the focus of recent concern, and the continuing personal and social difficulties faced by those young people who become care-leavers* (SIRCC, 2006, piv) – are challenges to quality care for all looked after children. Residential care remains an important and valuable placement option for some looked after children.

Kinship care/family and friends

At the point where it becomes necessary to remove a child from his or her immediate family, kinship care should always be considered. The variety of cultural practices within many communities throughout the world demonstrates that children are routinely placed within extended family placements during times of crisis as well as other circumstances without necessarily involving state services. Fahlberg (1994) highlights the value of this kind of placement for the child, especially in emergency situations, in terms of continuity of care, identity, attachments, and maintaining ongoing contact with significant others. Fahlberg also argues that *social workers should be aware of some of the possible pitfalls of such placements* (1994, p258), including: the parents believing the relatives are conspiring against them; the family dysfunction being more widespread within the extended family; and change in family relationships (the example she gives is grandparents needing to become parents in their 'new' role) (p259).

Home with parents

A number of children who are subject to a Care Order under section 31 of the Children Act 1989 are placed at home with their parents. Under this arrangement the local authority shares parental responsibility with parents.

Other

- **Boarding schools** There are a number of boarding schools which provide education provision for vulnerable children who may have challenging behaviour. Some boarding schools offer 52-week placements while others offer school term-time accommodation only.

People and agencies involved

There are a number of different people involved in the processes and decisions to place children in any given placement. These include social workers, social work managers, commissioners, legal departments, parents, children's guardians and the courts. Sinclair (2005, p59) comments that:

> These parties have different interests, do not necessarily agree and have varying degrees of experience of the system. The criteria against which decisions are made are loose and rarely written down. Plans change in response to shortages of resources and the actions of individuals. The meetings at which plans are 'firmed up' are not easy for children and parents…many decisions are made at short notice, as a matter of emergency and in a highly charged atmosphere.

What is clear from the research review undertaken by Sinclair (2005) is that the way in which placements were made and how involved children, young people and parents are in the planning of these placements makes a difference to the outcome of the placement. Placement choice is a complex process and should not be understood simplistically. He comments:

> Long-term placements face problems associated with undue delay, shorter-term ones are troubled first by rush and then by the difficulties of children overstaying their welcome as suitable longer-term placements are sought. There are genuine balances to be struck between waiting for the perfect match and losing a reasonable chance of permanence. Nevertheless improvements may be possible.

(Sinclair, 2005, pp64–5)

Commissioning

Each local authority has to plan and commission services for the looked after children it is responsible for. Many local authorities now have 'commissioning' and 'providing' elements in terms of the way in which their business and services are organised. They employ commissioners, brokers and contract officers to assist social workers in identifying suitable placements for children. They may have 'preferred providers' in the independent and voluntary sector. They may have commissioned 'block' services, such as respite care from particular providers.

Commissioning is one way that local authorities quality assures placements used (Hafford-Letchfield, 2007). Commissioned services are quality checked – service specifications and contracts should define the nature and standards of service provision – feedback from service users, social workers, and contract monitoring officers provides information to monitor and check the quality of services. Commissioned services also need to be assessed as providing the council with 'best value' for its money in terms of the resources being purchased for the child. 'Best value' should encompass quality and cost factors (i.e. not only the cheapest available). Commissioning is a significant means whereby the local authority ensures that the resources that it has go as far as possible, particularly when there is a high level of demand to be met within limited resources. Consequently, the requirements of local commissioning practice and cost effectiveness may affect the choice of placements available for a social worker to match against a child's needs.

When purchasing a service for a child, the social worker, or anyone involved in commissioning the service, should look at the relevant inspection reports from the regulatory authority. These are now available online from Ofsted (www.ofsted.gov.uk). Both 'in-house' local authority services as well as independent and voluntary sector services are subject to the same inspection and regulation regimes, whether fostering, adoption, residential, or respite services. The inspections are recorded, services are assessed and graded against clear performance standards, and the resulting reports are public documents. (It is worth noting that, if you have concerns about any service that is being provided for a child, there is an external regulatory body that you can raise these concerns with, as well as your own agency.)

Contact

There is a presumption of contact between children and their families of origin for all children who are in care. Research evidence shows that there are better outcomes for children if this occurs (Thoburn, 1994). The frequency of contact will be determined by the age of the child and the child's wishes and feelings, among other factors covered in an assessment relating to the relationship between the parent and child. Section 34 of the Children Act 1989 provides the necessary mandate for the court to deal with issues of parental contact. If an application has been refused by the court, then the applicant cannot reapply for six months. If a child has had infrequent communication with members of his or her birth family, the local authority should appoint an independent visitor to advise, assist and befriend the looked after child (paragraph 17 of Schedule 2 to the Act). This is a service which is relatively underused by many local authorities. Section 16 of the CYPA 2008 extended the group of looked after children for whom an independent visitor must be appointed, to include all children for whom such a visitor would be in their best interests (Brammer, 2010, p303).

CASE STUDY

Your manager gives you a piece of duty work to do. Two siblings, of mixed parentage (white Scottish and African–Caribbean), Chanelle aged six and Leisha aged four, were taken into care via an Emergency Protection Order just over a week ago. The local authority has successfully obtained an Interim Care Order today. However, the emergency foster carer cannot keep the children and they must be moved from the placement by this evening at the latest. You know from your work on duty that there are currently no foster placements available 'in-house', as another colleague has been searching for a placement for these siblings earlier in the week. Her advice is to now use an independent fostering agency placement. You ring the fostering team again, and are told that the placement situation has not changed, and is not likely to in the short term. You therefore begin to fill in the necessary paperwork for an independent fostering placement. This would ordinarily go to a divisional panel in order to obtain funding but due to the short time scale, you will have to present your case to the Head of Service to obtain interim funding. After the fostering team contacts an independent agency and finds an appropriate match, you present your case and rationale to the Head of Service who tells you that she will agree the placement on a short-term basis only, until such time as an in-house placement becomes available and the children will then have to move to the in-house placement.

Discuss the ethical issues arising in this case.

COMMENT

One of the main questions to emerge here is whether it is right that children are moved from their placement solely on grounds of cost to the local authority. You have to weigh up your responsibilities toward your clients, your professional ethical codes of conduct and your employer's wishes concerning your actions. Whilst limited resources may well be a significant factor for the local authority concerned, and should not be negated, the court will also have a view on these children moving placements without due regard to the effect this move will have on the children, as will the child's guardian. In order to limit the effect of multiple placement moves on the two children, who, because of their age, are likely to be significantly affected by two, possibly three, moves in quick succession, this may give you some leverage with your Head of Service concerning the timeframe for the children moving placements. If the children were to move again, it would be important that the next move would be the last move for a considerable period of time. You would also consider whether any kinship placements might be viable.

You are the allocated social worker for Simon, aged ten, whose placement with foster carers has just broken down. This placement was a long-term one where he and his older sister, Rachel, aged 12, had lived for two and a half years. Prior to this placement both children had lived in a small specialist children's home for two years. Both children have histories of severe neglect and sexual abuse. They came into care with significant difficulties arising from these experiences and after a psychiatric assessment the care plan involved both children living in a residential placement as the psychiatrist's advice was that the children's experiences of family life had been so damaging that at this point they could not function in a family environment. During their time in the residential placement, both children received significant therapy and support to enable them to move on to a long-term specialist foster placement at the end of the two-year period. Rachel's placement with these carers broke down a year before Simon's and she has moved on to another foster placement, where she is doing reasonably well. Simon's needs are so significant that you are considering another residential placement for him. He finds all peer and adult relationships difficult, and he needs constant supervision and guidance. Simon has a Statement of SEN and attends a special school.

What kind of residential or foster placement would you look for?

This is one case where you might ask for a specialist's view, in terms of looking at the various options you have for a long-term placement for Simon. In considering Simon's needs, a specialist therapeutic placement might provide him with the day-to-day therapeutic support he may need to make sense of the world around him and his difficult life journey and experiences to date. You would need to hold a disruption meeting with the foster carers and Simon to understand what went wrong in the long-term foster placement in order to plan effectively for his future in terms of matching his needs with his next placement. Simon should be involved in this as much as possible, according to his level of understanding. It would also be good practice to involve Simon's parents in the decisions that are made about Simon.

This chapter reviewed the legislative framework regarding pathways into care. The national data set on looked after children provided an overview of the national care context, patterns of placements and care pathways. This chapter has described the variety of types of placements children might be in while in care. The case study work allowed you to consider some of the complex issues arising when considering the options available for individual children. Finally we looked at the role of commissioning and regulation in this area.

On youth justice issues:

Pickford, J and Dugmore, P (2012) *Youth justice and social work* (2nd edition). Exeter: Learning Matters/Sage.

This book gives a general overview of youth justice and issues for social work practice.

On legal issues:

Brammer, A (2010) *Social work law* (3rd edition). Harlow: Pearson Education.

This textbook provides a comprehensive overview of the law as it pertains to social work. It is written in an accessible style and contains a number of case studies to enable application of the law to practice. A companion website has also been developed to support the material in the book.

The Fostering Network **www.fostering.net**

The British Association for Adoption and Fostering (BAAF) **www.baaf.org.uk**

Caldecott Foundation **www.thecaldecottfoundation.co.uk**

Childhood First **www.childhoodfirst.org.uk**

East Sussex County Council Fostering website: **www.eastsussex.gov.uk/childrenandfamilies/ childrenincare/fostering/default.htm**

Norfolk County Council Fostering website: **www.norfolk.gov.uk/Childrens_services/Adoption_ and_fostering/Fostering/index.htm**

Ofsted: **www.ofsted.gov.uk**

Tameside Council's Fostering website: **www.tameside.gov.uk/fostering**

The Centre for Excellence for Looked After Children in Scotland: **www.celcis.org**

Chapter 4
Assessment, care planning and contact

Introduction

This chapter follows on from Chapter 3, 'Pathways and placement types' and also links with Chapter 2, where we discussed the legal framework. The previous chapter describes how children become looked after either through voluntary accommodation or through care proceedings. There are specific requirements in relation to young people who are placed in secure accommodation where there is a restriction of liberty and freedom of movement. Section 25 of the Children Act 1989 gives details of when a child can be placed in secure accommodation and the regulations pertaining to looked after children. It is stated that looked after children can only be placed in secure accommodation by a local authority for a limited period; that means for no longer than 72 hours in a 28-day time period without referring the matter back to court (Brayne and Carr 2010; Johns, 2011). Further details regarding secure accommodation and youth justice can be found in Pickford and Dugmore (2012, Chapter 4). Whatever the route to becoming looked after, all children will require you, as their social worker, to undertake three key processes: assessment of their needs; care planning; and implementing plans in relation to contact. In this chapter we will explore the links between these processes, the tools that are available to help you undertake these tasks, and the underpinning theoretical models that will help to ensure that your focus remains on the individual child. This chapter will also discuss the connections between assessment, care planning and the promotion of placement stability.

Although there is great variation in the care histories and specific needs of children who become looked after, every child who enters care will be subject to a prescribed set of processes for care planning and reviewing their present and future care needs. This includes considering the child's immediate needs and also considering plans for their long-term care. By the four-month review there is a statutory requirement to consider permanence for the looked after child. This might be working towards returning the child to live with their family, or extended family or may mean looking for carers outside the family. Overall, when a child becomes looked after the local authority has a duty, as a corporate parent, to safeguard and promote the child's welfare.

Revised care planning, placement and case review regulations were issued in 2010 and the accompanying guidance (DCSF, 2010b) brings together in a single suite of documents the regulations; see Volume 2. The duties listed below are described as being *at the heart of effective corporate parenting* (DCSF, 2010b, p2) and are directly linked to improving outcomes by:

- placing the child at the centre of the work;

- effective care planning;

- ensuring that a child or young person is provided with accommodation which meets his/her needs; and

- ensuring that an effective review is conducted of the child's case within the specified timescales. (DCSF, 2010b, p2)

As stated in Chapter 12, updated guidance has also been published in relation to care leavers, see Volume 3 (DfE, 2010), and in relation to fostering, see Volume 4 (DfE, 2011d), with Volume 5 related to children's homes regulations (DfE, 2011i). New guidance has also been issued in relation to the work of IROs who hold a very important role in monitoring the local authority's responsibilities for looked after children (DCSF, 2010d). The guidance describes how *the intention is to enable the IRO to have an effective and independent oversight of the child's case to ensure that the care plan represents an effective response to the assessed needs of the child and that progress is being made towards achieving the identified outcomes* (DCSF, 2010a, p15).

Assessment is the first part of the care planning process and often the first point of contact between clients and their social worker, making it a central activity in social work practice with all client groups. Knowledge gained from undertaking an assessment forms the foundation of decisions and plans that are made about individual children's needs and how best they can be met. You may be drawing on previous assessments where issues of significant harm were identified and you are likely also to be drawing on assessments undertaken by other professionals. Knowledge of child development, attachment theory and the impact of poor parenting on children's emotional and social development should be central to your practice. This will help you in working directly with the child, their parents and foster carers using a relationship-based approach to practice (Wilson, et al. 2011, Chapter 16). However, you will realise from reading Chapter 3 that it is not always possible to undertake comprehensive assessments prior to children becoming looked after as they may become looked after following an unforeseen emergency. The numbers of children who are looked after is collected annually (see Chapter 1) and over the past four years these numbers have increased. This has in turn provoked debate about whether children are coming into care too quickly or whether in the past children were left for too long with abusive families. This has in part been linked to high profile media reporting and the 'blaming' and targeting of social workers following the death of Peter Connolly (Garrett, 2009). However, research undertaken by Cafcass (2011) *'The Baby Peter effect and the increase in s31 care order applications'*, and by Masson, et al. (2008) shows that applications to court should, in some cases, have been made earlier and that others came to the court system at the correct time. Full details of the specific regulations and procedures in relation to care planning processes, what they are, when the work should be undertaken and what the specific requirements are for children in a variety of different circumstances can be accessed from the DfE publications which are listed at the end of this chapter alongside the weblink. This chapter also examines some of the challenges involved, how social workers might respond to these challenges, and what the impact is on children when there are problems in care planning. There is then a discussion about contact, its purpose, the process for organising contact and issues arising from this part of the process.

The policy framework

A key concern in policy and practice for looked after children is placement stability. This issue was highlighted by the Social Exclusion Unit Report (2003) on educational opportunities for children in care, by research studies examining performance management data and placement stability (Ward and Skuse, 2001) and in *Care matters* (DfES, 2006f) and the subsequent White Paper, *Care matters: Time for change* (DfES, 2007). Placement stability remains a performance target for local authorities and is described as being key to ensuring children have a positive experience of care where they are given the same opportunities which are available to all children. Concerns about placement stability are focused on how important it is for all children to experience secure relationships and consistent care with loving, affectionate carers (Richardson and Joughin, 2000; Schofield, et al., 2000). Crawford and Walker (2007) discuss this in relation to developing attachments and highlight how *the relationships we develop and form with others, especially caregivers, are central to our emotional and social security* (p43). Following on from this, the social work role supports the emotional and social development of children through delivering high-quality assessment and care planning processes. Holland, et al. (2005, p37) identify this as a key component of the promotion of placement stability:

Respondents…noted that good quality social work, in the form of well-executed assessments and plans and skilled listening to children, was one of the most important ways of promoting stable placements.

In undertaking assessments and care plans you will be required to develop a relationship with the child and his/her family and carers using your communication skills and theories of emotional development to inform your interventions. You will also be required to adhere to legal processes and complete assessments and care plans within prescribed timescales (see Chapter 2). We will consider the impact of delay and poor decision-making below in the section on care planning.

RESEARCH SUMMARY

Assessment models

Before going on to discuss the specific features of assessment of the needs of looked after children, we review some relevant assessment models. Smale, et al. (1993) developed a model showing three different assessment types. The first is the 'questioning' model where the social worker, in the role of an 'expert,' shares minimal power with the client. The second focuses on a 'procedural' approach, which concentrates on ensuring key processes are followed, with less focus on examining issues in depth, for example the Framework for assessment of children in need and their families (DoH, 2000a). This approach favours the use of standardised assessment tools and systematic data collection. The third is described as an 'exchange' model, where power between the professional social worker and client is more balanced: clients are viewed as experts in terms of identifying their own particular needs. The exchange model encourages full participation of all parties in decision-making. Although it has traditionally featured in care management within adult social services, key features of empowerment and participation can be incorporated into working with looked after children.

Assessment models developed by Milner and O'Byrne (2002) and Parker and Bradley (2003) share common themes and processes, which highlight the different stages of an assessment. However, assessments are not necessarily sequential and in undertaking assessments you will have to constantly reassess and weigh up the information you have. Coulshed and Orme use the acronym 'CORE' to identify the core skills in assessment: communication, observation, reflection and evaluation (Coulshed and Orme, 2006, p25). They identify two theoretical approaches to assessment: positivist and constructivist, which can be linked to debates about whether social work is an art or science or a combination of the two (see Trinder, 1996; Webb, 2001). They suggest that the positivist approach is based on a diagnostic medical model whereas the constructivist approach is identified as being more reflective and accepts that there are no 'absolute' truths or certainties (Coulshed and Orme, 2006, p29).

In preparing to undertake an assessment of a looked after child you should have developed an understanding of different assessment models and their theoretical underpinnings as this will help you to plan and consider the following stages:

- *Preparation, planning and engagement.*

- *Data collection and creating a problem profile.*

- *Preliminary analysis of data.*

- *Testing the data, deep analysis.*

- *Use of data, creating an action plan.*

  (Parker and Bradley, 2003, p16)

Assessment and looked after children

All assessments require a focus on the service user's needs, presenting problems, a consideration of possible risk factors and an awareness that service users may sometimes be reluctant to give you information about problems they are experiencing. There may be deliberate concealment of critical information by adults, as in the case of many child-abuse inquiries (Reder and Duncan, 1999; Laming, 2003) or children may themselves be reluctant to discuss their personal history. It may be that they have told their story to previous social workers, who then left the authority, leaving them cautious about trusting new adults with their story. It may therefore take time for you to build a relationship with a child. Other children may have had previously harrowing experiences of loss and separation or faced the trauma of war, such as unaccompanied asylum-seeking children (Kohli, 2007). This area of practice is explored in Chapter 6.

Assessing looked after children involves collecting and analysing information about the child, including: their age; gender; developmental stage; ethnicity and faith; family history; significant relationships; education; plus their physical and emotional health. Careful planning, meticulous record keeping, consultation and liaison with other professionals, working in partnership with parents and ensuring that the child's views are elicited are integral to this process. If there are previous files you will have to read them and write a summary of key events. An ecomap or a genogram, showing important relationships and systems surrounding the child, can help to reveal family patterns across generations (Parker and Bradley, 2003, Chapter 2). They can also act as a powerful therapeutic tool, potentially uncovering the *family's unwritten rules, myths, secrets and taboos* (Coulshed and Orme, 2006, p204).

CASE STUDY

You are the allocated social worker for four children: Karen, 13 years old, John, 12 years old, Robert, 9 years old, and Amy, who is 7 years old, who live with their mother, Monica Edwards. The parents are separated but their father (Jeff) remains in contact with his family. He sees the children when he can, although he lives some distance away and is a long-distance lorry driver. The family have received a service from your office for some years as Monica has mental health difficulties (episodes of severe depressive illness) and has spent periods of time in the past as an in-patient in a psychiatric hospital. There has

CASE STUDY continued

been a recent mental health assessment and you have been informed that Monica is very unwell and needs to go into hospital as an in-patient. You have already completed core assessments on the four children, where you identified concerns about Monica's parenting capacity when unwell (DoH, 2000a, 2000b).

ACTIVITY 4.1

What action would you need to take if the children's father was unable to care for the children while their mother was in hospital?

What do you think might be an appropriate placement for the children?

COMMENT

If the children's father was unable to care for the children you would discuss other possible placement options within the family and friends (kinship network). If this was not possible then you may have to seek parental consent in order to accommodate the children under section 20 of the Children Act 1989.

You probably agree that if the children cannot be cared for within their family networks then the most appropriate placement would be with a local foster carer who could look after all of the children. If the children are placed with foster carers then the carers will have been fully assessed and will be subject to ongoing checks as part of the placement process.

In order to monitor and support the children while they are placed in foster care you will be required to undertake statutory reviews and plan and implement contact arrangements.

Completing assessments will help you to formulate decisions and construct care plans. If at some stage you go to court with a case, the written assessment records will form part of your evidence. In court, your work will be subject to scrutiny by a judge or magistrates, children's guardian, lawyers and possibly expert witnesses (Dickens, 2006, p24). It is therefore critical that you approach the assessment and planning processes methodically, that you use analytic skills to link key facts and events, look for patterns or reoccurring incidents and show that you reassess the care plan in the light of new information. Assessment is therefore an iterative process and not a one-off event; one where you are required to reflect and test emerging hypotheses. Brown and Rutter (2006) argue that it is helpful to consider how the processes involved in academic writing can be transferred to the task of writing assessments and reports. They suggest that *we learn more while we are writing as the process supports and develops reflective and critical abilities* (Brown and Rutter, 2006, p24). Therefore the skills you have gained in writing academic essays can be utilised in writing high-quality assessments, where knowledge can be clarified, key concepts linked and arguments presented coherently. This process, involving critical reflection, will mean that your assessments will require revisions and redrafts as new information becomes available.

Throughout your assessment the child should be held at the centre of your thinking. Theories of child development, attachment, loss and resilience will help you to understand the child's needs and perspective and will locate your assessment and care plans within a theoretical framework (Fahlberg, 1994; Crawford and Walker, 2007; Schofield, 2003). The importance of attending to the legal and procedural aspects of working with looked after children and retaining a focus on the emotional needs of the child is essential; but as Cooper states, *one of the hardest things to achieve* (Cooper, 2000, p3). He describes the tensions and dilemmas of being caught up in the vital aspects of planning meetings, conferences and writing reports, whilst balancing all this with the need to consider the everyday, emotional needs of the child.

Although looked after children share many of the same needs as children living with their own birth families, they will certainly have additional needs due to their adverse pre-care experiences (Dimigen, et al., 1999; Meltzer, et al., 2003; DfES, 2007). Therefore, your assessment must address their overall broad-ranging needs in terms of health, education, cultural needs and placement requirements and also their additional needs which are likely to have arisen due to experiences of abuse or neglect (Richardson and Joughin, 2000). The literature discussed in Chapter 9 highlights how children who become looked after are likely to have experienced serious difficulties in their family of origin which are often linked with concerns about parenting capacity (Dimigen, et al., 1999; Brophy, 2006; DfES, 2006f). These experiences are likely to have involved trauma and loss, resulting in serious emotional and behavioural difficulties for many children in care (Richardson and Joughin, 2000; Schofield, 2003; Meltzer, et al., 2004a, 2004b). The Green Paper *Care matters* describes how:

> ...*63% of children in care are there as a result of abuse or neglect; it is likely that the high incidence of mental health problems in the care population, and the high frequency of placement breakdown, is in many cases a result of pre-care experiences.*

> (DfES, 2006f, p16)

Therefore, in undertaking assessments you need to be able to draw on your knowledge of the impact of abuse and neglect on children, how this compromises their development, and what intervention is needed to promote their well-being. This will involve examining ways in which you can enhance the resilience of the children you are working with, focusing on their strengths and abilities through education, hobbies, and interests developed with friends and/or caring adults (Gilligan, 2000, 2001; Schofield, 2001; Wilson et al., 2011). Resilience can also be enhanced through providing emotional and practical support to children in their placement, helping them to develop new attachments and trust in adults.

Planning

In this section we will consider a key part of the care planning processes, statutory child care reviews, plus some of the challenges in care planning, and how you might respond to these challenges. Developing a plan for children in care is a statutory duty and essential in order to minimise drift and delay for children in care (DCSF, 2010b; Ivaldi, 1998). As previously stated, when a child enters the care system and becomes 'looked after', a number of regulations and procedures come into force. The Children Act 1989, Guidance and Regulations, Volume 2, (DCSF, 2010b) identifies key stages in the planning process for children in care with the child at the centre of all processes. They include undertaking a comprehensive assessment which is described as underpinning *the effectiveness of all subsequent actions and interventions and is essential to ensure improved outcomes for children. The process of assessment seeks to understand the complex interaction between the inner world of a child and his/her family or carers, and the outer world of social and environmental factors* (DCSF, 2010b, p15). This is followed by consultation and partnership involving liaison with all those concerned with the child and always ensuring the child is central. Thereafter, the information gathered is used to inform needs and decision-making, where the best course of action is decided.

Details of care planning for court proceedings are outlined by Brayne and Carr (2010, Chapter 11). They summarise the Public Law Outline although the recent Family Justice Review proposes significant changes to public law care proceedings. These changes include a six-month time limit for the duration of public law proceedings; minimising the use of experts; more support for parents and streamlining the justice system. The government's response (Ministry of Justice/DfE, 2012) states that action will be taken, *to raise the standards of social care practice'* and makes links to how *'the quality and timeliness of social care assessments put to the courts has a crucial bearing on how quickly cases progress. Poor or late assessments can lead to delayed or re-scheduled hearings and can result in courts commissioning evidence-gathering elsewhere* (Ministry of Justice/DfE, 2012, p13).

Delays in the court process and the negative impact this can have on children in terms of their development and emotional well-being have been documented and researched over a number of years, including as part of the *Prime minister's review of adoption* (Performance and Innovation Unit Report, 2000) and by McSherry, et al. (2006); Selwyn, et al. (2006); and Schofield, et al. (2007).

Parker and Bradley assert that *care plans are central to building on assessments and producing an effective map for the intervention to proceed* (Parker and Bradley, 2003, p70). Both Parker and Bradley (2003) and Thomas (2005) develop this analogy and liken this to the work needed to build a house or an aeroplane, in that the detail has to be correct, the pieces need to fit together and the correct materials need to be used. In developing a plan for a looked after child, you are required by law to find out what the views of the child are, taking into account the child's age and level of understanding (DoH, 1989, p52). You should also work in partnership with parents in developing a care plan. However, partnership working with parents should not take precedence over the child's best interests, as these are being paramount: to do so would be *both misapplying the law and bad practice* (Brayne and Carr, 2010, p241).

The challenge of working in partnership with parents when there are differences of view between professionals and parents is discussed by Clifford and Burke (2004). Although their study is focused on adoption practice, there are key messages for social work with looked after children in general. The study highlights the dilemmas of social workers trying to engage parents in partnership planning, while also considering permanence in new families. This can apply to partnership work with parents subject to different legal processes, including those for whom reunification with their birth families is the plan. Considerable skill is needed to undertake this work and the planning process should thus be collaborative.

Making decisions about a child's future is a significant undertaking and also a substantial part of the role of a child care social worker. However, you will not be making decisions alone but with other professionals and your manager, with involvement also from parents and the child(ren). In making decisions, it is important that you are able to reflect on and discuss your assessment and others' assessments in some depth. You also need to be open to being critiqued and questioned. Fahlberg discusses how the complexities around care planning require social workers to:

> ...achieve a delicate balance: on the one hand ... never minimise the life-long impact of the decisions they make; on the other, they must not allow themselves to become paralysed by fear of making a wrong decision.

(Fahlberg, 1994, p225)

We will now turn to consider key elements of care planning processes followed by a discussion of the role of statutory reviews in making plans for looked after children. In care planning for looked after children you will focus on the different developmental stages of children.

In developing a care plan information may be gained from:

- the child
- parents
- relatives
- foster carers
- social work, health and education professionals and their records.

Statutory review meetings are central to the planning process for all looked after children and are governed by the new DCSF (2010b) Regulations Volume 2. The first review should be held at 20 days, then the second review is held three months after that and thereafter reviews are held every six months. All review meetings are multi-agency and are chaired by an IRO. Their role is to chair the meetings, scrutinise and agree the care plan, invite contributions from a range of professionals who are involved in the child-care case and elicit the views of the child and parents as part of the process. Clear plans should be in place for the child(ren). The plan will obviously vary, depending on each individual child's age, circumstances and needs.

Parents will usually be invited to attend the meeting and should be offered assistance to ensure they can attend and contribute fully, for example, assistance with travel or the attendance of an interpreter. Similarly, the child or young person should be involved in the review. This might mean a young person chooses to attend their review, or part of it, or may want to give their views through talking to their social worker or foster carer but chooses not to attend directly. A child may not want to write down their views but might like to draw a picture, make a video or write a poem, which could be shared with the adults making decisions at the review meeting. Children may find it difficult to understand what the meeting means for them so it might help you to consider using the details in Activity 4.2, which offers a guide to explaining the review and planning process to children using clear language.

ACTIVITY **4.2**

Adapted from: Your looked after review: Information for children and young people who are looked after: London Borough of Barnet

What gets talked about at the meeting?

Some things we have to talk about because they are important for making sure you are being well looked after. You can add things you want to talk about as well.

These are some of the things we will talk about:

- *What you would like to happen.*
- *How things are going where you live.*
- *Your family's or parents' views.*
- *How long you will be in care and where you will be living.*
- *What help you may need when you leave care.*
- *Your religion, language and cultural needs.*
- *Arrangements for you to keep in touch with family and friends.*
- *Collecting photos of your family for you to keep.*
- *Your health and feelings.*
- *Arrangements for school and leisure activities.*
- *Your career ambitions.*
- *You may like to bring certificates or school work to show us.*

What happens after the meeting?

After the meeting the chairperson will write up notes of the meeting called minutes. You will receive a copy of the notes which will tell you what will be happening and who will do it.

COMMENT

You will have to adapt the points above in response to the specific age and circumstances of the looked after child you are working with.

Placing sibling groups

In developing care plans you may have to consider how to meet the needs of sibling groups if they cannot be placed together. This could happen when there is limited availability of foster carers for large sibling groups or it may arise due to the specific needs of the children, leading to the requirement that they are placed separately. Taking this action requires careful assessment of the implications of the separation and you will need to make judgements about the best options for placing children within available resources (DfES, 2007). This is discussed by Hollows and Nelson (2006) in relation to permanent placement, but many of the issues raised in terms of complexity in relation to decision-making apply also to children who are in short-term foster care. You will have to consider the relationship siblings have with each other, their previous history and periods of living with parents/carers plus who they have significant relationships with (Fahlberg, 1994). If you have to place a sibling group separately you will have to arrange contact so that the children can stay in touch with each other as well as their parents.

Contact

In order to explore contact for children in care we will work with the case study of the Edwards family outlined in Activity 4.1. The hospitalisation of Monica (the children's mother) resulted in the children being placed in foster care as their father Jeff was unable to look after them. However, just prior to Monica's returning home, he cared for them at their family home for approximately three weeks. Overall the children spent almost six months in foster placements, with the two girls placed together and the two boys placed together at some considerable distance from each other and from their local neighbourhood. The assessment showed that it was in the best interests of the children to be placed together in the same local foster placement but this was not possible as a local carer could not be found. The girls, although very sad at being separated from their mother, settled into their placement and developed a good relationship with their foster parents. The boys were less settled in their foster placement and became very unhappy; they reported feeling worried about what they could do in the foster home and said the carers were very strict and did not really talk to them.

Following a further assessment and concerns about the quality of care being offered by the foster carers, the two boys were moved to another foster placement where they were offered better quality of care although it was even further from their local neighbourhood and their sisters. Initially contact was every weekend between the sisters, brothers and their father, as their mother did not feel able to have contact. The children were upset about this but sent cards and letters, which she was unable to respond to for the first few weeks. As she became well, she started to talk to the children on the telephone and then direct contact was arranged. From the first review reunification was the plan and the contact arrangements supported this.

Contact is a legal requirement and a duty specified within the Children Act 1989 (s34). Where a child is under a care order there is a presumption that the child will have a reasonable contact with his or her parents... This also applies... under an emergency protection order or a child assessment order (Brayne and Carr, 2010, p284). For information about contact for looked after childen see DCSF (2010b) Volume 2. The guidance gives details about the legislative framework in relation to contact. The guidance is specific about the benefits to children of sustaining contact with those who are close to them, as it serves as an anchor and maintains important attachments at a time when children may feel bereft and distressed about being separated from those they are closest to. An issue in the Edwards family was ensuring contact was maintained between the siblings and their father: this was particularly important because of the initial distress they felt about being unable to see their mother. The importance of sibling relationships for looked after children is identified by Mullender (1999), who highlights how relationships between brothers and sisters can often be central to promoting children's emotional well-being as well as offering stability and continuity at a time of upheaval and uncertainty. Sibling contact is also discussed within Volume 2 of the Placement Regulations, with a specific requirement to set this out in the care plan. Fahlberg (1994, p260) refers to the unique and special relationship some siblings have with each other: *siblings may act as comforters, carers, role models, spurs to achievement, faithful allies and best friends*. Banks and Kahn (1982, in Fahlberg, 1994, p261) identify how the intensity of the sibling bond is greater through close contact, through lack of parental meeting of needs and through siblings seeking to have their identity needs met. If you consider the Edwards children in the context of this information you will see how relevant this is in terms of the importance of their sibling relationship.

Supporting and arranging contact

As a social worker you will be required to arrange and support contact, which will involve consultation and liaison with foster carers, parents and other significant adults and the children themselves (Cleaver, 2000; Sellick and Howell, 2003; DCSF, 2010b). In planning contact you should also undertake a risk assessment to ensure the contact is safe and meets the needs of the children. Once the venue for contact and the transport and escort arrangements are agreed, it is helpful to have a written agreement with the parent/s so that they are clear about the arrangements. Children will also have information from you about when contact will occur and who they will see; they should be consulted about this in an age-appropriate way. A contact agreement may need to specify what happens if the adults are late or fail to arrive for contact, so that the child's distress is minimised. It may also be important to ensure the child's day-to-day care is not undermined by adults making derogatory comments about the foster carer's routine and arrangements for the child.

The Edwards children and their father met every weekend at a family centre close to their home where they were able to enjoy being together and go on outings. Supervision and monitoring were provided from the family centre, which lessened as the months passed and the assessment showed that Jeff, the children's father, was able to care for his children. Support was given to the father about how to respond to his children's sadness and anger about their circumstances. A family support worker helped with contact visits and continued to offer support when the children had a short period in the family home being cared for by their father as well as after their mother returned home and resumed care of the children.

CHAPTER SUMMARY

In this chapter we explored assessment in relation to planning for children in care and considered different assessment models. We considered this in relation to the core underpinning theoretical knowledge, which is necessary in order to work with children in care. This includes theories of child development, awareness of the impact of separation and loss and attachment theory. We discussed the importance of integrating this knowledge with an in-depth understanding of legal and procedural processes. We then discussed how assessment is critical for making plans and decisions about where children will live, with whom, and what the long-tern plans are. This also involved a discussion about contact. The case study helped to highlight the importance of sibling relationships and the challenges in placements and contact when children cannot be placed together. Through reading this chapter and undertaking the activities the aim is that you will understand the importance of in-depth child-centred assessment and planning for looked after children.

FURTHER READING

Department for Children, Schools and Families (2010) *Children Act 1989 guidance and regulations, volume 2: Care planning, placement and case review.* Nottingham: The Stationery Office.

Department for Education (2011) *Children Act 1989 guidance and regulations, volume 4: Fostering services.* Nottingham: The Stationery Office.

Schofield, G (2003) *Part of the family: Pathways through foster care.* London: British Agencies for Fostering and Adoption.

This is an important and sensitively written account of the feelings and experiences of young adults who were in long-term foster care, with links made to theories of attachment and child development.

Sellick, C, Thoburn, J and Philpot, T (2004) *What works in adoption and foster care?* Barkingside: Barnardos.

This book summarises research evidence in relation to fostering and adoption and will help you to explore what counts as 'evidence' in child and family social work.

Chapter 5

Communication skills: Participation, children's rights and life story work

A C H I E V I N G   A   S O C I A L   W O R K   D E G R E E

This chapter will help you to develop the following capabilities from the **Professional Capabilities Framework**:

- **Judgement**
  Use judgement and authority to intervene with individuals, families and communities to promote independence, provide support and prevent harm, neglect and abuse.
- **Knowledge**
  Apply knowledge of social sciences, law and social work practice theory.
- **Values and ethics**
  Apply social work ethical principles and values to guide professional practice.
- **Diversity**
  Recognise diversity and apply anti-discriminatory and anti-oppressive principles in practice.
- **Critical reflection and analysis**
  Apply critical reflection and analysis to inform and provide a rationale for professional decision-making.

It will also introduce you to the following standards as set out in the 2008 social work subject benchmark statement
5.1.1 Social work services, service users and carers
5.1.5 The nature of social work practice
5.5.3 Analysis and synthesis
5.5.4 Intervention and evaluation
5.6   Communication skills
5.7   Skills in working with others

Introduction

In this chapter we focus on communicating with looked after children and examine the skills that you need in order to communicate effectively with children. Two key areas of practice are used in order to explore what it means to listen to and communicate with children. The first is life story work, where the focus is on individual casework, and the second concentrates on the active participation of children and young people in decision-making and service planning. Some authors use the term 'life journey work' (Romaine, et al., 2007) as opposed to life story work so that children do not become confused about their story being a fictional account. However, we take the view that children will understand more what a story means and through careful explanations they can be helped to connect with and understand their story in their particular context. There are many other areas of practice that we will refer to in terms of communicating with looked after children but we have chosen these two in particular as they give you the opportunity to understand in greater depth the differing approaches and theoretical frameworks that underpin them. The different approaches are identified by Luckock, et al. (2006a, p35) and are described as those using an empowerment model and those rooted in a psycho-social model. In this chapter, the theoretical frameworks underpinning communicating with children through undertaking life story work are based primarily on the psycho-social model and those underpinning work focused on the active participation of children cohere around the empowerment model. However, links are made between both approaches so that whenever possible elements of both can be applied as recommended by Luckock, et al. (2006).

It is important to start by defining what we mean when we discuss communicating with children. It seems obvious but it is important to recognise that communicating is a two-way process and involves giving out and receiving verbal and non-verbal messages. Most people use spoken and written language to communicate, although some people with communication impairments may use different methods involving symbols, signs, pictures, facial expressions and body language (Morris, 2002; Lefevre, 2010). Later on in this chapter, we discuss communicating with disabled children with communication impairments in greater detail. When communicating with others we use language in both written and verbal form and use our skills to listen and respond to verbal and non-verbal information (Jones, 2003; Koprowska, 2010). The SCIE review (Luckock, et al., 2006, p3) defines effective communication as reciprocal and states that it occurs when there is *a common language – words, emotions, behaviours, symbols, signs*. When we are communicating with looked after children it is important to remember that they may have had frightening or traumatic experiences that have left them with confused and angry feelings towards adults. So the work you do in communicating with children will require you to be patient, reliable and understanding. It is also important to remember that children and young people have different needs in terms of communication, which will depend on a number of factors: their age and developmental stage; their cognitive abilities; whether they have a disability; their language and culture; and their family history and current context. You will therefore need to have an understanding of human development, as children who are at different developmental stages will require your understanding and knowledge about their differing communicative abilities (Bee, 2000; Crawford and Walker, 2007). Having an understanding of the life-cycle and human development will strengthen your interventions and links to a relationship-based approach to practice (Wilson, et al. 2011).

ACTIVITY 5.1

Think about a time when you or your children had to spend a short period away from home. What were some of the issues that were of importance and who would you or your children talk to and confide in if either of you were unhappy?

COMMENT

This activity will help you to reflect on your own needs and those of your family when uprooted from familiar surroundings. It will help you to reflect on how it might be difficult to find someone to trust when we are removed from our personal networks. This exercise may help you to empathise with looked after children and how they might feel isolated and unsupported in new placements.

Legislative and policy context

Listening to looked after children, communicating with them and involving them in decisions about both their future plans and their daily living experiences is one of the core tasks in social work with looked after children. This is central in terms of good practice as it gives children, many of whom have been disempowered, the opportunity to actively participate in plans about their future and to have their voices heard and their views respected. Thomas (2005) outlines the importance of this in terms of increasing psychological well-being and goes on to say that decisions made involving looked after children, who are essentially the *experts in their own lives* (p27), are better as they are actually based on the views and knowledge of the children themselves. Respect for children is described by Brayne and Carr (2010) as pervading *all the questions of how the law looks at the child* (p238).

Specifically, the Children Act 1989 requires you, as a social worker, to ascertain the wishes and feelings of the child. The Adoption and Children Act 2002 specifies that children's views should be sought as part of the counselling process when adoption is planned. Communicating with looked after children and ascertaining their wishes and feelings is not a one-off event but should represent an ongoing dialogue linked to the care planning processes of assessment, planning, intervention and review (see Chapter 4). Additionally, Article 12 of the UNCRC states that children who are capable of giving their views should be allowed to do so freely, although their age and maturity should also be considered. The rights of looked after children to have a voice, the participation of looked after children in their own plans and in broader service plans only started to be given real focus and priority in the late 1980s and early 1990s. As discussed in Chapter 1, throughout this period there was an emergence of widespread concern about the safety of looked after children that led to government reviews. These include Warner (1992), where weaknesses in staff recruitment practices were identified; and Utting (1991, 1997) which revealed major concerns about the standards of care experienced by children living away from home. These reviews identified how the most poorly trained staff were often caring for the most severely disturbed children, with the children themselves having very limited opportunities to speak out about their experiences of being looked after (Colton, et al., 2001, p197; Stein, 2006c).

The widespread concern about the safety and well-being of looked after children resulted in the government responding positively to the many recommendations made by Utting (1997). This in turn provoked fundamental changes in services and increased support for looked after children, including the Quality Protects programme (QP) (DoH, 1999c). One of the central themes of this programme was to support listening to children, promote their active involvement, and it introduced the role of 'corporate parenting'. The role of corporate parenting was strengthened following *Care matters* and the publication of the White Paper in June

2007. It was stated that *a good corporate parent must offer everything that a good parent would, including stability* (DfES, 2007, p7). Children's rights and advocacy services are now well established and funded by local authorities and national organisations. These organisations have developed a range of services through the provision of mentoring schemes and support networks with the central aim of promoting the rights of children in care. Website addresses for national children's rights organisations are included at the end of this chapter. Overall, the enduring message and perhaps one of the most important lessons which emerged from the investigations into abuse of children in public care was the recognition that children need to be listened to, communicated with, and have their views respected.

The importance of communicating with looked after children is discussed as part of the consultation undertaken with looked after children, which informed the priorities within the Green Paper (DfES, 2006f, Appendix A and the White Paper, *Care matters*, 2007). This highlights a key message: the needs and ambitions of looked after children are similar to those of children living with their birth families. Two of the four key messages are critical in reference to participation and communicating with children: the first is that *children in care want to be treated as individuals, listened to, and helped to realise their ambitions*; the second is that *social workers should listen to children more, and take their views seriously in key decisions* (p104).

ACTIVITY 5.2

Consider the following questions.

1. *In the past, why do you think some looked after children were not believed when they told adults they were being harmed?*

2. *Can you identify particular contexts when you directly communicated with looked after children to ascertain their views?*

3. *What communication skills have you used and found helpful in your direct work with looked after children?*

COMMENT

You may have identified that societal expectations and beliefs about children's development played a part and many children were not empowered to speak out about their experiences. Many looked after children come from families with multiple problems and high levels of poverty and families may have felt they had limited power to intervene with powerful bureaucracies. Also, the concept of child abuse was not clearly defined as a social problem at this point in time.

You may have identified that you communicated directly with looked after children in meetings prior to statutory reviews, completing assessment records or during life story work.

Did you discuss the use of puzzles, books, toys and drawing with younger children? With adolescents you may have used the opportunity to talk and started by discussing straightforward issues before moving on to talk about more difficult areas. Communicating with adolescents and understanding their developmental trajectory is discussed by Briggs (2008), who focuses on psycho-social perspectives on adolescence.

Child and young person development

The SCIE review (Luckock et al., 2006) identifies three core conditions and their accompanying theoretical roots which are central to the development of communication skills with children and young people. These core conditions are discussed in more detail in the research summary below, a detailed discussion regarding capability and effectiveness in relation to practitioner skills is discussed by Lefevre (2010). It is identified that a number of key skills are required including the context of the work and the location, plus using observation skills, play, creative writing and music. Although knowledge of child development is extremely important in informing your work with children, this should not become rigid or deterministic as children develop at different stages and may follow different developmental pathways. Normative models of child development are critiqued by Sugarman (1986, p2), who argues against using overarching umbrella definitions of the different stages of human development, as these do not take into account unique, individual differences between children and young people. Therefore, in considering child development in the context of communicating with children, remember that information about child development provides a useful framework but it is for you to use your professional judgement in identifying and working with the communication needs of individual children (Bee, 2000; Jones, 2003; Lefevre, 2010).

The listening skills of social workers were also identified as being of key importance in the SCIE review (Luckock, et al., 2006), although listening to distressing or painful stories about children's lives was found to be *stressful both personally and emotionally for social workers* (p28). This is where reflection and professional supervision are critical in order to help you understand and manage difficult feelings and to ensure you are able to work sensitively and effectively in a way that holds the child's needs as central (Hughes and Pengelly 1997; Cooper, 2005; Knott and Scragg, 2007; Wilson, et al. 2011). If there is an absence of reflective practice there can be serious implications, and children's communications can be missed, as in the case of Victoria Climbié (Cooper, 2005; Butler, 2007).

RESEARCH SUMMARY

The core conditions are defined by Luckock, et al. (2006, pp17–31) as that combination of professional values and personal commitments that underpin skilled engagement with children (p17). The first core condition is defined as ethical and emotional engagement. This is described as a combination of upholding an ethical stance in respecting children for who they are and showing commitment to understanding the emotional needs of the child. This was shown to build trust and a strong working alliance. The second they identified as child-centred communication, where the importance of using child-centred language was emphasised, plus the use of play and other activities like drawing and painting to facilitate direct work, especially with younger children. The third core condition was identified as understanding the distinctive nature of child communication (p25), and was linked to the importance of knowledge about child development. These core conditions coupled with knowledge of human development (Sugarman, 1986; Bee, 2000; Crawford and Walker, 2007) will help you to understand the theoretical basis for your work with children in care.

Communicating with very young children

When you are communicating with pre-school children, incorporating the core conditions mentioned above is fundamental so that you remain child-centred in your work and are able to adjust your communication style to enable you to engage with a very young child. It is likely that young children will be most comfortable communicating with you through play, through doing activities together like painting, playing games, singing or reading books. Additionally children may use a 'third object' as a way of communicating with you, for example a cuddly toy or something else that is important to them. Daniel, et al. (2010) discuss the use of play when communicating with young children as a therapeutic intervention, which can help children express difficult feelings, for example fear, loss and uncertainty. They can therefore *use objects from the external world to symbolise their internal feelings and perceptions of their circumstances* (Hopper, 2007, p77). This will then help you to make sense of children's feelings and experiences. See also Bee (2000); Waddell (2002) and Chapter 3 of Crawford and Walker (2007), where details are given about the physical, cognitive, social and emotional development of young children. Lefevre (2010) refers to *hundreds of languages of childhood* (p64) and how practitioners should be responsive to a range of communication methods.

Children may say their first word when they are just over one year old followed by rapid increases in children using new words from around two years old, although the acquisition of vocabulary varies between children (Bee, 2000, p233). Jones (2003, p22) outlines how from two years old children's language and cognitive skills increase a great deal and at speed. Their language abilities extend from putting three words together at approximately two years old to constructing more complex sentences by the time they are four years old (Bee, 2000). Their ability to remember things also develops from three years old, although the author outlines how the exact source of the memory is not always clearly identified. This has implications for the direct work you undertake, as very young children may become confused about a particular event and the timing of it.

It is important to remember that many of the looked after children you will work with may have had experiences of abuse and neglect. Research shows this can have a significant impact on their health, well-being and development (see Chapter 10). The severe neglect of young children is shown to have *adverse effects on children's ability to form attachments and is associated with major impairment of growth and intellectual development* (DfES, 2006f, p185). The issue of impaired language development linked with children who have experienced emotionally harmful care is discussed by Koprowska (2010).

Communicating with primary-school age children

Children between the ages of five and 11 years are likely to have a range of communicative abilities involving play, creative activities and talking. They will usually have a good grasp of language and may learn to read and write between the ages of six and seven years (Daniel, et al., 2010). Jones (2003) states that children's vocabulary will be extensive by the time they are ten years old and they will understand subtle nuances in conversation like how to take turns; however, they are unlikely to correct or question adults. The following is a summary of key issues for communicating with primary-school age children and is taken from Walker (2005); Jones (2003); Daniel, et al. (2010) and Luckock, et al. (2006).

- Children want their social workers to be enthusiastic, humorous, caring and concerned as well as warm and friendly: these attributes were identified as essential for the development of trusting relationships (Luckock, et al. 2006, p20).

- Be authentic; this means being natural and avoiding a remote or stiff professional role (Walker, 2005, p67).

- Show interest and encouragement for the child's achievements and try to find something unique and special about the child (Walker, 2005, p68). This is described by Daniel, et al., (1999, p216) as locating *islands of competence*, which helps children to feel proud of their achievements and builds up their self-esteem.

- Be clear about the reasons why you are working directly with the child and be honest about the limits of confidentiality.

- Ask open, unambiguous questions and avoid correcting and interrupting children as this could 'close down' important aspects of the conversation (Jones, 2003, p30).

Jones (2003, p42) discusses the impact of adverse experiences for children in the primary school age group in terms of communication and states that there may be behavioural problems, emotional problems, self-blame and poor relationships with peers. All of these issues will require you to think carefully about how you can communicate with children in this situation. Additionally, it is recommended that particular care is taken in terms of offering reassurance through physical contact as children may have had their trust in adults and their behaviours severely affected. The issue of touch to convey comfort is discussed by Lefevre (2010). He explains that it is necessary to maintain professional boundaries while showing warmth and reassurance (affectionate touch is not normally sanctioned between field social workers and children and young people!) (p209).

Communicating with adolescents

Adolescence is sometimes described as a turbulent time, featuring stresses and challenges coupled with a period of huge bodily changes with the onset of puberty (Waddell, 2002). All adolescents have to manage the process of moving away from childhood and face the uncertainties of adulthood. For looked after young people, their earlier experiences of poor parenting may intensify adolescent conflicts as they are less likely to have experienced containing relationships with adults. Briggs (2008) discusses moving towards adolescence as a transition, involving loss and change, which can arouse strong feelings of anxiety in young people and which may result in risky and self-harming behaviour. During adolescence the relationships young people have with their peers becomes very important, as evidenced by increasing levels of intimacy and sharing. The issue of 'fitting in' with peer groups is likely to be central for all young people, including those who are looked after, with adults sometimes viewed as the 'enemy' and as people 'who just don't understand'. Adolescents who are looked after may therefore not want some people to know their family circumstances and looked after status, and want you as their social worker to assure them of discretion. In order to build a trusting relationship it will be critical that you outline the limits of confidentiality in your work and who you might have to share information with and in what circumstances.

Ward (2006) discusses how young people in care who are living in residential homes have particular needs due to the high proportion of them who have had very harmful experiences in their families of origin as well as multiple changes of placement and school. This is linked to high levels of mental health difficulties and the need for specialist therapeutic support. However, as a way of supplementing planned direct work, Ward (2006) suggests adopting an opportunistic approach. Thus in being responsive to specific moments or incidents you may be able to undertake some valuable work in communicating with a young person about issues that are of concern to them.

Many adolescents are likely to be very aware of the consequences of speaking to an adult about personal issues of concern (Jones, 2003, p30) and may be reluctant to talk to you about personal matters. It may take a great deal of time for a young person to build up trust in you, especially if there have been a number of changes in social worker. Young people raised concerns about this in a *consultation as part of the Green Paper saying that they wanted to have a consistent person in their lives* (DfES, 2006f, p104). Young people may be struggling with approaching independence, with issues of sexuality, their cultural identity, drugs and alcohol and issues of achieving in education. As their social worker, it will be important that you communicate with the young person about how you can help support them through these difficult issues, to challenge them about risky behaviours and to try to help them to reflect on the consequences of certain actions. You will need to work in partnership with the main carers, whether residential social workers or foster carers and access health and education advice as required.

Communicating with disabled children

In communicating with disabled children it will be important for you to identify what methods of communication the child uses. Parents, carers, the school, nursery or youth club who know the child should be able to advise you about the communication needs of particular children. In a study by Stalker and Connors (2003) they suggest that workers can learn basic skills and this accompanied by sensitivity and a positive attitude will facilitate the communication process with disabled children. Some tools and ideas you may find helpful are as follows and are summarised from Jones (2003); Stalker and Connors (2003); and Morris (2002).

- Some hearing impaired children may communicate using British Sign Language and will require the involvement of a qualified interpreter.

- Those children who have a learning disability may find sign-assisted language such as Makaton helpful.

- Some children may use an alphabetical or symbol-based communication tool including computer-aided programs and cards.

- Use of a 'spidergram' with boxes for names of important people (similar to a genogram) may help you to communicate (Stalker and Connors, 2003).

- Stalker and Connors (2003) recommend flexibility and creativity balanced by ensuring the child is familiar and comfortable with the method used.

- You may need to use a range of methods including observation of mood in different settings and situations as information may be difficult to draw on. You will need time and support to do this.

Additional information is given by Koprowska (2010, Chapter 8) about working with people with special communicative needs, including those who speak a minority language. Also, Morris (2002) has very helpful advice and practical information about how to communicate with disabled children and includes some key messages from young disabled children themselves, which are discussed further in Chapter 7 where we focus on looked after children who are disabled.

Children's rights and participation

Undertaking direct work with looked after children in care where the focus is on children's rights and active participation is consistent with an empowerment model of practice (Luckock, et al., 2006, p18; Leverett, 2008). This approach focuses on anti-discriminatory and anti-oppressive models of practice, linked with human rights and citizenship, where children are encouraged to think for themselves. Participation in the context of a children's rights framework is defined as *not simply taking part or being present* but as having some influence over decisions and actions (Kirby, et al., 2003, p5). There is a growing body of literature focused on this area of practice (McNeish, 1999; CYPU, 2001; Save The Children, 2003; Cavet and Sloper, 2004; Department for Constitutional Affairs (DCA), 2004). This approach to direct work with looked after children is mostly undertaken within a group-work context. The changing attitudes to looked after children in general, a focus on their rights as individuals, and government policy, including the Quality Protects programme, (DoH, 1999c); Every child matters (DfES, 2004); Care matters (DfES, 2006f); and Care matters: Time for change (DfES, 2007) has resulted in numerous strategies by local authorities to promote the rights of looked after children and engage them in participatory events. The requirement for Children in Care Councils has extended this further. Local authorities have written special booklets for looked after young people to ensure they receive information, and have created opportunities to ensure the voices of looked after children are part of the design and delivery processes for services. This can mean looked after children are involved in a range of forums and focus groups, or asked to complete questionnaires and surveys. Alongside this, group events may help to link looked after children with each other, giving the opportunity for mutual support and for sharing experiences.

If you are involved in developing group participatory events for looked after children, there are a number of issues you will have to consider. They may include some of the following: the age of the children; their developmental stage; whether they have special communication needs; and issues of consent. In order for the participation work you are engaged in to be meaningful, it will be important for you to be clear about the aims and objectives, both for the young people you are working with and for the organisation within which the participatory work is taking place. If information is being gathered, you should be able to give a clear account to the young people about how it will be used and how they will be kept informed of any outcomes (Morris and Burford, 2007). You will also have to reflect on how to maximise participation by using appropriate language or communication tools that are accessible for the specific group of children. You should also reflect on the organisational culture within which the participation is taking place, as this context is important in terms of identifying inhibiting or promoting factors in your work with looked after children. Kirby, et al. (2003, p25) suggest four stages of organisational change that may have to occur in order that meaningful participation with children is achieved. The four stages are:

- unfreezing existing attitudes through providing evidence of good practice and participatory strategies;

- establishing catalysts for change through providing clear rationale;

- internalising new ways of working through raising awareness and through acknowledging conflict and difference;

- institutionalising new ways of working through spreading good practice, and incorporating this into the mainstream.

In undertaking direct work with looked after children it is important that you do not adopt a *polarised position, with too narrow a focus* (Luckock, et al., 2006, p15) as you need skills and knowledge from both psycho-social and empowerment approaches in order to communicate effectively with looked after children. If you focus exclusively on one approach you are likely to miss what is being communicated. For example, if you are involved in a group participatory event, it will be important for you to not only use skills and knowledge associated with empowerment and anti-oppressive practice but to also understand and use skills and knowledge most commonly associated with the psycho-social model. The latter are identified by Luckock, et al. (2007, p198; Lefevre, 2010) as being emotionally attuned to the child; offering containment for difficult feelings; showing sensitivity; and being aware of how to care for individuals in a group process. Showing sensitivity is critical, as it may be difficult for some looked after children to participate in groups, due to negative experiences from other group settings such as school, or they may find it intimidating to discuss issues openly in group forums (Curtis, et al., 2004).

ACTIVITY 5.3

You are a social worker at a Leaving Care Team and have been asked to work with a colleague from the Children's Rights Service to develop a monthly participation forum for young people using the service. There have been concerns that looked after children have not been involved enough in service planning, so the aim is to consult young people about the service and develop a core group, who can be involved in a broader council-wide young people's participation and consultation group.

What steps would you take to develop participatory activities with young people from this service?

You may start with distributing leaflets to the young people and putting up posters in the Leaving Care office. You might also ask staff from the team to give information to the young people they are working with – this may be through text messaging or social media. On the leaflets you could give details of the time and place of the first meeting and if possible, try to provide food for the young people so that the event is relaxed and welcoming. It would also be important that you chose a time that fitted in with school and college commitments. A number of issues should be clearly discussed: why you want to develop a forum; issues of consent so that young people do not feel they are under any obligation to participate; what the time commitment is; and whether expenses will be paid for travel.

Life story work

You will undertake life story work with looked after children to help them understand their early life experiences, value their uniqueness, to aid the development of a positive sense of self and to support their future emotional development. Life story work has been defined as a means of *exploring co-operatively with a child or young person the story of his or her life so far* (Romaine, 2007, p47). For children who have experienced a number of moves and losses it is one way of helping them to make sense of who they are. In a guide to undertaking direct work with looked after children who are preparing for permanence the following objectives are identified:

- giving children information about their backgrounds and family circumstances;

- helping children make sense of their life history and present situation;

- offering children a safe and contained space to explore and express a range of emotions;

- ascertaining children's wishes and feelings;

- helping children develop a positive sense of self;

- helping children deal with family transitions.

    (Romaine, et al., 2007, p10)

Communicating with looked after children within the context of life story work will require you to: plan carefully; show sensitivity; and develop the capacity to engage in emotionally painful and difficult issues, where children may ask difficult questions about their past. Life story work will therefore require you: to be honest but not brutal (Ryan and Walker, 1993, p18); to use skills in active listening; to show empathy; and to be patient. We have linked communicating with children and undertaking life story work to the psycho-social model, where the emphasis is on *the therapeutic or reparative nature of communication* (Luckock, et al., 2007, p198). However, there are links also to the empowerment model and the rights of children to have their voices heard (Article 12, UNCRC). We agree with Ryan and Walker (1993, p5) that *all children are entitled to an accurate knowledge of their past and their family*.

What are the key issues in undertaking life story work?

Here is a summary of good practice points in undertaking life story work, based on Romaine, et al. (2007, pp11–55) and Ryan and Walker (1993).

1. You should discuss and consult with key people before, and if necessary throughout, the process, and ensure the child is aware of this. This will help you to prepare sessions with the child, reflect and take advice on difficult issues.

2. You should work in age-appropriate ways, which may mean communicating through play, using toys, puppets, drawings and games. Also, you should go at the child's pace. This may however, result in a dilemma, as the timescales might not fit with the momentum of family placement and court work.

3. Some children may find it very difficult to engage in one-to-one work as they have little experience of trusting adults, of having choices, or of thinking about their emotions. They may have very low self-esteem and show real ambivalence about the whole process because of the potentially painful feelings it arouses. This means that the work is likely to take time, and it is suggested that keeping accurate recordings will help you to keep abreast of progress.

4. Giving children difficult information about their past may sometimes result in workers feeling anxious, as they do not want to cause the child they are working with any distress. They may worry that they will not be able to respond to the child's emotions or answer questions in a way that the child finds manageable. However, if you cannot be honest with children you are working with and omit important details, then it may be that the child will presume there is something very wrong and unmentionable about their past (Ryan and Walker, 1993). Romaine, et al. (2007, p120) specifically say that the most important aspect in the work is the relationship you develop with the child. Further, they state that what counts are your listening skills, your honesty about what you know, and do not know, and your reliability. They also suggest identifying other adults who can support the child to focus on emotionally difficult issues. When giving difficult information, Romaine, et al. (2007, p46) suggest the following:

   - honesty and clear language;

   - giving the context;

   - clarity that you do not expect the child to react in a particular way;

   - ensuring children have the opportunity to express emotions with you at a time in the following days/weeks;

   - clarity that you will be able to help them manage and express their emotions in ways they are comfortable with;

   - helping children to feel they can ask questions.

5. You should create a life story book, a memory box or something else the child can keep and return to look at. Details of how to create a life story book with a child can be found in Fahlberg (1994, p354). You might also use an ecomap or a life graph with

photographs, cards or stickers plus symbols like sad/happy faces. However, it is not essential that a final product is made; what is important is that the child has a concrete representation of the process.

6. The child you are undertaking life story work with may also need expert therapeutic help to support them in healing from traumatic past abusive experiences.

7. Remember that every child and their experiences is unique.

CASE STUDY

Carolyn is five years old and has been living with foster parents for over one year. You are her social worker and are preparing to undertake life story work to help Carolyn understand her past and to help her move on to a new adoptive placement. Both Carolyn's parents had abused drugs and her father was in prison following a serious drug-related violent offence. Carolyn's mother continued to abuse drugs and had recently been hospitalised as her mental health had deteriorated. Carolyn had been neglected by her parents and on one occasion neighbours had found her locked outside the house late at night. She had started to talk to her foster carers about remembering being cold and hungry, and when playing with her dolls would repeatedly tell her doll not to be scared when people shout and get angry. She was also asking questions about why her best friend at school, Amber, had a mummy and daddy who looked after her and she did not.

1. *How would you plan your life story work with Carolyn and who would you consult?*

2. *What tools and skills would you use to ensure your work was age appropriate?*

3. *How would you explore with Carolyn some of the more difficult areas of her previous history?*

COMMENT

You would have to think about Carolyn's age and developmental stage. You may have started by considering the need to consult with Carolyn's teacher, foster carer, important family members and your team manager in planning the life story work. You may also have consulted with a play therapist from the local CAMHS about what communicative tools would help you in working with Carolyn. This may mean using painting/drawing, dolls, puppets, games and soft toys in guided play. Examples of communicating with children through play resources are: using toy telephones to speak through; using glove puppets to help children talk about difficult feelings; and using soft toys as imaginary people (Ryan and Walker, 1993, p42). Through play you could communicate with Carolyn how it was wrong that her parents had treated her in the way they had but you would explain that they were unwell through taking drugs that were very bad for them both. You might explain that sometimes adults get depressed and take drugs or alcohol and this makes them very confused and not able to look after themselves or their children very well. You would need to draw on theories of child development, attachment and resilience (Fahlberg, 1994, Chapter 7; Waddell, 2002, Chapter 6; Crawford and Walker 2007, Chapter 3) to help you understand what the impact of loss and separation could

COMMENT *continued*

have on Carolyn's emotional and social development. This will help you to plan for Carolyn's current and future needs. Communicating with looked after children is a central part of your role. It is important that you develop skills and knowledge to strengthen your practice and reflect on areas for your own development. For more in-depth analysis on theoretical perspectives and how you can develop your practice, see Chapter 6, Lefevre (2010). This chapter focuses on the skills needed to work with looked after children with links made to practice examples and exercises you can try.

CHAPTER SUMMARY

In this chapter we have explored communicating with looked after children, focusing on the practical application of skills and the use in practice of child and adolescent development theories. You were encouraged to reflect on ethics and values, and to relate this to key legislative frameworks. To strengthen links between theory and practice we examined two specific areas of practice: participation and children's rights and life story work. This gave us the opportunity to incorporate aspects of two theoretical positions, the psycho-social model and empowerment model, in communicating with children in a range of practice contexts. Through understanding different approaches to communicating with looked after children and through actively considering the importance of practice skills in building trusting relationships with children, you will be able to reflect on how to develop your practice in undertaking direct work.

FURTHER READING

Briggs, S (2008) *Working with adolescents: A contemporary psychodynamic approach.* Basingstoke: Palgrave.

This book uses psychoanalytic theory to explore the challenges of adolescence and gives helpful information about how to work directly with young people who are experiencing difficulties.

Fahlberg, V (1994) *A child's journey through placement.* London: BAAF.

This is essential reading for all social workers undertaking direct work with looked after children.

Lefevre, M (2010) *Communicating with children and young people.* Bristol: Policy Press.

This book provides both theoretical perspectives and skills development examples, with a focus on how to improve social workers' communication skills with children and young people.

WEBSITES

Scope, disability organisation: **www.scope.org.uk**

Voice for the child in care: **www.voiceyp.org**

A National Voice – website for young people who are looked after: **www.anationalvoice.org**

Chapter 6

Culture, ethnicity and faith: Working with children in care from diverse communities

This chapter will help you to develop the following capabilities from the **Professional Capabilities Framework**:

- **Knowledge**
  Apply knowledge of social sciences, law and social work practice theory.
- **Justice**
  Advance human rights and promote social justice and economic wellbeing.
- **Values and ethics**
  Apply social work ethical principles and values to guide professional practice.
- **Diversity**
  Recognise diversity and apply anti-discriminatory and anti-oppressive principles in practice.
- **Critical reflection and analysis**
  Apply critical reflection and analysis to inform and provide a rationale for professional decision-making.

It will also introduce you to the following standards as set out in the 2008 social work subject benchmark statement
5.1.1 Social work services, service users and carers
5.1.5 The nature of social work practice
5.5.4 Intervention and evaluation
5.6   Communication skills
5.7   Skills in working with others

Introduction

This chapter focuses on practice models, theory and legislation applicable to working with looked after children from black and minority ethnic communities and those who are unaccompanied asylum-seeking minors. We will highlight the importance of respecting diversity, of showing cultural sensitivity and of developing understanding about different religious practices. Many of the issues discussed will also be applicable to working with children from some white minority ethnic communities who have experienced discrimination and exclusion linked to their cultural practices, faith and language. This includes children from Irish travelling families, from Roma gypsy families and children from the Jewish community. Although children from minority ethnic communities and unaccompanied asylum-seeking young people are discussed together in this chapter, it is recognised that unaccompanied asylum-seeking children have particular needs in relation to their experiences of loss, trauma and uncertain legal status having arrived here from countries all over the world fleeing war and persecution.

In considering the needs of children who are unaccompanied and from minority ethnic communities, a helpful way of reconciling the complexities is offered by Thoburn, et al. (2005), who suggest it is legitimate to include unaccompanied asylum-seeking children within the broader discourse of the care of black and minority ethnic children *as they are currently subject to discrimination as if black* (Thoburn, et al., 2005, p14). In this chapter the histories of children from these communities is examined, necessitating an exploration of key terms and definitions, including the meanings attached to culture, ethnicity, linguistic traditions and faith. The chapter starts by discussing the policy context for practice in this area, making links to the emerging discourse about what it means to be 'British', notions about 'belonging' to a country and multiculturalism. We feel it is important that these concepts are understood as social workers are often working with people who are trying to make sense of their past and future, and trying to make links in new homes, in new communities and in new countries. Yet debates in the broader political and social arena about multiculturalism and diversity are sometimes tense, unsympathetic and uncertain. This discussion will be followed by statistical information about the profile of black, minority ethnic and unaccompanied asylum-seeking children within the looked after population. Key debates about practice, including contested issues regarding same-race placements, will be examined. The chapter then explores theoretical ideas which will help you to develop your practice in this area, including: cultural competence as a model; reflective practice; and the use of counselling skills within a multicultural framework (Miller, 2006).

What do we mean by culture and ethnicity?

The term 'ethnic' is subject to many and changing definitions. It has been described quite simply as being about *people who share some cultural or biological characteristics* (Hutchinson and Smith, 1996, p4). However, ethnicity is defined as, *a process of group identification…a sense of cultural and historical identity based on belonging by birth to a distinctive cultural group* (Bhavnani, et al., 2005, p130). The authors go on to define culture as involving the sharing of customs, beliefs and traditions with cultural practices passed on from one generation to another through family and community networks. This links to sociological articulations regarding culture and is captured by Giddens (1993), who states that culture *refers to the ways of life of the members of a society, or of groups, or within a society. It includes how they dress, their marriage customs and family life, their patterns of work, religious ceremonies and leisure pursuits* (p31). From these definitions you will see that all individuals have particular cultural waypoints they use to guide their lives, although some cultural groups are afforded less status and access to resources than others, due to stereotyping and discrimination, both overt and covert. In thinking about the meaning of culture to the young people you work with it is important to remember that an individual's cultural identity is not fixed but is fluid and interactive and will change over time in response to new situations, contexts and experiences.

Britain as a kaleidoscopic, multicultural country is built on many different communities and faiths. Therefore, some of the children you work with will come from communities that are different to your own in terms of ethnicity, faith, culture or language. Although Britain has been a multicultural country for many years, the impact of global mobility has *ushered in a new urgency requiring understanding of cultural differences* (Allain, 2007, p128). This requires you to develop skills in working with difference and diversity. Later on in the chapter you will see that the first step in this process entails looking at oneself in terms of culture, values and issues of power. This involves thinking about labels and how, for example, we relate to young people in care who are defined as 'unaccompanied asylum seeking'. This is explored by Kohli and Mitchell (2007, pxiv), who suggest that although labels such as these might be used by organisations to categorise needs, they can have the effect of airbrushing out the individuality and ordinariness of the young people themselves. Reflecting on your own values and beliefs and engaging in open discussions with fellow students and colleagues will enable you to explore the complexities of negative discrimination and stereotyping at a deeper level and help you to understand how the experiences of some young people can make them feel powerless, isolated and afraid about who they can trust.

Policy and legislative context

Some commentators describe how welfare services for black and minority ethnic communities have been characterised by either *fixed definitions of culture, a colour blind approach or an approach to disadvantage which constructs the groups as deficient* (Bhavnani et al., 2005, p80). In-depth analysis of the progress and challenges in social work practice over the past three decades working with multi-ethnic communities can be charted through the work of Ahmed, et al. (1986); Barn (1999); Barn, (1993); Barn, et al. (1997); Butt and Mirza (1996); Thoburn, et al. (2005); Kohli and Mitchell (2007); Bhatti-Sinclair (2011).

The broader policy context of practice in this area is contested and linked to political debates about 'Britishness' and the meaning of multiculturalism (Parekh, 2000; Baldwin and Rozenberg, 2004; Mason, 2000; Asthana and Hinsliff, 2004; Jasper, 2005). These debates are discussed in relation to there being a *renewed preoccupation with refugees and asylum seekers* (Solomos, 2003, p218) and notions of citizenship, belonging and identity. It is within this context that you will be working with children in care from diverse communities. In addition to the issues of loss, hurt and separation that all children in care are likely to experience, for unaccompanied asylum-seeking children questions of their citizenship exist as a deep and ever-present uncertainty corroding every aspect of their lives.

Britain's emergence as a multi-ethnic country is described as a process not led by conscious decision-making: *it has evolved as an unplanned, incremental process – a matter of multicultural drift, not of conscious policy* (Parekh, 2000, p14). If at the macro level the development of Britain as a multi-ethnic country is dominated by uncertainty and ambiguity then it could be argued that this is likely to be echoed in areas of policy. Disputes about multiculturalism and what it means to be British have intensified over the past few years. The head of the previously named Commission for Racial Equality commented that multiculturalism should be abandoned, as it is a dated concept, and no longer useful: this provoked concern from a range of commentators (Asthana and Hinsliff, 2004; Jasper, 2005). Their concerns centred on the possible divisiveness in communities if there was a rejection of the ideals underpinning the concept of multiculturalism. Government have also contributed to debates about what it means to be British, with political leaders arguing that we should move away from the model of multiculturalism and stop focusing on ethnicity and instead emphasise shared values across communities (Brown, 2007). This has been developed further with the current Conservative-led Coalition government introducing a stronger emphasis on the notion of 'Britishness' within citizenship tests. *Migrants applying for a British passport will soon have to be able to recite the first verse of God Save the Queen* (Travis, 2012). Overall practice is described as operating in an *increasingly harsh political climate towards asylum seekers* (Dixon and Wade, 2007, p125). This may in turn create anxiety for young people who are unaccompanied minors about their future and what decisions might be made about their legal status.

Legislation

Taking into account a child's religious and cultural needs is enshrined in the Children Act 1989 section 22(5)(c). The legislation states that, when making decisions, a local authority shall give due consideration to the child's religious persuasion, racial origin and cultural and linguistic background. Although there is not a duty attached to this section of the Act it would be considered good practice for local authorities to deliberate and reflect on the racial origin of looked after children plus their cultural, linguistic and religious needs when making plans for them (Barn, et al., 1997). In addition, the Race Relations (Amendment) Act 2000 aims to address the exclusion of certain groups in society and there is a specific duty for local authorities to promote equality and provide culturally appropriate services to their communities (Johns, 2011).

In Chapter 12 there is a more detailed discussion of the Children (Leaving Care) Act 2000 and specific issues for different groups of young people. Since the Hillingdon Judgement (2003) increased numbers of young people have received support under the Children (Leaving Care) Act 2000. The Hillingdon Judgement was a court case brought by four former unaccompanied asylum-seeking young people who asserted that they were entitled to after-care support although they had not been accommodated under section 20 of the Children Act 1989 but offered assistance under section 17 of the Act. The legal process established that section 17 should not be used as a matter of routine in supporting unaccompanied asylum-seeking young people. Guidance was issued to local authorities,

LAC (2003)13, outlining that in most instances unaccompanied asylum-seeking young people should be supported under section 20 of the Children Act 1989 (The Children's Legal Centre, 2005). Legislation and policy has grown and developed and there have been further High Court Judgements plus key policies relating to improving the care of unaccompanied young people. They include: the White Paper *Better Outcomes: The Way Forward – Improving the Care of Unaccompanied Asylum Seeking Children* (Home Office, 2008) and *Statutory guidance to the UK Border Agency on arrangements to safeguard the welfare of unaccompanied children* (Home Office (UK Border Agency) and DCSF, 2009). A new framework, *Volume 3: Planning Transition to Adulthood for Care Leavers (including guidance on The Care Leavers (England) Regulations 2010)*, published by the DfE in October 2010, came into force in April 2011. The guidance gives information about the *Care Leavers (England) Regulations 2010* which replaces some of the previous guidance and regulations associated with the Children (Leaving Care) Act 2000. Some of the issues raised and the framework *Planning Transition to Adulthood for Care Leavers* (DfE, 2010) are discussed further in Chapter 12.

Representation of black and minority ethnic children in care

The Green Paper Care Matters (DfES, 2006f) describes the diversity of the care population and highlights how there is an overrepresentation of some groups of children who are looked after. The overrepresentation of some communities in the looked after population has been a persistent trend in statistical data over a number of years. It was highlighted in research by Bebbington and Miles (1989), where it was shown that there was a greater likelihood of children becoming looked after from African, African–Caribbean and dual-heritage families (children with one black and one white parent). Barn (1993) also showed in a pre-Children Act 1989 study that black children were overrepresented and were more likely to enter care through a voluntary process. More current statistical data highlights how children from African, African–Caribbean and dual-heritage families are still more likely to be looked after: *18.5% of looked after children compared with 13% in the general population are of minority ethnic origin* (Thoburn, et al., 2005, p100). More recent research focusing on care pathways for minority ethnic looked after children has revealed that they are less likely to be placed for adoption (Selwyn, et al., 2010). The research considers issues of social work practice with black, Asian and dual heritage looked after children and explores issues of culture and ethnicity. The complexities of decision-making are explored and there is an examination of the debate regarding 'same-race' placements for looked after children. Due to increased recognition of the specific needs of black and dual-heritage children who are looked after, the British Association for Adoption and Fostering (BAAF) has set up the Black, Asian and Mixed Heritage Issues Project. The project offers advice, information and training and disseminates good practice guidelines. This work also importantly informs broader strategies and developments within BAAF. Details can be accessed from the BAAF website, www.baaf.org.uk.

In terms of the recruitment of foster carers, studies have highlighted how the recruitment of more black and minority ethnic foster carers has been largely successful, giving greater placement choice and the opportunity for children from ethnically diverse communities to be placed with families that meet their cultural needs (Sinclair, et al., 2004a). Other research demonstrates the importance placed by social workers and foster carers of meeting the cultural needs of children who are looked after through placements with families where their cultural needs are likely to be met (Waterhouse and Brocklesby, 1999; Allain, 2007).

The issue of 'same race' placements for black and minority ethnic looked after children has been a contested and highly controversial area (Gill and Jackson, 1983; Butt and Mirza, 1996; Barn, 1999). Academics and activists have campaigned to ensure the placement needs of black children are met through their being placed with families who share the same ethnic and cultural traditions wherever possible. However, there has been a shift in policy regarding adoption and ethnic matching and the Coalition government has stated that it plans to facilitate (where this is in the child's best interests) white couples being able to adopt black children. In an article in the *Guardian*, Malik (2012) presents the views of the Prime Minister who stated that there are moves against ensuring *ethnic matching being the primary consideration in the matching process*. Within short-term fostering, looked after children continue to be placed cross-culturally although their identity needs must always continue to be considered and integrated into their care plan. In a review of research in relation to kinship placements and black and minority *ethnic* looked after children it was concluded that *ethnic minority children were more likely than white children to be placed with relatives* (Thoburn, et al., 2005, p112). Research by Broad (2001) on kinship care has shown that this offers greater placement stability to children plus a feeling of 'emotional permanence'.

ACTIVITY **6.1**

Why are children from certain communities over represented in the care system? Consider how factors such as poverty, social exclusion and language differences might impact on this?

How can we work in a way which is anti-oppressive?

COMMENT

You may have considered that some groups of children are more vulnerable due to complex family problems that require intensive family support and the engagement of a range of agencies. The aim would be to assess parenting capacity so that interventions can be developed that strengthen families' abilities to care for their children. Parents from some minority ethnic communities may be isolated, have minimal local support and may not speak English. In order to work in a way that is anti-oppressive it would be important to understand the family's faith, culture and ethnicity and their parenting style. Although it is important to respect different cultural practices, if children are being harmed then child protection policies and legislation must be applied as they would be for all children.

Unaccompanied asylum-seeking looked after children

Unaccompanied asylum-seeking young people who settle in the UK arrive from all over the world and are usually fleeing war, conflict and persecution. They arrive here and try to find sanctuary, care and protection with carers who can support and guide them through to adulthood. Data from the DfE (2011a) government statistics shows that for the year ending March 2011 there were 2,680 unaccompanied looked after children, which is a decrease of 22% from 2010.

CASE STUDY

You are the social worker for two unaccompanied asylum-seeking young people, a brother (Habtai) and sister (Saba) from East Africa, accommodated under s20 of the Children Act 1989. They are both placed in foster care with a carer who is from the same cultural background as them and over the two years of their placement they have settled reasonably well. However, at a meeting where both young people attend it is revealed by the foster carer that she is very worried about Saba. At the meeting the young woman starts to cry and says she is worried that her brother soon has to leave the foster carers and move to a semi-independent leaving care unit. He is almost 17 years old and Saba is 15 years old. Saba and Habtai say they have always been together and want to stay together if possible. Also, the foster carer says that Saba has lost a lot of weight as she has not been eating very well and has been crying a lot. Saba agrees that she has not felt hungry and her brother says he is worried about her. At this point in the meeting Saba and Habtai show you a crumpled paper with a photograph of their father with details of the Red Cross on it and say this is all they have of their father's details and want help to try and trace him.

1. *What action would you take in relation to the possible separation of the siblings in terms of foster care for Saba and leaving care for Habtai?*

2. *How would you address the health needs of Saba? Who would you involve?*

3. *How would you respond to the request from Saba and Habtai to help them find their father?*

COMMENT

1. *To discuss placement options you would have to carefully review the issue of eligibility and the meaning of 'relevant children' in accordance with the Children (Leaving Care) Act 2000, as the local authority has a duty to assess and meet the needs of certain children. You could also seek support from management, outlining the particular circumstances of Saba and Habtai and how plans could be developed so that they can both remain with the foster carer.*

2. *In terms of health needs you may wish to discuss with Saba contacting the school nurse in the first instance and then perhaps the GP.*

3. *In terms of tracing their father you could support Saba and Habtai in contacting the British Red Cross international tracing and messaging service.*

Issues of practice in direct work with unaccompanied young people

A helpful and positive model of practice is offered by Kohli (2006), who identifies the strengths in social work practice with unaccompanied children through locating three domains of practice: cohesion, connection, and coherence (see Research summary). These domains give us a window into how to work practically, therapeutically and with compassion with unaccompanied asylum-seeking young people. They will help you to understand how you can support young people who are dislocated and removed from all that is familiar to them, their home, their language, their family and customs. The domains can also help you to support young people through the many difficult transitions they have to make. Having an emotional commitment to the young people is described by Kohli (2006, p4) as fundamental to effective practice in this area, alongside building trust through being honest, reliable and patient. The issue of trust is key. Many of the young people had secrets and remained silent about their past. This may be related to why they had been forced to leave their country of origin, what they had witnessed before and during their journey, and their fear about what might have happened to their families and loved ones. They may be holding onto their grief, sorrow and hurt and trying to manage this through remaining closed and silent.

A model of group work, using a psycho-social framework, which offers support to isolated, unaccompanied young people is discussed by Heaphy, et al. (2007, p78). There is recognition by the group leaders from the project that many of the young women may have experienced traumatic events in their own countries, leading to mental health difficulties such as post-traumatic stress disorder. While holding this in mind, they also engage with and listen to the young people about what they themselves want from the group. Through adopting a collaborative approach involving skilled professionals they devised an agenda led by the young women.

The main issues the young women wanted support with were: coping with stress; having the opportunity to talk with adults in a safe environment about their past and future; connecting with their culture through talking and sharing food from their country of origin; and socialising with other young people who shared some of their experiences. Through initial individual direct work with the young women it was revealed that many had witnessed the killing of family members and some of the young women had been sexually assaulted in their countries of origin. There was not the same level of open sharing in the group process, although through using life maps the young women had the opportunity to share information about their past in ways that was comfortable to them. They could choose how much of their personal history they wanted to reveal to the group. Using tools such as ecomaps and life maps can assist in undertaking direct work with young people although it is important to proceed sensitively and at the pace of the young person (Parker and Bradley, 2003, Chapter 2).

ACTIVITY **6.2**

You are working with a boy, 15 years old, who is an unaccompanied asylum-seeking minor who is looked after and placed with foster carers. His name is Bahir and he is from Afghanistan; he arrived in the UK three years ago. He has always been hesitant to talk about his past and you have been asked to undertake direct work with him regarding his needs and what his views are about his future.

What assessment tools might help you in working with Bahir?

COMMENT

You may have decided that starting the work using a genogram may be too intrusive as young people who are unaccompanied asylum-seeking minors may not be ready to reveal painful aspects of their past and need to maintain a degree of privacy as a way of protecting themselves (Kohli, 2006). However, you might have considered using a culturagram: a tool developed specifically to assess the cultural needs of people who have experiences of immigration and settling in a new country (Parker and Bradley, 2003, p50). Another useful way of starting an assessment with unaccompanied asylum-seeking young people which a social work student discussed in a seminar, is through using a map of the young person's country of origin. A student gave an example of bringing a map of Afghanistan to a session involving direct work with a young person from Afghanistan, which really opened up discussions. The young person started to identify places on the map he knew, talked about where he was from and what his country meant to him. You may find these approaches helpful in your practice.

RESEARCH SUMMARY

The three domains identified by Kohli (2007, p154) are:

* *cohesion, where resettlement meant bringing order to the outside world;*

* *connection, where resettlement of their internal worlds was sought and sometimes found;*

* *coherence, where resettlement allowed whole histories to be carried forward safely into the new land and into a new future.*

Kohli (2006) outlines how as a social worker you will work across the three domains as the needs of the young people will ebb and flow and change over time. He describes the domain of cohesion as one where the focus is on practical matters of finding a place to stay, food, health care and education, links to community members and ensuring good legal representation. Social workers, when practising within this domain, are referred to as 'Humanitarians' (Kohli, 2007, p155). It is likely that working within this domain will predominate in the initials stages of the intervention with a young person.

Continued

*The domain of connection is referred to as practice where the focus is on working thera-
peutically, where you are required as a social worker to respond to the emotional needs
of the young person. This entails being able to help young people manage their feelings
of emotional pain and loss. Social workers, when practising in this domain, are referred to
as 'Witnesses' as they help the young people to make connections between the past and
the present and their inner and outer worlds. In undertaking this work it is important that
you also receive supervision where you are given the opportunity to discuss any issues
that arise from your practice.*

*The domain of coherence is described as one where the young people were living ordinary
lives although they continued to experience extraordinarily adverse circumstances (Kohli,
2007, p157). Workers in this domain were described as 'Confederates' who describe
the young people as resilient and speak of them with affection. They were workers who
were skilled at navigating the system on behalf of the young people and seemed to go
'the extra mile' in offering support and companionship, thus helping the young people
to build new lives. Although Kohli's work (2006, 2007) is focused on the needs of unaccompanied asylum-seeking young people in the care system, many of the principles of
good practice outlined in the domains can be transferred to working with children who
are looked after from all communities. All looked after children, wherever they are from,
benefit from social workers who are committed to them, who know and understand their
individual needs and can help them build new relationships within new families.*

Applications of cultural competence in practice

There are a number of models of practice that might help you when working in contexts
of difference and diversity. A useful model offered by Walker (2005) and O'Hagan (2001)
is the concept of culturally competent practice (Walker, 2005). The model has also been
used within medicine and nursing (Papadopoulos, 2003) as it offers a framework for facilitating reflection and interventions with service users from diverse communities.

Walker (2005) suggests that a number of theories can be used to assist social workers and
therapists in working in a way which is 'culturally competent.' He asserts that sociological perspectives offer us an understanding of the socially constructed nature of childhood
and how this differs across countries. He suggests this theoretical knowledge can be integrated with knowledge of child development and systemic and psychodynamic ideas,
giving practitioners the opportunity to link *the context of the presenting problem...to the
family context, wider...socio-economic and cultural context* (Walker, 2005, p47). Taking
this approach will enable you to understand the links between individuals, their immediate
families, their broader networks and communities, and their positioning in terms of class,
ethnicity, faith and culture.

However, the cultural competence model has been critiqued as being superficial and formulaic when the focus is only on learning about other cultures (Dogra, 2005). We advocate taking a broader approach linking political empowerment perspectives (Korbin, 2002) with self-awareness and cultural knowledge as advocated by Papadopoulos et al., (2004). This then means the focus is on cultural sensibility, which is:

> *…not about acquiring expertise about others, but of recognising that we need to be aware of our perspectives and how they affect our ability to be open to other perspectives.*

> (Dogra, 2005, p235)

To work in a culturally sensitive way with young people who are looked after, you should be respectful about differences between you and them, although this does not mean ignoring the law in relation to working within a context of diversity. It may mean considering issues of language and how you will communicate with the child you are working with, the pronunciation of their name and whether their traditions of second names is different to that which you are used to. You should also consider issues of faith and how you can support the child to carry on accessing their religious practices in their new placement. Miller (2006) suggests that in order to work within the context of diversity it is essential to examine our own cultural traditions and beliefs.

The idea of cultural sensitivity is introduced by Miller (2006). She refers to Palmer (2002, cited in Miller, 2006, p8) and how cultural sensitivity relates to the practical skills we develop through increasing our cultural awareness and knowledge, which can then be communicated in our work in sensitive and respectful ways. In essence, to understand the cultural needs of a young person you need to work in partnership with them and their families. Additionally, in order to gain insight about their lives you may also have to discuss their religious and spiritual beliefs. Cultural practices linked with language, traditions associated with food and issues of faith and worship are key facets of culturally sensitive practice and must be actively considered in order to practise in a culturally competent way (Walker, 2005, p119). Walker goes on to outline some important themes in relation to direct work with children and young people where religion and spirituality are part of the child's life. It is suggested that by taking the following issues into account the child will be supported through the process of direct work, with trust more likely to deepen thus leading to discussions about other more complex areas of their lives. The key points that he raises are as follows:

- The worker should allow discussions about faith to develop with the child leading (although the exception to this might be that you initiate the discussion if you think the child feels it is taboo to discuss certain matters).

- The worker should be aware that children may spontaneously introduce issues of religion and faith.

- The worker should create an open and accepting environment.

- Be respectful to and value the child's religious beliefs.

    (Walker, 2005, p129)

The practical application of culturally sensitive approaches to practice with looked after children will differ in response to the specific developmental stage of the child. Overall, the child or young person should have access to their culture and ethnicity through the adults who care for them in their placement. The placement experience should mean that they are able to continue eating the food of their community, speak their language and continue to share the cultural celebrations and cultural references that are familiar to them. Living in contexts where diversity is understood and respected will help the child negotiate the complexities of their lives in terms of identity and belonging. Also, having adults around them who can support them through the many different expressions of racism and discrimination is central. The complexity and new forms of racism are described by Bhavnani, et al. (2005) as the *culturalisation of racism where racism has increasingly been linked with culture – meaning a way of life, with religion, dress and rituals* (p16).

The position of bi-racial or dual-heritage children in child welfare systems has been the subject of recent research interest as the demography of Britain has changed and there are increasing numbers of children represented in this group (Census, ONs, 2001). In addition, children of dual-heritage are overrepresented in the looked after population. Issues of identity development are discussed by Robinson (2007), where it is suggested that, although some children may experience conflicts in relation to their identity, many will not. It is felt that achieving a positive identity means the child acknowledging and integrating comfortably both aspects of their heritage. Robinson (2007, p66) cites a study by Tizard and Phoenix (1993) to show that many dual-heritage children *had high self-esteem and positive identities*. Prevatt-Goldstein (1999) challenges the negativity surrounding issues of identity development for dual-heritage children and discusses how social work intervention must take into account their uniqueness as individuals. Prevatt-Goldstein (2002) explores the complexities in terms of placement decisions for dual-heritage children, emphasising that a skilled assessment is critical in order to establish what culturally the most meaningful thing is for a particular child, in their context, given their age, stage and trajectory of life. In terms of being culturally sensitive it is also important that the broader community context and environment is taken into account. It is suggested that both black and white substitute foster carers will have strengths and strong abilities in certain areas although black carers will *potentially be a positive resource for enabling the child to feel positive about black people and resisting racism* (Prevatt-Goldstein, 2002, p561).

The main message from this chapter and from reviewing the research is that working with difference and diversity involves being reflective and respectful about the different cultural beliefs, faith and traditions of the looked after children you will work with. It means focusing on strengths as well as being realistic about the challenges. It means managing complexity and using a range of models and skills so that children and young people from diverse communities can thrive in homes and within communities where they feel understood and feel a sense of belonging.

CHAPTER SUMMARY

In this chapter we explored the position of black and minority ethnic and unaccompanied asylum-seeking young people who are looked after. We started by reviewing the policy and legislative context for this area of practice and explored key definitions in terms of ethnicity, culture and faith. The rationale for having a specific chapter in this area of practice was given and is linked to the impact of globalisation and the multicultural society in which we now live. We explored different models of practice and showed that the starting point for intervention is respect, openness and reliability plus the ability to reflect on one's own values and culture.

FURTHER READING

Kohli, RKS (2007) *Social work with unaccompanied asylum seeking children*. Basingstoke: Palgrave.

This book gives detailed information about the experiences of unaccompanied asylum-seeking young people and offers helpful models of social work practice.

Robinson, L (2007) *Cross-cultural child development for social workers: An introduction*. Basingstoke: Palgrave.

This book gives an overview regarding issues of culture, ethnicity and identity development with a focus on working cross-culturally using psychological theories in relation to child development.

Thoburn, J, Chand, A and Proctor, J (2005) *Child welfare services for minority ethnic families – the research reviewed*. London: Jessica Kingsley.

This book offers excellent research summaries regarding child care social work with children and families from minority ethnic communities.

Chapter 7
Disabled children

This chapter will help you to develop the following capabilities from the **Professional Capabilities Framework**:

- **Knowledge**
  Apply knowledge of social sciences, law and social work practice theory.
- **Values and ethics**
  Apply social work ethical principles and values to guide professional practice.
- **Diversity**
  Recognise diversity and apply anti-discriminatory and anti-oppressive principles in practice.
- **Justice**
  Advance human rights and promote social justice and economic wellbeing.
- **Critical reflection and analysis**
  Apply critical reflection and analysis to inform and provide a rationale for professional decision-making.
- **Contexts and organisations**
  Engage with, inform, and adapt to changing contexts that shape practice. Operate effectively within your own organisational frameworks and contribute to the development of services and organisations. Operate effectively within multi-agency and inter-professional settings.

It will also introduce you to the following standards as set out in the 2008 social work subject benchmark statement
5.1.1 Social work services, service users and carers
5.1.5 The nature of social work practice
5.5.2 Gathering Information
5.5.4 Intervention and evaluation
5.6   Communication skills
5.7   Skills in working with others

Introduction

This chapter focuses on social work practice with disabled children who are looked after. Some disabled children become looked after for the same reasons that many other looked after children do, which may be related to child protection concerns, poor parenting or absent parents/carers. However, there are significant differences for many disabled children in terms of their routes into becoming looked after, which are linked to their disability and care needs and not always primarily about abusive and neglectful care. To address these differences, we explore two aspects of looked after children services: respite care away from home, which is sometimes referred to as 'short breaks'; and longer-term residential school placements and foster care. We are concentrating our discussions on these areas as they form a central part of a spectrum of services used by disabled children and their families.

Respite care is part of a broader range of family support services offered to families of disabled children, and residential school and foster placements are used when disabled children are looked after away from home for longer periods. When children receive respite care for over 75 nights, or from two separate placements, or overnight respite care, they are subject to looked after children procedures, although for most of the time they remain living at home. In this chapter we also discuss the legislative framework, policy context and the broader debates about the circumstances and needs of disabled children and their experiences of exclusion and discrimination. Through case studies and activities we examine the key debates regarding support for disabled children and their families and explore good practice in relation to transition planning. In this chapter we are using the term 'disabled children' as it is used *within the disabled people's movement* (Priestley, 2003, p3)

Definitions of disability

There are numerous and varying views about the definition of 'disability', which are linked to two main and often opposing theoretical models. The first is the 'medical model' or individual model (Oliver and Sapey, 2006, p22) of disability where the focus is on treating the disability as an impairment or medical condition. The second is the 'social model' of disability where the focus is on how societal barriers and unequal access creates and perpetuates disadvantages for disabled people. The medical model is critiqued as upholding the idea that the disability is a problem for the individual disabled person and they need to be helped to adjust to their situation (Oliver and Sapey, 2006).

The social model of disability was developed by activists in the 1970s and 1980s to challenge the predominance of the medical model. It focuses on how the problem lies not with individuals but with the *physical and social environments* and how *they impose limitations upon certain groups or categories of people* (Oliver and Sapey, 2006, p29). A critique of some of the problems with the social model of disability has also emerged and is discussed by Hingley-Jones (2011) who examines how this can result in minimisation of the individual impact of the impairment on the child and their family. This may then lead to parents being seen as *potential oppressors* of their child (p320) if their experiences do highlight the personal problems they and their child are experiencing. The research undertaken by Hingley-Jones (2011) focusing on the experiences of severely learning disabled young people highlights this and offers *observations of ordinary families coping in extraordinary circumstances* (p331). To address these dichotomies a closer integration of the social model with relationship-based approaches to practice is suggested.

In thinking about the practical application of the social model of disability, Oliver and Sapey (2006, p31) suggest that it could be used to create alternatives to residential, foster and respite care for disabled children if services were designed and provided within a social model of disability.

ACTIVITY 7.1

Reflect on your views regarding the social and medical models of disability. What types of services and housing would need to be provided to families caring for a severely disabled child? Would the provision of the right sort of services help parents to care for a severely disabled child at home or might they still need respite care away from home?

COMMENT

There is no easy answer to these questions as in some situations where children have severe and complex needs, residential or respite care away from home might always be needed. This might not necessarily be a negative option for the child and the family but would depend on a number of factors including the age of the child, the location and quality of the substitute care and contact arrangements.

Legislative framework

As well as having knowledge of the specific areas of law in relation to looked after children in the Children Act 1989, you should also be aware of the Carers and Disabled Children Act 2000 as parents may be commissioning services for their child through direct payments. In addition, the Equality Act 2010 replaced previous anti-discrimination legislation and has a specific section on disability. This legislation impacts on many areas of the lives of disabled children and their families, with the overarching aim of removing disabling barriers, so that disabled children and their families can receive the support and services they need. The requirements are:

- not to treat disabled children less favourably; and

- actively make 'reasonable adjustments' for disabled children.

The Children Act 1989, section 17 (10)(c), defines disabled children as children in need. As a disabled child is automatically considered to be 'in need', they are entitled to an assessment of their needs and a range of services. Part 3 of the Children Act 1989 has provisions for disabled children with some duties and powers also in Schedule 2, although the entire Act applies (Middleton, 1996).

Provision for disabled children and the requirements of local authorities to deliver services are specified in the Children Act 1989 (Schedule 2, Part 1, section 6), where it is stated that:

Every local authority shall provide services designed –

(a) To minimise the effect on disabled children within their area of their disabilities; and

(b) To give such children the opportunity to lead lives which are as normal as possible.

Local authorities are also required to maintain a register of disabled children in their area, which aids service planning and commissioning (Children Act 1989, Schedule 2, Part 1, section 2). The Children Act 1989, section 17 (11) definition of disabled children has been amended in response to the updated definition in the Disability Discrimination Act 1995, and is as follows:

For the purposes of this Part, a child is disabled if he has a physical or mental impairment which has a substantial or long-term adverse effect on his ability to carry out normal day to day activities; and in this Part 'development' means physical, intellectual, emotional, social or behavioural development; and 'health' means physical or mental health.

Defining disability in this way helps the state to target often scarce resources to those who are deemed to be eligible, based on legal definitions. As you can see from Schedule 2(6) of the Act, it is stipulated that disabled children should have access to local services that help them to live as others do in their local communities. These local services may involve respite care or 'short breaks', with overnight stays with paid carers, or in residential care homes (SCIE, 2004a). New guidance was issued regarding legislative and policy changes with respect to short-break provision for disabled children (DCSF, 2010e). Prior to changes to the Care Planning, Placement and Case Review Regulations 2010 disabled children who received overnight respite were subject to care planning regulations as looked after children. However, this was amended as the regulations did not meet the range of needs and placement requirements of all disabled children; especially given that respite can be delivered in and out of the home and may also be purchased through direct payments. The guidance issued by the DCSF (2010e) explains how short breaks can now be provided under section 17 of the Children Act 1989 where the focus is on children in need and children are not deemed to be looked after. Whereas if children receive respite under section 20 of the Act they are deemed to be looked after and are subject to Care Planning regulations; details regarding the regulations and procedures can be found in the DCSF (2010e) statutory guidance document. Additional support has also been made available for parents of disabled children in the Breaks for Carers of Disabled Children Regulations 2010. This means that from 1 April 2011 there is a new duty on local authorities to provide *breaks from caring to assist parents and others who provide care for disabled children to continue to do so or to do so more effectively* (section 25 Children and Young Person Act 2008). When children are accommodated they are subject to the whole range of regulations and procedures applicable to looked after children.

With regard to transition planning, the Children (Leaving Care) Act 2000 places duties on local authorities for the ongoing care needs of children who have been looked after post-18 years of age. How this interfaces with Community Care legislation for disabled young people leaving care will be discussed in the 'Transitions' section of this chapter.

ACTIVITY **7.2**

You are working with Anna, who is ten years old and has a learning disability. She enjoys going to visit Margaret, her respite carer, every month, where she has daytime respite on Saturdays. Anna's parents have requested an increase in respite care, so that every other month Anna has an overnight stay with her respite carer. What would you need to consider and what processes would you need to follow to arrange overnight respite care for Anna?

You would need to undertake a further assessment to establish whether the circumstances have changed in the family and review the overall package of support services. If it is agreed with the family and the carer that Anna should have additional respite, then you could discuss with the parents and the respite carer how to talk to Anna about this. You would need to develop a new care plan involving Anna, her parents, Margaret the respite carer and other professionals who are involved in Anna's care. Following the first respite care stay it would be good practice to communicate with Anna about how she felt about the stay as well as with the carer and parents. You might do this through using a picture book and symbols (Morris, 2002).

Policy context

The main policy focus in terms of services for disabled children is on providing local services to enable parents to care for their children in their own communities. This is linked with the other important policy driver to develop integrated and collaborative working across agencies in order to better meet the needs of disabled children. Legislation supports this, with both the Health Act 1999 and the Children Act 2004 containing powers to establish joint services with pooled budgets aimed at creating more seamless service provision. The issue of seamless services for disabled children has been recognised as important for some years. In 2005 the Prime Minister's Strategy Unit in a policy report *Improving the life chances of disabled people* identified this as one way of tackling the *fragmentation, complexity and bureaucracy of service provision ... for families of disabled children* (Prime Minister's Strategy Unit, 2005, p15).

A number of policies link with and support the Every child matters agenda (DfES, 2004). Starting in early years with *Together from the start* (DfES and DoH, 2003), the National Service Framework for Children, Young People and Maternity Services, Standard 8 (DfES and DoH, 2004c) and the White Paper *Valuing people* (DoH, 2001b) focused on improving services for people with learning disabilities. In response to concerns that Every child matters did not sufficiently address the needs of disabled children, a group of charities formed an organisation to champion change for, and improvement in, services for disabled children and their families, Every disabled child matters, www.edcm.org.uk. The campaign influenced policy-makers, and a policy document *Aiming high for disabled children: Better support for families* (HM Treasury and DfES, 2007) gave important new funding commitments in a range of areas including transition planning, child-care provision and short breaks for disabled children. These policy objectives are also discussed in *The children's plan, building brighter futures* (DCSF, 2007c) and in *Care matters: Time for change* (DfES, 2007, p38). Additional guidance regarding respite care and short breaks is available from the DCSF (2010e) guidance document.

The policy framework includes specific policies regarding disabled children, as well as general policies aimed at all looked after children. These shape the current landscape for social work practice with disabled children and their families. The key policy imperative is to encourage integrated practice, led by a lead professional or key worker. The key worker role is particularly important for disabled children and their families as they have so many professionals involved in their lives and having a key worker or lead professional helps their care needs to be co-ordinated (Greco, et al., 2006).

Respite care

Respite care for disabled children is part of the range of family support services which are provided by local authorities in line with the requirements of the Children Act 1989. The respite can take place in a range of different ways including day care in or out of the home or short-term overnight placements in residential care or with a family. We will be focusing on the issues regarding overnight respite care as this is when a child is deemed to be looked after in some cases when they receive services as part of section 20 of the Children Act, 1989. In the literature you will also see the term 'short breaks' often used instead of 'respite'. This name change is linked to the greater variety of respite provision available now, compared to the past where the focus was on giving parents a break from caring. Now respite is seen *to benefit the child as well as the parent* (McConkey et al., 2004, p62).

Despite the government pledging support for local short-break services, parents themselves, and findings from research, have highlighted chronic problems in this area. These are in relation to underfunding; a high demand for services resulting in lengthy waiting lists; lifting and handling issues; plus difficulties in recruiting carers (Prewett, 1999; McConkey and Adams, 2000; Flynn, 2001; McConkey, et al., 2004; SCIE, 2004a). This can result in frustrations for parents, who then have to use services in crisis situations as the support is not there when they need it (SCIE, 2004a, p2). Flynn (2001) discusses in particular the issues in relation to black families and the availability of respite services, as research shows less access for some minority communities.

Research undertaken by McConkey, et al (2004) examines how short breaks benefited both the child and the family, as the child was able to be with friends and participate in fun activities. Parents identified the friendliness and consistency of staff as important but wanted more frequent and longer breaks. Prewett's (1999) study identified that teenagers in particular valued the break away from home. They describe how they enjoy going swimming and bowling with the carer's children; the fun they have taking part in everyday experiences with other young people; how they enjoy going on trips to restaurants, adventure playgrounds, bowling, shopping and discos.

ACTIVITY 7.3

You undertake an initial visit to a family who have moved into your area from abroad and find a single mother living in a small, cramped flat with three children, Anna who is 13 years old, Peter who is seven years old and Michael who is two years old. Mrs Russell tells you that she has been living in the Middle East and, following her separation from her husband, she has moved back to the UK. She tells you that Peter has special needs and is autistic and says she wants help to settle in. You find out that she has visited her GP and Peter has been referred to the local Child Development Centre. What might some of the issues be in relation to this family and how could you help them to access support services?

You may have contacted the Education Department and advised Mrs Russell how she could proceed with accessing schools for Anna and Peter; the Education Department would then advise Mrs Russell about a specific assessment of Peter's needs.

Did you discuss respite care or 'short breaks' for Peter and did you think about some home-based family support? You may have come to the conclusion that given Peter's age, home-based respite care would be preferable, although given the cramped accommodation, this would have to be carefully planned.

What about the needs of the other siblings? Anna may wish to join a youth group or a local young carers' group, where she can have fun with other young people. You may also have discussed with Mrs Russell finding a part-time nursery place for Michael. Mrs Russell is likely to be experiencing a great deal of pressure, given the extent of her caring responsibilities, separation from her husband and relocation in the UK. You would need to act as a co-ordinating lead professional so that Mrs Russell does not become overwhelmed with the many responsibilities she has.

RESEARCH SUMMARY

It may also be helpful for you to consider how you can offer further support to parents. The factors below have been identified as important in supporting the parents of disabled children.

- *Improving material and economic conditions.*

- *Social support from family, friends and the local community.*

- *Providing clear explanations of the nature and character of the child's disability and how it is likely to affect the child's ability to communicate needs and emotions.*

- *Helping parents understand their child's disability, which increases their resilience and improves the sensitivity of their interaction.*

- *Helping parents resolve issues of loss and trauma in terms of the diagnosis of disability.*

- *Helping insecure parents reflect on and reprocess attachment issues relating to their own childhood experiences (Howe, 2006, p103).*

Residential and foster care

Disabled children may have to be accommodated in residential or foster care, if they have high levels of need, and limited access to respite or 'short breaks' or other local support. This can place a considerable strain on their families. In addition, disabled children who are in need of protection may also have to be accommodated. Data from the 2001 Children In Need Census shows that disabled children are *more likely than non-disabled children to be looked after because of abuse or neglect* (Miller, 2003, p21). Miller (2003) goes on to discuss the particular vulnerabilities of disabled children and identifies three main groups of factors. First, assumptions that disabled children would not be hurt or abused and that abuse may be mistakenly attributed to their impairment. Secondly, *inadequacies in service provision* (Miller, 2003, p21), leading to social isolation, lack of communication with disabled children and lack of independence and choice for disabled children in some circumstances. Thirdly, *factors associated with their impairment* (p22) may mean they receive intimate personal care from a number of carers and do not have the ability to tell others what is happening to them. Disabled children living away from home are seen as particularly vulnerable. If you are the social worker for a child who is accommodated, it will be very important that you get to know the child, understand their routines and how to communicate with them, ensuring you seek their views and thus give them choices. In order to improve safeguarding for disabled children, Miller (2003, p24) advocates changes on four levels:

societal level – to recognise the equal rights of disabled children;

community level – to provide disabled children with supportive and safe environments and a choice of services;

carer level – better support and consultation with disabled children and their carers plus awareness-raising about abuse;

individual level – empowerment of disabled children, seeking their views and acting on them plus sex education and safety-awareness work.

There is a long history of disabled children being sent to live away from their families. McConkey et al. (2004) discuss how up until the 1970s many children with profound learning disabilities, physical disabilities and severe medical conditions were cared for in long-stay institutions. They describe also how many children with sensory impairments were cared for in residential boarding schools, away from their families. Although much has changed and there is now a greater focus on local support, disabled children (31%) are still more likely to be in residential care than in family placements, compared to non-disabled children (23%) (Miller, 2003, p23). A study by Abbott, et al. (2001) highlights how there are still many disabled children living in specialist residential school placements, with many placed a significant distance from their home. More recent research presents detailed profiles of disabled children in residential placements, stating that approximately *two-fifths of disabled children looked after by social services in residential placements, are boarded in special schools* (Pinney, 2005, p1). It is important to remember that not all disabled children in residential schools are looked after; some are placed there by education departments with no involvement from social services. This is discussed in the Green Paper (DfES, 2006f, p52) and local authorities were asked to consider, in consultation with parents of disabled children, whether all disabled children in residential placements should have looked after status. Responses to the consultation found that parents wanted to be supported and not undermined although the importance of safeguards and the vulnerabilities of children placed away from home were recognised. To ensure children's needs are met, guidance about visits to children in residential placements has been issued, as outlined in *Care matters: Time for change* (DfES, 2007, p61).

> ## ACTIVITY 7.4
>
> *Why do you think some parents might be reluctant to agree to their child becoming 'looked after' if they are placed in a residential boarding school?*
>
> ### COMMENT
>
> *A review by the DfES/DoH (2004b) highlighted this issue and found that some parents feel that their child being looked after is a stigma. Do you think this links to the stigma some parents might attach to being involved with social services? Do you think there might be some other issues in relation to regulations, policies and procedures and some parents may find this off-putting?*
>
> *Abbott, et al. (2001) found that many social services authorities were confused about applying the looked after children regulations when children were in residential establishments and in many cases did not support parents in maintaining contact. Findings from their study show that it was difficult for allocated social workers to get to know the disabled children they were responsible for due to having to travel long distances to undertake visits, and workers needing additional training to work with children with communication impairments. When working with children with communication impairments, Morris (2002, p8) gives good practice guidance and suggests that social workers can prepare for the first meeting by asking the referrer or the parents how the child communicates. Also, she reminds professionals that it takes time to build up a relationship with a child and it takes time to understand how they communicate.*

RESEARCH SUMMARY

Morris (2002, pp7–8) lists some messages from young people with communication impairments, concerning things to avoid.

- *Don't assume it's okay to finish their sentences.*
- *Don't be impatient, wait for the young person to finish, it might take longer when using other methods of communication apart from speech.*
- *Don't pretend to understand if you don't.*
- *Don't act like the young person is a baby.*
- *Don't ask more than one question at a time.*
- *Talk directly to the young person and not only their carer.*

If a disabled child is looked after, they should receive regular social work visits and have statutory reviews, in line with all other children in care. When a child is first placed in a residential education placement it is important to discuss these issues so that there is clarity about your role, which is focused on ensuring the child receives good care and ensuring their emotional and social needs are met. We are reminded by McGill, et al. (2006) of the importance of this, given that we know children who are vulnerable and isolated are known to be at greater risk of abuse. Parents should also be supported to visit their child in school and maintain contact; this might mean you have to become involved in practical arrangements and offer financial support. We know that contact between children in care and their families is important in terms of promoting children's emotional well-being and mental health, and this is the same for disabled children.

A study has shown that when disabled children were placed in foster care they too had lower levels of contact with relatives than non-disabled looked after children (Baker, 2006). There were attempts made to ascertain disabled children's views about contact, but similar to the issues raised in terms of residential care, social workers and foster carers found it difficult to access information. The barriers they identified related to the severe disabilities and associated communication impairments of some children. However, some carers acknowledged they needed further training in order to develop their skills in communication with severely disabled children.

Transitions

Transition planning work is an important but complex and challenging area of practice with disabled children and their families. Many local authorities in Wheatley's (2006) study of Pathfinder Children's Trusts identified this as an area of their service they wanted to improve. Children and young people between the ages of 14 and 25 are the focus of transition work across children's and adult services.

Good practice in relation to transitions focuses on understanding the interface between different legislative and service frameworks in adult and children's services, the key developmental stage of adolescence and what the issues are for disabled young people in moving towards independence.

A summary of the legislative and policy framework

- Prime Minister's Strategy Unit (2005) *Improving the life chances of disabled people*: Cabinet Office.

- DfES and DoH (2004c) *National service framework for children, young people and maternity services* (standard 8, pp37–9).

- DoH (2001b) *Valuing people: A new strategy for learning disability in the 21st century*.

- DfES (2004) *Every child matters: Change for children.*

- Legislation: Children Act 1989; Children (Leaving Care) Act 2000; Community Care (Direct Payments) Act 1996; National Health Service and Community Care Act 1990.

- Fair Access to Care Services (FACS) LAC (2002), 13.

- www.transitioninfonetwork.org.uk gives information about transitions.

- DCSF (2010e).

  (adapted from Wheatley, 2006)

For many young disabled people there are many barriers to overcome on their transitions journey to adulthood. (Priestley, 2003, Chapter 4). You will remember from the introduction to this chapter and the discussion about the social and medical models of disability, that many of these barriers are in fact related to inequalities in society, making it more difficult for disabled people to access housing and employment than non-disabled people. The transition to adulthood for disabled young people is described as *one of the most challenging times for securing the support needed to make their experience positive and successful* (Wheatley, 2006, p38).

The difficulties encountered by young people experiencing transition services were discussed more than ten years ago by Morris (1995), who claimed that young disabled people were not having their needs met through the traditional leaving care services in the same way as non-disabled looked after children were. It was argued that the term 'leaving care' was meaningless for disabled young people as it simply meant being *passed over to adult services* (Morris, 1995, p81). Despite improvements in legislation and policy guidance, more recent studies highlight ongoing concerns from parents about future service provision and the issue of transition, particularly for young people with severe and complex needs moving from residential placements (Ward, et al., 2003; Pinney, 2005; McGill, et al. 2006). In the study by McGill, et al. (2006), where data from 73 parents whose children were placed in residential schools was analysed, it was reported that *75 per cent were 'extremely worried' about the availability of suitable, future services* (McGill, et al., 2006, p610). They reported that some young people who were soon to leave school still had no future placement. Another study interviewed young people themselves about what supported them most in making the transition to adulthood and found it was having *exceptional parents* (Pascall and Hendey, 2004).

The views of disabled children

Involving disabled children and reporting their views in relation to the services they receive is seen as important and was a central tenet of the government's *Quality protects* programme (Franklin and Sloper, 2006). Studies by Watson, et al. (1999) and Watson, et al. (2006) explore and present the views and experiences of disabled children. The Watson, et al. (2006) study gathered views from young people with complex healthcare needs, a group where very little research has been undertaken. The findings highlighted how children with limited verbal communication had few friendships, although their parents were keen to help them to develop communication systems. Positive reports were given about school, although one child thought it was *silly and boring* that they had to see so many professionals (Watson, et al., 2006, p93). The children enjoyed doing things that most children enjoy but needed additional parental or carer support to access most activities. They wanted to feel included and like most children did not like feeling left out. The study by Watson, et al. (1999) involved a group of 300 young people aged 11 to 16 years with a range of different disabilities. Some of the issues they raised are summarised below.

- They felt they did not have enough privacy from adults and lived under a high degree of surveillance.

- They felt they had limited opportunities for social interactions.

- They often felt 'labelled' as disabled and were resistant to this.

- They described the disadvantages of going to schools outside their own neighbour-hoods, which resulted in lost friendships at school.

The impact of having a disability on life course development is discussed by Crawford and Walker (2007, p106). This is a very important issue in relation to working with young people in transition to adulthood and some of the frustrations and challenges are identified by the young people themselves in the study by Watson, et al. (1999), where they identify feeling constrained and limited in what they are able to do. There may be conflict within families about the levels of care and support young people need, with young disabled people themselves wanting to have greater levels of independence than their parents feel is right for them. The development of intimate adult relationships may be hampered or not allowed if it is felt a young adult cannot fully express their wishes and is deemed to be vulnerable (Crawford and Walker, 2007, p106). As the social worker it will be important for you to engage with the young person and find out from them what their wishes and feelings are so that you can advocate for them and also ensure safeguards are in place.

CHAPTER SUMMARY

This chapter has explored issues in relation to practice with disabled children who are looked after. We started by outlining the legislative and policy framework and explored the intersections and links with practice and policy across children's and adult social services. We examined the meanings behind the term 'disability' and how both the social and medical models impact on the position of disabled children in society. Through exploring three specific services: overnight respite care, residential and foster care and transition, we focused on the experiences of disabled, looked after children. In reviewing the issue of transition planning we highlighted the complexities and challenges, and showed how it was critical that you as the worker reached across the bridge to adult services, so that the young person themselves felt supported on their journey to adulthood. We ended the chapter by highlighting the views and experiences of disabled children and young people themselves showing both their ongoing needs and their strengths.

FURTHER READING

Ahmad, W (2000) (eds) *Ethnicity, disability and chronic illness*. Buckingham: Open University Press.

Middleton, L (1999) *Disabled children: Challenging social exclusion*: Oxford: Blackwell.

Read, J and Clements, L (2001) *Disabled children and the law: Research and good practice*. London: Jessica Kingsley.

WEBSITES

Information about the Council for Disabled Children can be accessed through NCB: **www.ncb.org.uk**

Contact a Family provides information for families with disabled children: **www.cafamily.org.uk**

The Equality and Human Rights Commission was created in October 2007 and includes the previous Disability Rights Commissions: **www.equalityhumanrights.com**

Chapter 8

Attachment, adversity and resilience

A C H I E V I N G   A   S O C I A L   W O R K   D E G R E E

This chapter will help you to develop the following capabilities from the **Professional Capabilities Framework**:

- **Judgement**
  Use judgement and authority to intervene with individuals, families and communities to promote independence, provide support and prevent harm, neglect and abuse.
- **Knowledge**
  Apply knowledge of social sciences, law and social work practice theory.
- **Critical reflection and analysis**
  Apply critical reflection and analysis to inform and provide a rationale for professional decision-making.
- **Contexts and organisations**
  Engage with, inform, and adapt to changing contexts that shape practice. Operate effectively within your own organisational frameworks and contribute to the development of services and organisations. Operate effectively within multi-agency and inter-professional settings.

It will also introduce you to the following standards as set out in the 2008 social work subject benchmark statement
5.1.1 Social work services, service users and carers
5.1.2 The service delivery context
5.1.3 Values and ethics
5.1.4 Social work theory
5.1.5 The nature of social work practice
5.5.1 Managing problem solving activities
5.5.2 Gathering information
5.5.3 Analysis and synthesis
5.5.4 Intervention and evaluation

Introduction

Attachment, adversity and resilience are terms often used by social workers in their work with children. But what significance do they have for work with looked after children? Within the psychological literature a significant amount is known about attachment theory, and the related concepts of adversity and resilience. A number of contemporary social work authors synthesise a number of psychological theories and concepts for social work practice (e.g. Newman 2004; Howe, 2005; Gilligan 2007). Schofield (2001, p11) describes attachment theory as *probably the most popular developmental framework for family placement practice*. This knowledge base is one of the drivers underpinning such developments as the DoH (2000a) publication, *Framework for assessment of children in need and their families*. However, in the case of adversity and resilience in particular, there is still much to learn. For example, we still do not fully understand why it is that some children can experience adversity (difficult life experiences which can have a harmful effect on a child's overall development) and can seemingly make adjustments to this in terms of negating the impact that these experiences could then have in other areas of their life. This is the development of 'resilience' that Fonagy, et al. (1994) describe as *normal development under difficult conditions*. Looked after children often have additional hurdles to negotiate in their lives, for example, breaks in significant attachments, experiences of loss, so in thinking about how these concepts apply to looked after children, it is important that the particular context and circumstances of looked after children's lives and experiences are considered.

This chapter covers a number of issues:

1. the importance of understanding child development;

2. what is attachment theory?

3. what are adversity and resilience and how do they relate to attachment?

4. why are these concepts important in relation to looked after children?

5. what difference can a social worker make to the resilience of a child they are working with?

This chapter will define attachment, adversity and resilience and make links to practice through a number of activities and case studies which you can use to reflect on the information provided. These will help you think about how this links with your practice, and your work with individual children.

The importance of understanding child development

This chapter will not present an overview of the current debates within child development literature, nor go into detail concerning the major theories explaining human development, such as: Erikson – model of life stage development; Freud – psychoanalysis; Piaget – cognitive development; Skinner – behaviourism; Bandura – social learning theory; Bronfenbrenner – ecological development. It is important that social workers have a comprehensive understanding of the various theoretical perspectives underpinning child development, including knowledge about age stage development (for further information see Berk, 2003; Crawford and Walker, 2003; and the Mary Sheridan developmental charts appended to the Assessment Framework documentation (DoH, 2000a)). The DoH requires this information to be taught to students on qualifying programmes (DoH, 2002a; Boylan and Ray, 2012).

Having a wide-ranging understanding of these theories enables social workers to communicate effectively with children, and translate this theoretical knowledge into their practice. For those children who experience abuse and neglect, it is quite possible that some aspect of their overall development will be affected. Unless social workers know what is age-appropriate behaviour and development, they will not be able to easily identify atypical development in those children who have experienced abuse and neglect. Additionally, it will be very difficult for social workers to recognise the more subtle but equally important signals, expressions of distress and worrying behaviours of abuse and neglect, which can often present as abused children failing to meet their developmental milestones.

In understanding the many different theories which exist in child development, Berk (2003) suggests that clarification can be gained from exploring each theory's relationship to three questions. First, is development continuous or discontinuous? Continuous development is a smooth, constant process which sees children regularly develop skills as part of their ongoing development, whereas discontinuous development sees children change rapidly as they 'step up' to a new stage in development, but sometimes little change occurs in between; while children process they change 'step'.

Secondly, is there one course of development or many? How does the theory characterise development – one path for all, or many different paths depending on the context? Perhaps it is a combination of both.

Finally, is nature or nurture more important? This is an ongoing debate within the field, with the argument centring on identifying the role of genetics versus that of environment in terms of children's development. How do they collaborate? What is the link between early experiences and later life patterns of behaviour, and is it possible to overcome early experiences of adversity?

In terms of the relevance of the child development literature for social work, criticisms have been levelled within social work education concerning a lack of emphasis on developmental theories being taught to social work students in a critical manner. Taylor (2004) is very critical of what she sees as social work's uncritical assimilation of child development theory. In particular she notes that child development theory makes a number of universally valid claims about children but fails to locate these claims historically and culturally. Such theories treat children as developing adults rather than persons in their own right and competent social actors. Taylor believes that child development theories are individualistic in focus. This potentially negates the influence of culture on different children's development, as well as misinterpreting social realities of some children's lives. *Instead of poverty, unemployment and frustration we have evil children, bad mothers, absent fathers and broken homes* (Burman, 1997, p142, cited in Taylor, 2004). These have become the social constructions of parenting. They are based on a 'deficit model', concentrating on limitations and lack of competence. However, it is this deficit model that is in danger of defining social work, as it is the lack of competence and limitations in parenting capacity that are looked for and ultimately will determine the actions of a social worker.

Critiques of ethnicity and family structures

Robinson (1995) believes that child development theories do not understand black children's experiences and how these differ from those of white children. She believes that, *it is necessary to analyse black behaviour in the context of its own norms* (1995, p18). She thinks that the entire field lacks a black perspective and that research conducted in this arena is *based largely on white middle-class children, which is assumed to be (or defined as) generic to all children. The behaviours and patterns of development in non-white children are then viewed comparatively against this 'norm' and defined as 'exceptions' or 'deviations' from the norm* (1995, p67), and that more broadly, *child psychology does not usually consider race and race awareness as an important variable in the child's mental, emotional and personality development* (1995, p67). We will return to this point later in the chapter. Robinson's suggestion of moving from a deficit model to one which acknowledges strengths and competencies remains a challenge for us all in our practice, even with the DoH's Assessment Framework (DoH, 2000a) adopting an ecological, strength-based approach (Bronfenbrenner, 1986).

Golombok (2000) found in her studies into non-traditional family structures (including a longitudinal research project examining outcomes for children raised in heterosexual single-parent families and lesbian families) that:

> the experiences of children raised by single mothers, lesbian mothers or by parents with whom they have no genetic link are not alike and it cannot be assumed that the consequences for children growing up in these family types will be the same. Neither can it be assumed that the consequences for such children will necessarily be bad.

(p100)

Further, she comments: *it is what happens within families, not the way families are composed, that seems to matter most* (2000, p101).

So how important is all this for practice? In conducting a significant number of serious case reviews over the past 20 years, the Bridge Child Care Development Service has identified a number of actions as assisting the multi-agency community in recognising neglect and emotional abuse. These include:

- detailed information about the developmental history, including health and social development and family interactions for all children in the family, should be available to all professionals working with children in the family;

- formal inter-agency discussion should occur about the needs of all the children in the family;

- keeping careful records, summarising files and regularly sharing relevant information with other agencies; a willingness to explore a hypothesis about the existence of neglect when dealing with developmental delay. (Bridge Child Care Development Service, 2000; Jeyarajah Dent and Cocker, 2005).

Working together with other professionals is important in this regard as other professionals bring different knowledge and experience to situations where knowledge of child development is crucial. Additionally, the main tool of assessment used in the UK by social workers assessing families, the Assessment Framework (DoH, 2000a), is built on an ecological model, and assumes that practitioners have a comprehensive knowledge of child development.

What is attachment theory?

Over the last 40 years, following the publication of Bowlby's three volumes on attachment, separation and loss, attachment theory has become the central psychological theory for understanding the social and emotional development of children of all ages in its broadest sense. Shemmings (2004, p300) comments that *attachment theory is impressive in terms of the scope of its research endeavours and it can justifiably claim to have become a truly interdisciplinary field of study (one of Bowlby's original aspirations).*

Bowlby says of attachment: to *say of a child that he is attached to, or has an attachment to, someone means that he is strongly disposed to seek proximity to and contact with a specific figure and to do so in certain situations, notably when he is frightened, tired or ill* (1969, p371). Bowlby makes a distinction between this and attachment behaviour, which refers to *any forms of behaviour that a child commonly engages in to attain and/ or maintain a desired proximity* (1969, p371). Bowlby's view is that the child's attachment behaviour is dependent on the situation and context present at any given time and will be present or absent accordingly, whereas the attachment that a child has with a main caregiver is *an attribute of the child...which changes only slowly over time and which is unaffected by the situation of the moment* (1969, p371). Attachment theory explains both these phenomena.

RESEARCH SUMMARY

Attachment

Mary Ainsworth's work is important because she operationalised the theory of John Bowlby and made it measurable, which is vital for practice. Ainsworth's classic observational studies using the 'strange situation' test identified three patterns of attachment present within toddlers and young children from approximately one to three years (see Ainsworth et al., 1978). These are called Type A, Type B and Type C.

Type A: Anxious, avoidant, insecure attachment, where toddlers experience their caregivers as consistently rejecting, and themselves as insecure but compulsively self-reliant. They show little distress when the caregiver leaves, and avoid contact with the caregiver on their return – some will avoid the caregiver completely. Toddlers with an avoidant attachment will react to a stranger in the same way that they do with their caregiver (Daniel, et al., 2010).

Behavioural characteristics of the main caregiver are described as controlling, rejecting or dismissing, not of the child but of the behaviour, but the child cannot make this distinction and therefore adapts to this by downplaying and holding back their feelings of need, so as to behave in a way which meets with their caregiver's approval (Howe, 2005).

Type B: Secure attachment, where toddlers experience their caregiver as available and they see themselves positively. They explore when their caregiver is present, show upset at the caregiver's departure and stop exploring. They show interest in reuniting with the caregiver upon return but then want to explore. They will cling to their caregiver in the presence of a stranger (Daniel, et al., 2010).

The behavioural characteristics that the main caregiver exhibits in early months of life which have been documented as crucial for developing secure attachments is availability, mutual reciprocity, sensitivity, loving, responsiveness, attunement and accepting (Howe, 2005). Two-thirds of children demonstrate this type of attachment.

Type C: Anxious resistant or ambivalent insecure attachment, where toddlers experience their caregiver as inconsistently responsive and themselves as dependent and poorly valued. They are anxious before their caregiver leaves, distressed while their caregiver leaves and will demonstrate a mix of resisting and seeking contact with their caregiver on return (Daniel, et al., 2010).

Behavioural characteristics of the caregiver are described as warm but not consistent or sensitive to the child's needs, often because the caregiver's own needs take priority over those of the child. Children will then increase their displays of anxious and distressing behaviour in order to gain their caregiver's attention.

Main and colleagues (Main and Hesse, 1990, cited in Schofield and Beek, 2006, p38) identified a further group of children who were insecurely attached and yet did not fall into either Type A or C. This further type of insecure attachment is Type D.

Type D: Disorganised, disoriented insecure attachment, where toddlers experience their caregivers as either frightening or frightened, and themselves as helpless, angry and unworthy. Toddlers' behaviours are contradictory and high levels of negative emotions are expressed.

Behavioural characteristics of caregivers are described as ineffective, helpless, hostile or scary (Daniel, et al., 2010). Atwool (2006) comments that there is general agreement in the literature that Type D attachments are more likely to emerge in abusive situations. Abusive and hostile carers hurt and frighten their children. Depressed, drunk or drugged parents can appear helpless and this can also frighten children (Howe, 2005, p37). Those caregivers who are so affected by unresolved losses and traumas from their own unhappy childhoods will find it difficult to meet the needs of and empathise with the distress of their own children because it highlights all of their own unmet and unresolved needs (Howe, 2005).

Ainsworth's findings have been verified many times. Van Ijzendoorn and Kroonenberg (1988) conducted a meta-analysis of all studies undertaken using the 'strange situation' and found that while there were some similarities in cross-cultural patterns, there were also a number of differences. Type A classifications emerge as relatively more prevalent in western European countries and Type C classifications are relatively more frequent in Israel and Japan (cited in Yeo, 2003, p295). However, they also found that there was more intra-cultural (within cultures) variation than inter-cultural (between cultures) variation (Holmes, 1993).

So what is the relationship between children having an insecure attachment of an either ambivalent or avoidant form or a disorganised attachment and the likelihood of that child developing problems of some sort in later life? The work of Sroufe, et al. (2005) via the Minnesota study would suggest a strong correlation; the work of other theorists isn't so clear, including those that think that 'the strange situation' assessments completed on children is not a test for attachment but a test of a child's temperament. Crawford and Walker (2003, p79) describe temperament as *individual difference in the basic psychological processes – the apparent in-built tendencies in relation to reactions and behaviours.* Theories exploring temperament suggest that these responses are biologically or genetically determined (Buss and Plomin, 1989; Thomas and Chess, 1977, cited in Crawford and Walker, 2003, pp79–80).

Children develop multiple attachments over time. Rutter (1981, cited in Fahlberg, 1994, p14) contends that, if 'mothering' is of high quality and provided by figures who remain the same during the child's early life, then at least up to four or five multiple parenting figures need have no adverse effects.

Golombok (2000, p101) contends that:

> *The opportunity to form attachments to parents or other caretakers is fundamental to children's psychological wellbeing. But it is not just whether or not attachments are formed but the type of attachments that children have to their parents that affects how they will function in childhood and in later life…whether children are raised by one parent or two, whether or not a father is present in the home, whether the child is genetically unrelated to one or both parents, and whether the parents are homosexual or heterosexual makes little difference to children's wellbeing.*

Other concepts you will come across within the attachment literature are: 'bonding' and 'internal working models'. Although Fahlberg uses as her definition of attachment one provided by Klaus and Kennel (1976, cited in Fahlberg 1994, p14): *an affectionate bond between two individuals that endures through space and time and serves to join them emotionally*, this is more closely linked with bonding behaviour than that of attachment. Fahlberg (1994) talks about an *arousal/relaxation cycle* – attachment-seeking behaviour as initiated by the child – and the *positive interaction cycle* – interaction between a caregiver and child as initiated by the adult – as examples of bonding and attachment behaviours in action. The adults' responses to these cycles will have implications for how reliable and available babies and children view their caregivers.

Attachment theory holds that, within close relationships, young children acquire mental representations, or internal working models, of their own worthiness based on other people's availability and their willingness to provide care and protection (Ainsworth et al., 1978, cited in Howe, et al., 1999, p21). It is through the world of relationships that children begin to understand themselves and their relationship with others (Howe, 1996). Atwool (2006, p317) states that *although internal working models have a strong propensity for stability they are not templates…in childhood it is possible that internal working models can only be altered in response to changes in direct experience.* The importance of this for Rutter's work on self-esteem, self-efficacy and children's ability to develop social problem-solving skills will be explored in the next section.

However, the work of Hodges, et al. (2003) using the attachment assessment technique 'story stem' would suggest that templates are not so much changed, but that a second, competing model is established for the child which is more adaptive. There are a number of other attachment measures that different CAMHS assessors use. Examples of these include the adolescent attachment interview and the mid-childhood attachment interview. Minnis, et al. (2002) have also developed a scale for measuring attachment disorders.

ACTIVITY *8.1*

For those already working with looked after children, identify two children that you are working with. How would you describe their attachments to current main caregivers and to birth family members?

For those not working with looked after children, identify two children you know who have experienced significant loss. How would you describe the manifestation of this loss on the children? Was it the same for both children?

To help you think about this in a structured way, use the DoH's Assessment Framework triangle (DoH, 2000a). Identify and describe the strengths as well as areas for development in these children's attachments and relationships with their family and within their wider community.

COMMENT

Often people mistake a strong attachment for a healthy one and it is misread as an indicator of security. Think about the loss these children have experienced in their lives and look at the list you have written which demonstrates the ways in which these children have coped with this loss. How do the children's responses differ from one another? There will be strengths and factors of resilience for each of the children. Can you identify these?

What are adversity and resilience and how do they relate to attachment?

Daniel, et al. (2010, p105) define adversity as the *experience of life events and circumstances which may combine to threaten or challenge healthy development*. Newman's comprehensive description of resilience draws heavily from the work of Rutter. *Resilience refers to the positive ability of people to respond to stress, but also to 'hope and optimism in the face of adversity'* (Rutter, 1987, p317, cited in Newman, 2004, p3). This positive adaptation generally occurs in circumstances where personal, familial or environmental difficulties are so extreme that a person's functional or cognitive abilities are usually impaired (Garmenzy, 1983, 1985, 1991; Rutter, 1985; Masten and Coatsworth, 1998, cited in Newman, 2004, p4).

Schofield (2001) believes that resilience is a difficult term to clearly define because of its interrelatedness to a number of other key concepts: stress, adversity, coping, risk and vulnerability (Garmezy and Rutter, 1983; Haggerty, et al., 1994, cited in Schofield, 2001, p8). She favours the definition provided by Masten, et al. (1990, p436, cited in Schofield, 2001, p8):

> *Resilience refers to the process of, capacity for, or outcome of successful adaptation, despite challenging or threatening circumstances. Psychological resilience is concerned with behavioural adaptation, usually defined in terms of internal states of well-being or effective functioning in the environment or both.*

RESEARCH SUMMARY

Resilience

In his review of relevant literature, Newman (2004) concludes that we know a great deal about the processes through which resilience can be identified. However, positively influencing these processes is more difficult (Rutter 1993, cited in Newman 2004, p5).

Rutter (1985) identifies three key factors associated with resilience which are intrinsic to the child, which are:

- *a sense of self-esteem and confidence: to feel good about;*

- *a belief in own self-efficacy and ability to deal with change and adaptation; and*

- *a repertoire of social problem-solving approaches.*

Atwool (2006) expands this by identifying four factors from the literature associated with resilience, where only the first is related solely to the child: individual characteristics of the child (temperament, competence, self-efficacy and self-esteem); family support; support outside of the family; and culture. Atwool cites the work of Ungar (2003); Harwood et al. (1995) and Carlson and Harwood (2003). These works not only challenge some of the assumptions underpinning attachment theory in terms of the main caregiver's sensitivity and competence, but also examine the role of culture in determining values and influencing the caregiver's mental representation and interpretation of relationship experiences (Atwool, 2006, p324).

None of the researchers working in this field see resilience as exclusively individual traits which are somehow separated from the family and environmental context in which the child is situated. Research now identifies a combination of internal and external dynamics as relevant and necessary to expanding our understanding of resilience (Atwool, 2006), reiterating that resilience is a process, not a state of being, and is something that can change over time (both positively and negatively) depending on circumstances (Newman, 2004).

Theories of resilience are not without their critics. Newman (2004, p78) highlights a number of issues: it excessively simplifies the positive responses of different people to different stimuli (Kaplan, 1999)...it under-emphasises structural causes of oppression and inequality (Barton, 2000). *Practitioners may recognise the value of promoting resilience, but find it hard to distinguish its implications from strategies they might be using already. Atwool (2006, p315) comments:* there is a danger, however, that we rely too heavily on the evidence that children can achieve positive outcomes in the face of adversity without fully understanding what enables these children to do so.

Resilience and attachment

In relation to attachment, Atwool summarises the degree of interplay between resilience and the four different types of attachment that we discussed earlier (see Research summary pp110–111). She comments:

> The implications for resilience are clear. A secure internal working model encompasses all of the factors that relate to resilience. The avoidant [Type A] and ambivalent [Type C] patterns are adaptive and demonstrate a degree of resilience in less than optimal circumstances, allowing children to manage relationships and emotions. Those children with a disorganised attachment [Type D] are the most vulnerable, lacking a coherent strategy for managing relationships, feelings or experiences.
>
> (2006, p320)

Schofield (2001) identifies three conceptual links between attachment and resilience. First, internal working models are critical in reflecting the child's belief about how loveable they are, how much say they feel they have in the living of their life, the predictability of important relationships and the degree of care and protection afforded the child through these relationships. Secondly, the concept of adaptation is important in terms of the child being an active participant in adapting to their environment as opposed to a passive recipient. It is important to realise that children with insecure attachments can adapt to their environment as a way of survival; however, this adaptation, although functional as it informs survival, may be destructive or maladaptive. Thirdly, Schofield highlights the importance of systems theory as a framework for understanding the complexities of both concepts in terms of outcomes for children. If both frameworks are correctly interpreted, then social workers will understand the importance of attachment and resilience for not only the internal world of the child but for the external caregiving environment and beyond – taking into account all levels of an ecological model.

Why are these concepts important in relation to looked after children?

Schofield (2001, p6) believes that *the themes of risk and protective factors, vulnerability and resilience in children's lives need to be understood within [a] developmental framework. This is particularly true of the complex lives of adopted and looked after children.* In this regard, the professional network surrounding the looked after child should be used to support the child within their placement. Howe (2005, p274) states: *the mark of a caring society is to ensure that children who might otherwise become lost along tortured pathways of increasing developmental despair encounter others who can understand, value and contain them.* The best way to do this is by supporting the caregiver responsible for providing the day-to-day care for the child, and recognising the importance of other significant adult and peer friendships for the child. Fahlberg (1994, p6) highlights:

> the significance of interpersonal relationships, the necessity of building alliances with children and adults by enhancing communication skills, increasing the individual's knowledge of self, and the importance of developing a plan for continuity of relationships throughout a lifetime.

Leonie is six years old and her older sister Michaela is eight. Both children have been looked after for one year now. They have an older brother who is 11 years old and is in another placement. All three children were removed from their father's house following allegations of neglect, sexual and physical abuse. Their mother lives locally but has remarried and has two other younger children, who are also looked after, but not placed with the girls.

Leonie is in Year 2 and is significantly behind her peers at school. An example of this delay is that she cannot recognise or read many words unaided and her numeracy skills show she is also trailing her peers by a wide margin. Within a matter of months, the school placed Leonie on the SEN register, at 'school action plus' (please see Chapter 10 for further information about education), so she is receiving additional help with her learning within the classroom. However, she has made some progress since becoming looked after, chiefly because her relationships with peers have improved. At her previous school she was constantly teased for being dirty and smelly and children would not sit next to her in class. She is involved in a number of after school activities – African drumming and art.

Michaela is in Year 4, and she appeared at least initially to settle well into the placement and new school but problems are now beginning to emerge. Recently she has begun stealing money from her foster carers, and they are concerned that she is unhappy in the placement. She has been getting into arguments at school and alienating peers. Also, things are going missing in the classroom. Michaela is attending a swimming club two nights a week, which she is enjoying.

As these children's social worker, how might you offer support to these children, and which other agencies and professionals would you work closely with?

Leonie's and Michaela's early life experiences have had a considerable impact on their overall development as well as their ability to make and maintain relationships with peers and others outside of the immediate family. Both children have different needs. It is important to understand that both children will have experienced adversity in different ways and the support offered to them must reflect the different ways in which their early experiences have been understood by them, both consciously and unconsciously. Both children will also have exhibited different responses to the loss and separation they have experienced in entering care. Remember also the insidious nature of neglect and the effect that this can have on children's development.

Getting to know these children separately is important. What kind of attachment do these children have with their father and mother? What kind of attachment do they have with their current caregivers, with each other, with other siblings, important adults and extended family members in their lives? What is each child good at? What does each child enjoy? What does each child dream about for their life? Do they have goals or ambitions?

Involving the foster carers and the school is critical in supporting these children with their separate needs. Newman (2004, p78) comments that *it is widely acknowledged that resilience is most effectively promoted as part of a broader strategy, which is likely to involve a range of agencies and institutions as well as communities and ordinary individuals.* The practical and emotional availability of the school, foster carers and social worker in times of quite testing behaviour will be important in demonstrating the importance of positive relationships to these children, where people work at supporting one another when this is required. Small successes are to be celebrated, because they can and should be built on, and the importance of a 'sleeper' effect should not be underestimated either, where the benefits of a particular activity for a child may not be immediately obvious but may 'kick in' at a later stage.

Schofield (2001, p9) comments that the life of an adopted or fostered child is constantly evolving and changing:

> *The developmental consequences of their early life experiences will not always be known or be predictable, which is why it is so important not to see resilience as a fixed trait in a child. Children who appear to be vulnerable can and should be encouraged to gain certain coping strategies.*

Attachment and resilience are not static concepts – children's attachments to key caregivers, their skills in adapting to new environments, their self-esteem, their understanding about the influence they have in their life, all can and will change over time. It is important that social workers do not become locked into a static interpretation of the above but understand how best to encourage this change over the long term. This is where little steps are important. For example, for a four- or five-year-old child to be given the school register by the class teacher to take to the school office can be a significant event. Being trusted to undertake this task can do wonders for a child's self-esteem and might be the first time they have ever been trusted to undertake an important task.

How do social workers use attachment theory?

Howe (1998, p136) believes that:

> *Attachment theory has shown itself to be very useful to child welfare and adoption workers. It offers a framework that classifies different behaviours and relationship patterns...it can be seen as a provisionally useful and relatively effective theory, at least for the while.*

However, an exclusive focus on attachment may well limit responses to difficulties. Rushton and Dance (2002, p28) comment that: the *attachment explains all; the approach may miss other available well tested interventions to target the problem directly.* Scott (2003, p311) also concurs with this: *narrowly defined attachment problems often come with a host of other difficulties that could usefully be addressed using other approaches from developmental psychopathology,* but he also believes that *a wide range of clinical problems might be better understood and treated if attachment theory were applied.* Even with these and other difficulties, including *no systematic evidence-based approach for treating children with attachment disorder* ... and *the misguided use of attachment theory and research by some clinicians working with highly vulnerable children and their parents (often adoptive)* (Steele, 2003, p219), there is still an important role for attachment theory that cannot be underestimated. Attachment theory does not need to remain the prerogative of child therapists or CAMHS assessors. There are many ways in which this theory can be of benefit to social workers, including through observation and assessment, and in view of the Public Law Outline (HM Courts and Tribunal Services, 2008), you will have to write court reports which demonstrate competence in this area.

One of the most powerful tools and skills that a social worker can develop is that of observation: to be able to differentiate between a secure and insecure attachment can be useful in assessing the quality of the attachment to the caregiver and recognising any areas of difficulty. This is one of the key skills in the assessment task (see Chapter 4 on assessment). Assessments are key tools used by social workers in working with children and families. Since 2000, with the introduction of the Framework of assessment for children in need and their families by the DoH (2000a), there has been more rigour attached to the assessment process, both in terms of content and period of time in which an assessment is undertaken. This framework borrows heavily from a developmental perspective, as do the corresponding materials used with looked after children called the Looking After Children (LAC) materials, including age-related Action and Assessment Records. The work of Garrett (2003) provides a critique of the LAC material and the role of the 'corporate parent' inherent within this.

The importance of life story/life journey activity as a tool for children to begin to understand their past experiences cannot be underestimated. Constructing a narrative around significant life events for the child is a powerful way of the child being able to acknowledge and process feelings and emotions related to their life story. A social worker's role in this is crucial in offering the child a secure base from which to explore potentially difficult events and related emotions (Schofield and Beek, 2006). See Chapter 5 for further information on life story work.

Schofield and Beek (2006) believe that attachment research has assisted in giving practitioners ideas about how the effects of adversity in early life experiences, including managing separation and loss (which are common to all looked after children) can affect children's developing minds, emotions and behaviour. *It is this potential for change in children's thoughts, feelings and behaviour in the contexts of new relationships that needs to be understood in order to promote successful adoption and fostering practice* (2006, p9). It is therefore possible through building formative relationships with vulnerable children to model new patterns and introduce and strengthen healthier attachments with caregivers and significant others. Howe (2005, p277) believes that attachment theory can guide practitioners:

> *towards effective interventions in cases where children's development has been seriously affected by abuse and neglect. By understanding how competent, integrated, emotionally literate minds are built, professionals can help maltreated children and their carers capture these same constructive ingredients, facilitating healthy development and aiding recovery.*

What difference can a social worker make to the resilience of a child?

In considering the interplay between resilience and the child and wider social context, it is useful to recognise a number of risk and protective factors identified in the literature, which are spread across the child, family and social/environmental areas. These factors are not exhaustive and should not be used as a 'shopping list' – countering one risk factor with a protective factor. *It is difficult to demonstrate conclusively a cause and effect relationship between interventions and changes, particularly with children and families who have severe and longstanding difficulties* (Wallace, et al. 1997, cited in Audit Commission, 1999, p64).

The literature identifies a number of risk factors that apply to the social environment, family and child (NHS Health Advisory Service Thematic Review, 1995; BMA,1999, p124; and Mental Health Foundation, 1999, pp8–10; Rutter, 1985; Gilligan, 2001). Social risk factors identified include: socio-economic disadvantage; homelessness; isolation; and discrimination. Family risk factors include: poor parenting skills; inconsistent or unclear discipline; hostile and rejecting relationships; failure to adapt to the child's changing developmental needs; abuse; parental conflict; family breakdown through divorce or death; death and loss – including loss of friendship; parental mental illness; large families; and parental criminality, alcoholism and personality disorder. Risk factors for the child include: genetic influences; difficult temperament; chronic physical or neurological illness; low IQ and learning disability; specific developmental delays; communication difficulties; academic failure; and low self-esteem.

The literature also identifies a number of protective factors that apply to the social environment, family and child (NHS Health Advisory Service Thematic Review, 1995; BMA 1999, p124; and Mental Health Foundation 1999, pp8–10; Rutter, 1985; Gilligan, 2001). Social protective factors identified include: family-friendly government policies; social support systems that encourage personal effort and coping; adequate standard of living; good housing; access to good quality child care; high morale school, with positive policies for behaviour, attitudes and anti-bullying; schools with strong academic and non-academic opportunities; range of positive sport/leisure activities. Family protective factors include: affection; supervision; promotion of self-esteem; authoritative discipline; mentally healthy parents; family compassion, warmth and absence of parental discord; at least one good parent–child relationship; and support for education. Child protective factors include: easy temperament; high self-esteem; being female; higher intelligence; secure attachment; good communication skills; humour; religious faith; a capacity to reflect; and positive attitude, problem-solving approach.

> *In each case it is important to recognise that the individual qualities of the child, the state of the family as a whole, and the wider environment can interact in ways that protect the child.*

(Koprowska and Stein, 2000, p172)

Daniel and colleagues have produced a two-dimensional framework for assessing the vulnerability of a child, identifying aspects of adversity, resilience and protective factors which are a part of each child's life (Daniel, et al., 2010, p14). The concepts of resilience and vulnerability are at different ends of a vertical spectrum, while adversity and protective factors are at different ends of an intersecting horizontal spectrum.

ACTIVITY 8.2

Think about where you would place Leonie and Michaela (from the previous case study) on the model developed by Daniel et al. (2010, p65). Can you identify protective factors and areas of resilience for both children? What are the overriding areas of adversity and vulnerability? After you have charted these on separate frameworks for each child, identify actions you could take to assist with boosting resilience for these children. The work of Daniel and Wassell (2002a, b, c) will assist with ideas for how to undertake this work.

In thinking about implications for practice, Schofield (2001) concurs with Golombok (2000) concerning the quality of the caregiving environment and associated relationships. Both argue that these have the most important effects on the outcome for the child, rather than the age of the child when placed permanently, the length of time a child has been in placement or the legal status of the placement in question. Rutter (1985, p608, cited in Schofield, 2001, p17) comments that:

> the quality of resilience resides in how people deal with life changes and what they do about their situations. That quality is influenced by early life experiences, by happenings during later childhood and adolescence and by circumstances in later life. None of these is in itself determinative of later outcomes, but in combination they may serve to create a chain of indirect linkages that foster escape from adversity.

The role of social workers in looked after children's lives is crucial. Many of the discussions in this chapter have direct relevance to social workers as, while they might not be acting as an everyday caregiver for a child, they are making important decisions which will have long-term implications for children. The relationship between a social worker and a looked after child is very important and many of the qualities within positive caregiving relationships discussed earlier apply here. Such relationships are *challenging to build and sustain through difficult times, but are extremely valuable in bringing together inner and outer worlds and as a source of potential continuity* (Schofield and Beek, 2006, p368). This is especially challenging given the high turnover of social work staff, and high use of agency social work staff in some parts of the country.

Schofield and Beek (2006) also highlight the importance of listening to children. This might sound rather obvious; however, there are still many examples of children's voices not being heard and routinely recorded despite expectations that this is undertaken as a part of practice (Jeyarajah Dent and Cocker, 2005). This is critical for children's sense of self-efficacy concerning their own lives and is a necessary part of social workers making decisions and planning effectively for children.

There are resources available which provide information about 'key messages' and suggested interventions for resilience promoting activities with children of various ages. See Newman (2004) Chapters 3, 4 and 5; and Daniel and Wassel (2002a, b, and c) for further information.

CHAPTER SUMMARY

Having a critical and comprehensive understanding of the various theoretical perspectives underpinning child development, and knowledge about age stage development is important. For social workers, integrating attachment theories and models into their work with looked after children is important, as is working with other professionals who are also knowledgeable in this area (e.g. health visitors, GPs, CAMHS workers). Critically applying attachment theory to the assessments which are now such a mainstay activity of a social worker's role will also ensure that looked after children are given all opportunities to build resilience and prevent mental health deterioration throughout their childhood and into their adult lives.

As the evidence base for effective practice develops around resilience, the challenge for social workers is to continuously keep abreast of any new findings and incorporate these into practice. If these developments are productive, the quality of life and life chances for looked after children can be improved, and that should be the main aim of the child-care system.

FURTHER READING

Comfort, R L (2008) *Searching to be found: Understanding and helping adopted and looked after children with attention difficulties.* London: Karnac.

An excellent guide to some of the attention difficulties looked after children and adopted children can exhibit at home and at school.

Daniel, B, Wassell, S and Gilligan, R (2010) *Child development for child care and protection workers* (2nd edition). London: Jessica Kingsley.

A 'must have' for social workers working in child and family social work.

Howe, D (2005) *Child abuse and neglect: Attachment, development and intervention.* Basingstoke: Palgrave.

David Howe has written a number of books on attachment theory and social work which are well liked and well utilised by both practitioners and students. This is his latest book.

Luckock, B and Lefevre, M (eds) (2008) *Direct work: Social work with children and young people in care.* London: BAAF.

An edited volume that brings together many academics writing about direct work with looked after children and young people.

Newman, T (2004) *What works in building resilience?* Ilford: Barnardo's.

This book is published as part of the well-respected Barnardo's 'What Works' series, and reviews existing research in this area.

Schofield, G and Beek, M (2006) *Attachment handbook for foster care and adoption.* London: BAAF.

An excellent guide that examines the importance of attachment theory for social workers (and others) working in the area of fostering and adoption.

Schofield, G, Simmonds, J and Hill, M (eds) (2009) *The child placement handbook: Research, policy and practice.* London: BAAF.

An edited volume that examines many aspects of the care system.

Chapter 9

Looked after children and mental health

Introduction

A growing body of research shows that looked after children are vulnerable in terms of poor health and mental health outcomes. This chapter defines some terms and examines the main debates in this field, provides you with an overview of current research, looks at what we know works with this group of children, and examines issues arising in multi-disciplinary working. The chapter will also look at the contribution of social workers to improving the mental health of looked after children, both in children's physical environment as well as their relational world. The structure of the chapter covers these areas:

1. What is mental health?

2. What do social workers need to know about the mental health of looked after children?

3. What kinds of mental health problems do looked after children have?

4. What contribution can social workers make in this area?

5. How do social workers make informed recommendations about appropriate interventions?

6. Multi-disciplinary working.

What is mental health?

In this section you will find an extended glossary of terms that are frequently used in relation to child and adolescent mental health. After completing Activity 9.1, look at the glossary to explore the differences in terminology, and think about the impact that this terminology might have upon the child or children to whom these terms apply. There are positives and negatives in using such terms, and this is recognised by the researchers, policy-makers, clinicians and other professionals working in the field.

A major issue raised by practitioners when discussing their reluctance for children to receive mental health assessments is the labelling and stigma attached to having a mental disorder. Scott and Lindsey (2003) outline a number of concerns that exist about applying a diagnostic label, with counter-arguments to allay fears that professionals may raise: parents and young people can be relieved to have an explanation for their feelings and behaviour; once the behaviour stops, then the diagnosis no longer applies; a diagnosis should not obscure the uniqueness of the individual; and diagnostic systems may not capture the range and types of difficulties seen particularly in adopted children and looked after children.

The NHS Health Advisory Service (1995, p16) comments that:

> *such terms can be stigmatising and mark the child as being different. However, unless children with mental health problems are recognised, and some attempt is made to understand and clarify their problems, in the context of their social, educational and health needs, it is very difficult to organise helpful interventions for them.*

Another issue often raised is that the medical model and corresponding terminologies and interventions often describe the child as the 'problem', rather than seeing the child, and working with the child, within a broader context and environment. Thankfully such views are now changing.

> *In reality disorders may arise for a variety of reasons, often interacting. In certain circumstances, a mental or psychiatric disorder, which describes a constellation or syndrome of features, may indicate the reactions of a child or adolescent to external circumstances, which, if changed, could largely resolve the problem.*

(NHS Health Advisory Service, 1995, p16)

Many CAMHS and local authority children's services now offer jointly commissioned and managed services for looked after children (i.e. health, social service and education, CAMH service). There are many different models for service delivery, including community-based services, with outreach available, rather than requiring the child and carers to go to a clinic setting.

ACTIVITY **9.1**

Have a go at answering the following questions:

* *What is a mental health problem?*

* *What is the difference between a mental health problem and an emotional or behavioural difficulty?*

* *What is the difference between a mental health problem and a mental disorder?*

* *How many children in care have diagnosable disorders?*

A summary of definitions and key concepts

There are many concepts and terms used in this work and many different definitions exist for each of the words listed in this section. Where possible the definitions below are from relevant government guidance. This will give you an opportunity to become familiar with some of the key policy documents in this area. Other definitions are from other published work. Please see the reference list at the end of the book for further information.

Mental health

The following definition of mental health is comprehensive and widely used (NHS Advisory Service, 1995, p15)

The components of mental health include the following capacities:

* *the ability to develop psychologically, emotionally, intellectually and spiritually;*

* *the ability to initiate, develop and sustain mutually satisfying personal relationships;*

* *the ability to become aware of others and to empathise with them; and*

* *the ability to use psychological distress as a developmental process so that it does not hinder or impair further development.*

Within this broad framework, and incorporating the developmental nature of both body and mind in childhood and adolescence, mental health in young people is indicated more specifically by:

- *a capacity to enter into and sustain mutually satisfying relationships;*

- *continuing progression of psychological development;*

- *an ability to play and learn so that attainments are appropriate for age and intellectual level; and*

- *a developing moral sense of right and wrong.*

Mental health problem or emotional and behavioural difficulty

'Emotional and behavioural difficulties' and 'mental health problem' are terms that are used interchangeably and frequently to describe many different situations. Even though these terms are rooted in different social and medical approaches to mental ill health, it is assumed that these are both broad categories that refer to the same things. However, it is important to note that different definitions and thresholds for what constitute 'problems' have produced very different estimates of the number of children with emotional or behavioural difficulties (Scott, 2004).

Mental disorder

A mental disorder is a diagnosable mental illness which is internationally recognised in one of two classificatory systems. The *Diagnostic and statistical manual of mental disorders*, Fourth Edition (DSM-IV) is published by the American Psychiatric Association, Washington, D.C. (1994). This is the main diagnostic reference of mental health professionals in the United States of America. The *International classification of diseases – mental health disorders*, Tenth Edition (ICD-10, 1993) was endorsed by the forty-third World Health Assembly in May 1990, and came into use in World Health Organization Member States as from 1994. The classification of 'mental disorders' has become increasingly sophisticated. The original DSM published in 1952 listed 60 types and subtypes of mental disorder, while DSM-IV, the current edition, contains well over 200. Difficulties experienced by children and young people represent one of the areas of classificatory expansion that has both reflected and inspired research interest in the field (Cocker and Scott, 2006). Assessments undertaken using the DSM-IV and the ICD-10 are multi-axial assessments. Carr (1999, p66) comments, *as multi-axial systems, they allow for complex information about important facets of a case to be coded simply and briefly without the drawback of over-simplification that characterises single-axis categorical systems*. This means that both systems can assess the impact of complexities inherent within some families, such as family functioning and school-based difficulties.

Specific mental disorders

Within the DSM-IV and ICD-10 classification systems there are a number of broad categories within which mental disorders can be classified. For a more in-depth look at the classification systems, see Carr (1999, pp68–9). For the purposes of this chapter we have used the list of specific disorders that Meltzer, et al. (2003) identify in their prevalence study of the mental health of children looked after by local authorities in England.

- Anxiety disorders. Examples include separation anxiety; specific phobias; panic; agoraphobia; post-traumatic stress disorder (PTSD); and obsessive–compulsive disorder (OCD).

- Depression.

- Conduct disorders. Examples include oppositional defiant disorder; conduct disorder (family context); unsocialised conduct disorder; and socialised conduct disorder.

- Hyperkinetic disorder. Examples include attention deficit hyperactivity disorder (ADHD).

- Less common disorders. Examples include pervasive development disorder (e.g. autism); psychotic disorders; tic disorders; eating disorders; and other psychiatric disorders.

This list is not exhaustive – they are examples only of some of the most common, and there are many others not included.

CAMHS

The term CAMHS (child and adolescent mental health services) is used in two different ways. One is a broad concept embracing all services that contribute to the mental health care of children and young people, whether provided by health, education or social services or other agencies. It includes those services whose primary function is not mental health care, e.g. GP practices or schools (referred to as tier 1 or 'universal services'; see Table 9.1). The other applies specifically to specialist child and adolescent mental health services at tiers 2, 3 and 4, and also includes specialist social care, educational, voluntary and independent provision for children and young people with mental health problems. The primary function of these services is to provide mental health care to children and young people, staffed by a multi-disciplinary workforce, with specialist training in child and adolescent mental health (National Service Framework for Children, (NSF) DfES and DoH 2004a, p44).

Table 9.1 The four-tier strategic framework (from NSF for Children, DfES and DoH 2004a, pp46–7)

Tier	Professionals providing the service:	Function/service
Tier 1: A primary level of care	• GPs • Health visitors • School nurses • Social workers • Teachers • Juvenile justice workers • Voluntary agencies	CAMHS at this level are provided by professionals working in universal services who are in a position to: • identify mental health problems early in their development • offer general advice • pursue opportunities for mental health promotion and prevention
Tier 2: A service provided by professionals relating to workers in primary care	• Clinical child psychologists • Paediatricians (especially community) • Educational psychologists • Child and adolescent psychiatrists • Child and adolescent psychotherapists • Community nurses/nurse specialists • Family therapy	CAMHS professionals should be able to offer: • training and consultation to other professionals (who might be within tier 1) • consultation to professionals and families • outreach • assessment

Tier 3: A specialised service for more severe, complex or persistent disorders	• Child and adolescent psychiatrists • Clinical child psychologists • Nurses (community or in-patient) • Child psychotherapists • Occupational therapists • Speech and language therapists • Art, music and drama therapists • Family therapy	Services offer: • assessment and treatment • assessment for referrals to T4 • contributions to the services, consultation and training at T1 and T2
Tier 4: Essential tertiary level services such as day units, highly specialised out-patient teams and in-patient units.		Child and adolescent in-patient units: • secure forensic units • eating disorders unit • specialist teams (e.g. for sexual) abuse • specialist teams for neuro psychiatric problems

Interventions

Definition taken from NSF for Children (2004a, p45):

CAMHS cover all types of provision and intervention from mental health promotion and primary prevention, specialist community-based services through to very specialist care as provided by in-patient units for young people with mental illness...Interventions may be indirect (e.g. consultative advice to another agency) or direct (e.g. direct therapeutic work with an individual, child or family). Services for children, young people and their families...will focus on the initial assessment and identification of difficulties and may include advice or the provision of therapeutic help that does not require intensive specialist training or onward referral. The nature, severity, complexity and specificity of the child's mental health problem will help determine where the child is best seen and by which service. Specialist services may be offered in a range of settings according to need and availability, often in partnership with other agencies, including in community locations, out-patient clinics, day and in-patient units and the family's home. Specialist CAMHS will provide a range of assessment and treatment options singly or in combination, utilising the skills of multi-disciplinary teams.

Standardised tests of assessment

Standardised tests are instruments such as scales or questionnaires that are used to measure data gathered through an interview with a child, young person or adult. Standardised tests have been through a rigorous process of development, including publication of data in peer-reviewed sources that detail the reliability and validity of tests in measuring whatever the test is specifically designed to measure. The test will have been used on different (large) samples of the population in order to create 'normative' data against which individual test scores can be compared. A standardised test will not necessarily be diagnostic (i.e. tell you when someone has a mental illness) but might be a screening tool (the Strengths and Difficulties Questionnaire (SDQ) is a screening tool developed by Robert Goodman at the Institute of Psychiatry in London, which identifies those children and young people at higher risk of either having a mental illness or having mental health problems that significantly affect their life).

Standardised tests are routinely used by clinical psychologists in their clinical work, and by other health service professionals in assessment. They are also used by health science researchers when undertaking research. Some of these tests can only be used by clinical psychologists or by other professionals who have been specifically trained in using these tests. Their use by other professionals renders the results invalid.

There are a number of standardised tools that social workers can use, and a number of these are contained in the pack of information supplementing the DoH Assessment Framework materials (DoH, 2000a), including the Strengths and Difficulties Questionnaire. Although these tests are fairly straightforward to use, it is recommended that a practitioner using the tests for the first time seeks advice from someone who has experience of using the test, so that support is given when administering the test and in analysing the data generated from the test. (Please see Chapter 10, p159 for further information about how the SDQ is currently used by local authorities to monitor the health of looked after children.)

Non-standardised tests of assessment

These are tests that do not have the evidence around reliability and validity that standardised tests have. Non-standardised tests rely much more on the subjective evaluations of the assessor. Most of the assessments undertaken by social workers fall into this category. Using non-standardised assessments can be positive, as the different demands of practice and the complexities of situations that social workers are required to assess may necessitate the use of non-standardised tools.

Examples of assessment tools that fall into this category include: the Assessment Framework (Initial and Core assessments); the Action and Assessment Records (AAR) for looked after children; Common Assessment Framework; home visits; and observations.

As mentioned above, the definition of these terms shows the magnitude of the medical contribution to this topic. Current assessment methods are heavily reliant on health colleagues taking the lead in assessment using standardised tests. However, there are ways in which social workers should be participating in the debates and assessments undertaken on children for whom they have responsibilities. The next section will expand on some of the ways social workers can begin to make more of an informed contribution to this area of work.

What do social workers need to know about the mental health of looked after children?

Mental health is something that affects each of us. For social workers and carers working with looked after children, having an understanding about the issues which affect the mental health of these children is crucial in ensuring that if children have more serious needs in this area, they can access the services they need as soon as possible. There are behaviours that looked after children may exhibit which will immediately be of concern to carers and social workers (for example: uncontrollable anger and outbursts; self-harming behaviours; physically hurting other children; smearing faeces; fire starting; killing pets). Looked after children may also be traumatised by their experiences but present this trauma in different ways (for example: not be able to make and/or sustain friendships at school; lack of concentration at school affecting their ability to learn; very quiet and withdrawn; not engaging with foster carers, teachers, friends; sleeping and eating problems).

Every child has basic needs that should be met in order to reach their potential for physical and emotional growth and development. Examples of these needs are: basic physical care, affection, security, stimulation of innate potential, guidance and control, responsibility and independence (Talbot, 2002, pp84–5). However, there are many factors which can influence how children will respond to difficult life circumstances. Please see Chapter 8 for further discussions about factors of attachment, adversity and resilience and their relevance for looked after children.

A child's mental heath is not 'fixed' – if children develop emotional and behavioural problems, then it is quite probable that, with support and treatment, much can be done to alleviate the symptoms children exhibit. However, understanding the cause of these problems, including the implications of abuse and neglect on the mental health of looked after children, is also vital to a social worker's role with children in care. The experiences of loss and separation are common across all looked after children (Fahlberg, 1994) and yet the impact of these life experiences can affect individual children very differently.

Howe (2005, p278) believes that *if relationships are where things developmental can go wrong, then relationships are where they are most likely to be put right*. In the majority of instances, the people with the most contact with looked after children are their carers (either foster carers, residential carers or extended family members), their social worker and their teacher. In recognising the role of teachers, mentors and other significant professionals, Werner (2001) describes a moving account of a follow-up study of 24 child survivors of the Nazi Holocaust. As children these survivors were sent from concentration camps to a therapeutic nursery in England at the end of the war. *Excerpts from follow-up interviews after 30–40 years reveal an extraordinary affirmation of life. Furthermore, all of the resilient survivors considered one woman to be among the most potent influences on their lives – the nursery school teacher who provided warmth and caring and who taught them to behave compassionately* (Moskovitz 1983, cited in Werner, 2001, p126). Howe's views are that *those who can stay with and touch these children, emotionally and psychologically, have the capacity to heal young minds* (2005, p278).

CASE STUDY

Ben is ten years old and is of white UK origin. He was placed with foster carers, Mr and Mrs Smith, when he was four years old. His birth mother has long-standing alcohol dependency issues and Ben has recently been diagnosed with foetal alcohol syndrome. Ben experienced substantial neglect while in the care of his mother. When he was first placed with Mr and Mrs Smith, Ben was a withdrawn child, who didn't show much emotion. He never cried. He was small for his age (on third centile) although he was born on the 50th centile. He didn't really know how to play with toys. The nursery reported that when Ben was living with his mum, he would come to nursery and spend quite a lot of time on his own curled up on a mat on the floor. He had to be strongly encouraged to play with other children. On more than one occasion Mrs Smith found Ben taking food out of the rubbish bin to eat, even though he had eaten a full meal a short time before.

Continued

Ben does not have any contact with his birth mother but does see his older sister (aged 18) regularly. She has recently left care and is living in a flat of her own. The local authority has a Care Order and the permanency plan is for Ben to remain with his foster carers. They are applying for a Special Guardianship Order (Adoption and Children Act 2002). Ben finds it difficult to concentrate in school (he is statemented and receives ten hours of support a week), he has no friends within school, and has begun to steal money from the foster carers. They are worried about Ben's recent behaviour and have asked you to refer Ben for counselling in order that someone can talk to him about his behaviour.

From the information above, and in your reading so far:

- *What do you think the problems are for Ben?*

- *What other agencies would you contact about Ben, and what kind of information would you be seeking?*

- *How do you think that you would respond to Ben, to the foster carers and other foster family members? What role is there for the birth family?*

COMMENT

Ben has had a difficult start in life and it is likely that the attachment he has to his carers might have been affected by his experiences in his early years with his birth family. Separation and loss might also be issues for Ben. The foster carers will have a lot of information about Ben and his development over the six years they have cared for him. Asking them questions such as who Ben approaches for comfort when he is upset, who will he talk to when he has a problem, and who does he talk to when he has good things to share, will give the social worker some ideas about how Ben relates to different people within the foster family.

Some of the issues for Ben that you might have identified are: attachment – is it secure or insecure; peer relationships – he has no friends; academic delay and impending transfer to secondary school; the recent spate of stealing – what does Ben say about this? It would be important to meet with Ben and ascertain his views about the current situation. Does he think there is a problem? Completing an observation of Ben at school might also be useful.

It would be equally important to engage the foster carers. The placement is secure but the foster carers are clearly asking for help in managing this situation.

As a social worker you will need to think about whether Ben has the capacity to give informed consent for the referral to the CAMHS or other services.

We know that one of the most effective ways to positively affect the lives of children and young people in care is through the relationship they have with their foster carers.

RESEARCH SUMMARY

One of the most important factors in enabling children to remain engaged with education (itself protective, and predictive of, mental health) is placement stability. Evidence is accumulating that shows the effectiveness of appropriate training, involvement and support of foster carers in improving placement stability and reducing emotional and behavioural difficulties in the children. Rushton and Minnis (2002, p35) comment that the only interventions with demonstrated effectiveness in reducing the emotional and behavioural problems of looked after children are those delivered either in close liaison with foster carers, or directly through foster carers.

In addition, securing and reinforcing a relationship with a main carer represents current best wisdom in relation to attachment problems: placement stability and permanence are important proxy indicators (Howe and Fearnley, 1999). However, despite the recognition of the importance of improving attachments with looked after children and their carers, we lack an evidence base supporting interventions in relation to older children with attachment difficulties. Additionally, there is as yet no research that effectively unpacks the different elements in interventions, based on enhancing training and support to carers, which make a difference to stability of placement and improved outcomes (see Minnis and Del Priore, 2001), but our knowledge base is growing in this area. There have been a number of randomised controlled trials (RCTs) undertaken in the UK in recent years examining foster care training interventions (Minnis and Devine, 2001; Macdonald and Turner, 2005) and other evidence-based foster care interventions (Pallet, et al., 2005), as well as Multi-Dimensional Treatment Foster Care (Biehal, et al., 2011) and enhancing adoptive parenting (Rushton and Monck, 2009).

What kinds of mental health problems do looked after children have?

Over the last ten years our knowledge about the mental health needs of looked after children has improved markedly, due to research and specialist clinical practice in local integrated teams. Some research has shown (McCann, et al., 1996; Dimigen, et al., 1999) that the number of children in care with a diagnosable mental disorder is much higher than the national average for all children. Although this finding is not necessarily surprising, what is concerning is the number of children who are in care who have undiagnosed psychiatric disorders (McCann, et al., 1996) and the number of children in public care who face lengthy delays in accessing much needed mental health services (Audit Commission, 1999).

RESEARCH SUMMARY

The first prevalence study (a research study with a large enough sample size to give an indication of the total number of cases of diagnosable disorders in a given population at a specific time) was published in 2003, which provided much needed data on the mental health needs of looked after children in England. Similar studies were also undertaken with looked after children in Scotland and Wales (Meltzer, et al. 2004a, 2004b).

This research, undertaken by Howard Meltzer and colleagues for the Office of National Statistics (ONS), compared the mental health (as identifiable 'disorders') of children looked after by the state and children in the overall population. In The mental health of children and adolescents in Great Britain *(Meltzer, et al., 2000), information was collected on 10,000 children. It found:*

- *among 5–10 year olds, 10% of boys and 6% of girls had an identified disorder;*
- *among 11–15 year olds, 13% of boys and 10% of girls had an identified disorder;*
- *conduct disorder accounted for half of all cases – boys were twice as likely as girls to be identified as having a conduct or hyperkinetic disorder.*

In The mental health of young people looked after by local authorities in England *(Meltzer, et al., 2003), information was collected on 1,039 children. It found:*

- *among 5–10 year olds, 50% of boys and 33% of girls had an identified disorder;*
- *among 11–15 year olds, it was 55% of boys and 43% of girls;*
- *conduct disorder was identified in 42% of boys and 31% of girls.*

Research evidences that 1 in 10 of all children display behaviours of the same magnitude as those currently being accepted and treated by CAMHS. This rises to almost half of all looked after children being in need of mental health services. The answer to this need is sometimes conceived in terms of more child psychiatrists, psychologists, in-patient beds and primary mental health care workers. However, in relation to the mental health needs of children in state care, such provision, even if it were forthcoming, is unlikely to provide a complete solution. The reasons for this lie in the origins and causes of most emotional and behavioural difficulties in looked after children, as well as issues of the appropriateness and accessibility of traditional mental health services (Cocker and Scott, 2006).

The work of Meltzer, et al. (2003, 2004a, 2004b) is particularly helpful because it includes information about looked after young people's physical health, use of services, placement type, educational achievement, social networks and lifestyle issues alongside the prevalence of mental disorders. Two-thirds of all looked after children were reported to have at least one physical complaint, the most common being eyesight, speech and language problems, co-ordination difficulties and asthma. Forty-four per cent of those identified as having a mental disorder were in touch with child mental health services.

About 60% of all looked after children had difficulties with reading, spelling or maths. Children identified as having a 'mental disorder' were more than twice as likely as other looked after children to have marked difficulties, and a third were considered to be three or more years behind in their intellectual development. These children were also four times more likely than their looked after peers to report not spending any time with their friends. Such correlations remind us that emotional and behavioural difficulties are inseparable from numerous other aspects of life. However, they also raise numerous questions. Policy-makers, professionals and carers need to know precisely how such difficulties are interrelated, what is the direction of cause and effect (where such exists), what are the priorities for intervention, and how are interventions in one domain likely to impact in another? (Cocker and Scott, 2006).

CASE STUDY

Leaving care

Akim is about to leave care. He turns 18 in two weeks. He is originally from Sierra Leone, and moved to the UK when he was seven. His mother was already living in the UK at this time and he joined her. Their relationship has always been fraught. The local authority has known Akim since shortly after his arrival in the UK. He has been accommodated since he was 13, when his mother contacted the local authority and said that Akim was out of her control, and she could no longer care for him. She has since disappeared and Akim has not heard from her for four years. Akim has been in a number of different placements since being in care, including eight foster placements and two residential placements. During the first two years of Akim being in care he went through six placements in very quick succession because of violence towards others in the placement and in the final foster placement he set fire to his bedroom. He saw a child psychiatrist from the local CAMHS service after this episode and since then has worked with a clinical psychologist for a couple of years, who continues to see him every couple of months, and sees him as vulnerable. He is currently placed in a semi-independent unit, where he receives a limited amount of support from the staff on the unit. In the next month he will move to his own flat. You are Akim's social worker, and you have known Akim for 18 months. You have a number of concerns about whether Akim is ready for this move.

COMMENT

One of the major gaps in the current arrangement in mental health services for children and young people is the link and transition between child mental health and adult mental health services, called community mental health teams (CMHT). This can often be difficult for professionals to negotiate, never mind service users.

Late adolescence marks an important point within a young person's development – where they are moving on to independence. This is a pretty bumpy ride for most teenagers. However, for looked after young people, moving on to independence at 18 can appear rather early for such tremendous change to occur, especially as some young people are still vulnerable and will continue to require considerable support throughout early adulthood. Although attention has been paid to improving services to young people

Continued

COMMENT *continued*

leaving care via pathway plans and specialist leaving care services, the evidence from a large number of studies (Stein, 1997, 2004) points to a care leaver's journey to adulthood being steeper, quicker and occurring within a shorter timeframe than is the experience of young people not in care. The outcomes for many young people with care histories are not good:

> just over a half move regularly and 20% experience homelessness in the two years after they leave care; they have lower levels of educational attainment and lower post 16 further education participation rates; they have higher unemployment rates, more unstable career patterns and higher levels of dependency on welfare benefits; they enter parenthood earlier and they experience more mental health problems.

(Richardson and Joughin, 2000, p98)

What contribution can social workers make in this area?

Child and family social workers are one of the key groups of professionals involved with looked after children. They are required to act as corporate parents, and in so doing make many decisions about looked after children, many of which have far-reaching conse-quences for these children. Often such decisions are life-changing, for example: matching children who have experienced abuse and neglect with permanent substitute families and carers; arranging therapeutic support to children who have experienced trauma; sup-porting children through many changes in their personal situations; supporting children in education; and arranging appropriate health care. A lot of these tasks are undertaken competently by social workers. A social worker can be a real 'lifeline' for a child who is negotiating his or her way through the quagmire that is the 'looked after' system. The skill base required to undertake this role is mixed and varied and borrows heavily from the knowledge base of colleagues in health-related professions.

So what does this mean for practice? There are a number of points to discuss.

In order to support children and young people it is necessary for social workers to iden-tify the different factors which may determine life chances (or lack of them) for a looked after child, recognise the effect of abusive experiences on that child, and support the child through the difficult process of change in relationships and behaviours necessary for indi-vidual children to achieve better outcomes. This is made all the more difficult by the many placement moves that looked after children and young people experience. This potential for chaos in both the inner (emotional) world and external (physical) world of the child has a knock-on effect for the kind of support (including therapeutic support) offered to children by the professional network. This is a point we will return to later. However, there is a lot now written about resilience among children who have experienced early adversity (Gilligan, 1997; Werner, 2001; Daniel and Wassell, 2002a). This material is more optimistic about outcomes for these children.

Gilligan (1997, p14) believes that resilience – *the capacity to transcend adversity – may be seen as the essential quality which care planning and provision should seek to stimulate as a key outcome of the care offered*. See Chapter 8 for further discussion on this topic.

Once recognised and identified, what do social workers do about mental health difficulties?

First, social workers should be able to recognise different kinds of mental health difficulties that looked after children might experience. Historically, low referral rates of looked after children to CAMHS services do not reflect the large numbers of children that research tells us (McCann, et al., 1996; Dimigen, et al., 1999; Meltzer, et al., 2003) are experiencing emotional difficulties and not receiving treatment and support, where this might be indicated. Every looked after child shares the experiences of loss and separation. Aldgate, cited in Fahlberg (1994, p133), points out: *the importance of adults involved with children in the care system recognising that separation involves fear, which needs to be mastered, and that loss involves grief which needs to be expressed.* (See Chapter 10, p159 for further information on how the DfE monitors the mental health of looked after children.)

Secondly, a shortage of qualified child and adolescent mental health practitioners, who specifically understand the experiences of looked after children, and long waiting lists mean that it can be a long time before children access supportive services. The DoH's target is that all children should be seen within 13 weeks from the point of referral (DoH, 2004). Waiting list times have improved over recent years. However, when children are seen, do social workers understand the role and remit of the different mental health specialists and interventions? It is imperative that social workers understand this area to effectively advocate for their child and discharge their corporate parental duties.

Thirdly, there are a range of issues and tensions between referring and receiving organisations at points of referral. Some of these have already been discussed (labelling and stigma of a diagnosis of a mental illness; the complex nature of looked after children's lives and the impact of this on assessment and interventions; difficulty of children being seen quickly by specialists) and some will be discussed later in the chapter (understanding therapeutic work – what it can do and what it cannot do; the effect of transition for young people leaving care; and supporting foster carers). Other difficulties can include: a lack of recognition of the seriousness of a situation for a child or young person exhibiting troubling or disturbing behaviour; other priorities for social workers impeding referrals to CAMHS; crisis-led referrals from social services; and inflexible service provision offered from CAMHS (Talbot, 2002).

Finally, social workers should consider their own relationship with the child, and how that relationship could potentially become a catalyst for change for the child. Issues that will affect this are frequency of visits to the child – including reliability and punctuality; and undertaking some kind of direct work with the child to get to know them. Direct work includes: life story/journey work (see Chapter 5); arranging an outing with the child to support a school project; supporting a skill that the child or young person has; responding to the child's interest; or any number of other activities which engage the child and enable the social worker and child's relationship to move beyond the perfunctory 'hello' and 'how are you?' Talbot (2002) uses the word 'containers' as a metaphor and an acronym for identifying key skills that people working with looked after children should have. These skills and traits are: Consistency, Observers, Negotiators, Task setters or thinkers,

Awareness of self and owning one's authority, Investment (in a relationship with the child/young person), Novelty and creativity, Experience, Responsibility, creating Structure (including predictability and safety).

In relation to the two case studies above, what essential information is needed by the CAMHS service when you are referring Ben and Akim respectively?

COMMENT

Usually social workers will have a great deal of information about a child or young person and their history on their files. It is worth taking the time to read through this information and pass on a comprehensive summary of the key events in a child or young person's life to the CAMHS service. This will ensure that the CAMHS worker has a full account of early life experiences, family background, physical health, details of any change in circumstances that children and young people may have experienced, an educational history of the child, any previous referrals to CAMHS services and as much information as possible about birth parents, including any mental health issues, drug and alcohol dependency issues and other relevant information.

How do social workers make informed recommendations about appropriate interventions?

CASE STUDY

Marinda is nine years old and is currently the subject of an interim care order. She is a black British child. She lives with experienced foster carers, and has been in the same placement since being placed in care two years ago. Marinda came into care because of physical injuries received from her mother's boyfriend. Her arm was broken by her stepfather and she had a number of other bruises over her body. This family was known to social services over a number of years. Marinda has two other younger siblings, who are half-brothers (Samuel who is four and Joshua who is six). The boys were also taken into care, but they are placed with other foster carers. Marinda has recently disclosed that while living at home she was subjected to repeated sexual abuse. The foster carers are providing Marinda with a safe and supportive environment and she has become particularly close to her foster mum. However, the foster mum is worried that Marinda does not have any friends at school, is not doing very well academically, and she has recently started wetting her bed two or three times a week. Marinda's social worker has recently changed – you are the new social worker and you have met Marinda once. You recently received a telephone call from a child psychotherapist at the local CAMHS service, who was responding to a referral made by the previous social worker for Marinda to start *having therapy to help her talk about her experiences while living at home. The child psychotherapist does not think that it would be wise for Marinda to receive any therapy until she is in a permanent placement. You disagree.*

How do you respond to the child psychotherapist?

COMMENT

When should children receive therapeutic support?

There is an ongoing debate within CAMHS services about when a child is most receptive to therapeutic support, with some practitioners believing that children who are 'in transition' or not in permanent placements, should not receive therapy, whereas others do not support this view (Wilson 2001, cited in Hunter, 2001). This links to whether children whose inner (emotional) and outer (physical) worlds are in turmoil, are able to make use of therapeutic experiences. Hunter (2001, p1), herself a psychotherapist, believes that psychoanalytic work with deeply mistrustful, traumatised children requires modification of therapeutic practice. The process has to be adapted to reach these otherwise unreachable children, and she believes this work can be done with children in transition.

Psychotherapy is not the only kind of therapy or intervention that children referred to a CAMHS service can receive. Social workers do need to engage with these debates and ensure that they are not part of the problem in enabling their clients to access services in an appropriate and timely manner. Providing accurate and detailed health, educational and social histories of children to CAMHS teams at the point of referral is essential. Being available for consultation and having realistic expectations about what the therapy or a number of sessions with a psychotherapist, family therapist, art therapist, play therapist, mental health nurse, clinical psychologist or psychiatrist can achieve is essential.

Treatment/interventions

This section will give you a very brief definition of the different kinds of talking therapies available. Some of these theoretical approaches (solution focused; task centred, person centred) will be more familiar to social workers than others listed below. While a working knowledge of the differences in therapeutic approaches is important, the literature also recognises the importance of the quality of the therapeutic relationship between the child or young person and the therapist (Cooper, et al., 2005).

- Psychoanalysis: *a method of psychological treatment, developed from the work of Freud, which focuses on uncovering the unconscious conflicts by mainly verbal means. It is classically a lengthy and intensive therapy lasting several years although briefer and less intense forms have also been developed.* (Richardson and Joughin, 2000, p105)

- Psychotherapy: *any of a large number of related methods of treating mental and emotional disorders by psychological techniques rather than a physical approach.* (Richardson and Joughin, 2000, p106)

- Psychodynamic therapy: *this form of therapy has its origins in Freud's work. It also concentrates on the inner world of clients and helps clients relate this to their background, upbringing and development.* (Richardson and Joughin, 2000, p106)

- Person-centred therapy: this therapeutic approach is usually associated with Carl Rogers. According to Trevithick (2005, p269), Rogers based his approach *on the humanistic belief that human beings have an innate motivation to grow, develop and change....[this] non directive, non-judgemental, accepting, warm and caring approach has strong links with counselling.*

- Cognitive behavioural therapy (CBT): *describes the combination of behaviour therapy and cognitive therapy in which, usually, behavioural procedures are used to change cognitive processes.* (Richardson and Joughin, 2000, p105)

- Behavioural therapy: *This therapy uses psychological principles to achieve behavioural goals, as opposed to achieving personal insight or personality change.* (Richardson and Joughin, 2000, p105)

- Cognitive therapy: *any of the methods of treating disorders that help a person to change attitudes, perceptions, and patterns of thinking from rational to realistic thoughts about self and situations.* (Richardson and Joughin, 2000, p105)

- Brief therapy and solution-focused (strengths-based) approach: this approach moves away from focusing on problems, toward encouraging change to occur by identifying solutions and looking at desired outcomes. This is a different perspective than most of the other therapies, which rely on the therapist and service user understanding the problem and working on this over a period of time through the therapeutic relationship (Miller, 2006).

- Family therapy: family therapy uses systems theory to understand the shared relationships (positive and negative) between groups of people who have emotional ties and connections with each other (Miller, 2006). Family therapy works with the many understandings and viewpoints expressed by various family members in terms of particular difficulties the family might be experiencing, in order that better communication can result.

- Group work: this involves participants working in a group, rather than discussing a problem within an individually based therapeutic relationship. The social aspect of groups requires participants to engage with other group participants in a communal way. This can bring out tensions in the group's working processes, but this is seen as a part of the group learning about how to work effectively together.

Other types of therapeutic interventions
- Play therapy, art therapy, drama therapy, music therapy: these creative therapies use a specific medium to access the subconscious or inner thoughts as a vehicle to working through emotional issues. Children can have difficulty engaging with 'talking therapies', or expressing emotions, thoughts and feelings verbally. Music, art, play and drama become tools for non-verbal communication and can be a helpful way for children to express their sadness and distress (Cooper, et al., 2005).

Medication

In particular situations, psychiatrists will recommend that children and young people with specific mental disorders (e.g. psychotic disorders) should be prescribed medication, as well as receive other talking therapies, to assist with relieving/controlling some of the symptoms that they might experience. This would occur when medication is known to have a positive effect for the particular disorder the child or young person has. Medication can be a source of contention between social services and health colleagues. Social workers are concerned about inappropriately labelling and stigmatising children and young people. Discussion between professionals can help work through these tensions. These differing perspectives, if not resolved, can potentially affect the intervention received by the child or young person and ultimately cause further harm. Social workers should feel able to express their views and should request information from child and adolescent psychiatrists about recommended treatment options for specific disorders and the implications of this (including side effects) in order that social workers can support children/young people in their role as corporate parent.

Sometimes children may not be able to instantly accept and respond positively to support and therapy. Instead the results of a whole range of clinical and other interventions may only be seen through the course of time and developing maturity. Archer (2003, p91) suggests that forming therapeutic relationships with looked after children who have experienced trauma is likely to be difficult because the foundations upon which relationships are based have the capacity to be *rocky … the child may share few common perceptions of the world with the therapist: lacking fundamental self awareness and possessing distorted 'road maps' by which to negotiate his [her] healing journey*. Archer outlines some of the difficulties of children engaging in *the talking cure*, commenting that children's *poorly developed reflective capacities will also interfere with the acquisition of appropriate insights through dialogue*. In these circumstances there may be other appropriate activities that can be suggested and done with key adults in children's lives, including social workers, which may involve raising self-esteem (for example, engaging the child in some kind of sports activity), or practising key skills such as sharing, concentration and modelling behaviour through a range of everyday activities (for example, play, sand play, doing practical activities such as cooking and baking, reading with the child – all of these activities should positively build on the relationship between the child and adult). For other ideas see Archer, 1999a, b).

Multi-disciplinary working

Multi-disciplinary work is an integral part of social work. Often social workers for looked after children are working with a range of different agencies, including CAMHS, in setting up appropriate care plans for the children. It is important that social workers understand what services are available locally, and can liaise with a number of different professionals. The case study below provides an example of one local project.

The Brownwood Looked After Children Project

This project was set up five years ago to work with the local community of looked after children, comprising over 550 children, including children recently placed for adoption. It is a jointly funded and jointly managed project between health services and the local authority, and is based in a health community setting. The project employs a number of mental health specialists to work solely with looked after children. Specialists include: one child psychiatrist (part-time); two clinical psychologists; three social work specialists; three family therapists; one psychotherapist; and a play therapist. This team have all completed 'Theraplay' training (www.theraplayinc.com) and use this technique to work with young children, along with other interventions, including: clinical psychological interventions; CBT; narrative techniques; trauma work; play therapy; psychotherapy; art therapy (via sessional art therapist); and integrative therapists, drawing on a number of treatment modalities based on the needs of the child and what is assessed as being best to affect change for that child. Each year the team see between 50 and 80 children and/or their carers, and in addition to this will offer a series of consultations to other professionals to discuss specific looked after children and adopted children. At the point of referral children do not wait longer than 13 weeks before receiving an initial appointment.

Describe the ways in which you could you use a service such as this to support your work with looked after children.

Specialist CAMHS projects for looked after children

Local jointly commissioned and funded CAMHS projects developed specifically for looked after children are now seen by the DCSF as 'good practice'. Over the last ten years there has been a large increase in the development of such projects. The benefits include flexibility of service design and delivery – the projects can adapt quickly to local needs and be more flexible about when and where children are seen. This means on a very practical level that children do not need to miss school to attend appointments at hospital or community outpatient services. CAMHS project staff can also offer regular consultations to district social work teams and residential children's homes, building relationships with individual team members whilst promoting discussions about potentially troubling or disturbing behaviour that children or young people might be exhibiting. As a result, more children may benefit from these consultation sessions.

ACTIVITY **9.3**

Make a list of the different kinds of professionals represented in a child and adolescent mental health service (CAMHS). How do their respective roles differ from each other?

COMMENT

Each member of a multi-disciplinary team has a different professional role when working with a child or young person. For example, a psychiatrist (who is a medical doctor) can make a diagnosis of a specific disorder – and can prescribe medication, if necessary. Other professionals are not able to undertake this role. A clinical psychologist (who is a doctor of clinical psychology but does not have medical training) is able to assess a child or young person using a range of standardised and non-standardised tests (see earlier section for a definition of these terms), many of which other professionals cannot use. Other professionals have relevant specialist training in this area, of at least two to three years in addition to their original professional qualification (family therapists). Some professionals have longer training periods (child psychotherapists).

Despite what we know about the emotional and mental health problems that looked after children face, we know very little about what is effective. Research evidence now gives us an indication about the numbers of children affected (prevalence rates) and identifies some of the risk factors for morbidity (the rate of incidence of a disease) or co-morbidity (other diagnoses and disorders – sometimes related – that occur at the same time). However, it does little to assist in identifying what interventions are effective in improving mental health with this client group. Efforts now need to be made by practitioners, policy-makers and researchers to collectively concentrate on filling some of the gaps in our knowledge. This includes making better use of the evaluations of current services to inform the development of these services to ensure they remain fit for purpose.

There is also an important role for many of the specialist services to evaluate the work they are doing and share the results of their work, both in terms of the numbers of children that are seen and the outcomes that are achieved (Cocker and Scott, 2006).

CHAPTER SUMMARY

One in ten children in our society has a diagnosable mental disorder and this rises to nearly 50% for children who are looked after. There are not enough specialists from many professional backgrounds working in this area currently.

We do not know what works best for improving the mental health of looked after children. We know placement stability and education are important factors and we know that the best way of 'holding' a child and 'containing' them within their community once they are looked after is to provide a good level of support to the foster carer.

Continued

CHAPTER SUMMARY *continued*

We do know what works best for many of the disorders and phobias which affect children. However, often children within the general population are faced with one problem, not multiple problems, which is often the case for looked after children. This 'co-morbidity' and complexity are what makes finding 'what works' for looked after children (and all children) so difficult.

Multi-disciplinary working is essential, which means that you have to be a good advocate for your child and you need to know a little bit about this field so that you are not inadvertently silenced by the jargon and technical language of other professions; you need to know what you can do to make a difference. Do not be afraid to concentrate on the little things – use small steps to raise a child's self-esteem in their own eyes as well as in the eyes of their peers. Small changes may often have other positive and unimaginable/ unintended outcomes for the child. Change is not instant so do not expect immediate, large changes, and remember the 'sleeper effect', where changes can occur after a longer time period and have a cumulative effect. Think about your relationship with a looked after child and think about the small things you can do with the child that will build on this relationship and model good practice (being reliable and consistent in your contact with the child; thinking about how to best communicate with the child in a way that is meaningful for the child; engaging in activities with the child which are of their choosing).

Know what different therapeutic approaches are about and have a view about which might be appropriate for the child you are working with. Do not expect a therapist to 'change' or 'fix' a child in order to make her/him 'adoptable' within a short time period. The responsibility for this is more complicated, involving the entire professional community working together, and change will take time. This might involve things getting worse before they get better, as therapeutic work is painful.

FURTHER READING

Archer, C (1999a) *First steps in parenting the child who hurts: Tiddlers and toddlers.* London: Jessica Kingsley.

Archer, C (1999b) *Next steps in parenting the child who hurts: Tykes and teens.* London: Jessica Kingsley.

These two books by Caroline Archer are written in a very accessible manner and include a number of practical ideas and exercises to guide direct work with looked after children.

Fahlberg, V (1994) *A child's journey through placement (UK edition).* London: BAAF.

This book is an absolute 'must have' for all social workers working with looked after children. Although it is somewhat dated now, it is very good.

Golding, K (2008) *Nurturing attachments: Supporting children who are fostered or adopted.* London: Jessica Kingsley.

This book provides guidance for foster carers, adopters and social workers in caring for looked after children.

Hunter, M (2001) *Psychotherapy with young people in care: Lost and found.* Abingdon: Brunner Routledge.

This book is written by a psychotherapist who believes that looked after children who are in transition can receive psychotherapeutic support.

Richardson, J and Joughin, C (2000) *The mental health needs of looked after children.* London: Royal College of Psychiatrists.

This book is specifically written with social workers in mind and is a very useful text.

Simmonds, J (2011) The making and breaking of relationships: organisational and clinical questions in providing services for looks after children? *Clinical Child Psychology and Psychiatry* 15(4), 601–12.

Walker, S (2011) *The social worker's guide to child and adolescent mental health.* London: Jessica Kingsley.

This book is a good general tool on a social worker's role in working with children and young people with mental health problems.

EBSITES

A range of voluntary-sector organisations exists, all of which contribute to this area of practice. Visit the following websites.

- Young Minds: **www.youngminds.org.uk**
  The voluntary-sector organisation Young Minds is very well respected. As a part of its services it produces an excellent bi-monthly magazine for professionals (Young Minds magazine) dedicated to mental health issues for all children.

- Who cares? Trust: **www.thewhocarestrust.org.uk**

- Care Leavers Association: **www.careleavers.org**

- A National Voice: **www.anationalvoice.org**

Chapter 10
Education and health of looked after children

Introduction

This chapter will examine two areas which are important to your work with looked after children. The first area is education. The poor educational outcomes of looked after children are often used as the benchmark to measure the 'success' of the looked after system generally. It is vital to both understand the facts and figures as they are presented, and to think about the issues for practice. Educational achievement is a complex area, and the low GCSE results mask a range of issues: this chapter explores some of them to assist you in understanding the significance of your interventions.

The second area is health. This is also a very important topic. Chapters 8 and 9 in this book examine issues that are concerned specifically with mental health, including attachment and resilience. This chapter will therefore concentrate on physical health issues for looked after children.

Education

In 1998 when the Quality protects initiative was launched by the Labour government, Frank Dobson (then the Secretary of State for Health) commented that educational achievement was *the single most significant measure of the effectiveness of local authority parenting*.

At that time a number of key articles had identified that looked after children were underperforming in this area (e.g. Jackson, 1988). Over the following ten years more studies showed that looked after children and young people underachieve regarding education (for example, Jackson and Sachdev, 2001; SEU, 2003; Harker, et al., 2004; DfES, 2006a), with some researchers (Harker, et al., 2004) suggesting that the care system itself contributes to this educational underachievement. There is still significant debate among researchers, academics, civil servants and politicians about the causes of the low attainment (see the Research Summary in this chapter). It is important that these differences are aired because the solution to changing and improving these outcomes is complex.

Legal context

The Education Act 1996 (EA 1996) provides the basic framework of the law relating to education. Other Acts supplement this provision and set out the framework for governing the management of schools and pupils, notably the School Standards and Framework Act 1997 and the Special Educational Needs and Disability Act 2001. Additionally, further Education Acts (1997, 2002, 2005) support broader duties, but this chapter will not be reviewing them. Please see Brammer (2010) or Horner and Krawczyk (2006) for detailed information.

Section 7 of the Education Act 1996 states that parents have a duty to ensure their children are suitably educated. The term 'parent' is defined in the Act:

> *'Parent' means anyone who has parental responsibility for or care of the child.*

> (EA 1996, s576(1))

Children are required to attend school from the school term in which they turn five until the end of the school year where they turn 16. Pupils should not be absent from school without a legitimate reason and parents have a duty to comply with this. All secondary schools must provide sex education (EA 2002, s80); however, at primary schools this is not mandatory (EA 1996, s404). Governors will ensure there is a policy on the content and teaching of sex education. Section 403 EA 1996 states that schools must give due regard to moral considerations and the values of family life (Brammer, 2010). Parents can withdraw their children from sex education classes without the need to give reasons (EA 1996, s 405).

The Special Educational Needs and Disability Act 2001 amended the Education Act 1996 regarding the assessment of SEN. In addition, local authorities must have regard to the Special Educational Needs Code of Practice (DfES, 2001b). The legal requirements governing SEN support and provision are complex (Brammer, 2010) and it is important to ensure that you have clear information about the needs of the child, understand the SEN processes and stage that a child is at, and have a clear idea concerning the support a child is entitled to. Brammer (2010, p357) comments, *parents have sought statements to obtain additional specialist help for their children but LAs are, because of limited resources, not always keen to incur the expenditure required to meet those perceived needs.*

Section S2 of the Children Act 2004 places a statutory obligation on local authorities to promote the education of looked after children. This duty is added to the general duties promoting looked after children's welfare contained in section 22 of the Children Act 1989. This is also in addition to the duty that social services have under section 28 of the Children Act 1989, to consult with local educational authorities so that appropriate provision can be made for a looked after child's education.

The Children and Young Persons Act 2008 (CYPA 2008) also introduces changes to emphasise the importance of education for looked after children. Section 20 deals with designated teachers in schools where looked after children are on roll; section 21 deals with care leavers who attend higher education provision; and section 22 deals with care leavers pursuing other education or training opportunities. These changes add additional duties to s23 of CA 1989. In addition, Schedule 1 of CYPA 2008 makes changes to 22C of CA 1989, stating that placements should not disrupt education whilst students are completing GCSEs.

The Education (Admission of Looked After Children) (England) Regulations 2006 came into force on 21 Feb 2006, and make certain that local authority community schools, voluntary aided and foundation schools ensure looked after children are prioritised by admissions authorities in the school's oversubscription criteria. Faith schools must give first priority to looked after children of their faith ahead of other applicants, and are permitted to give priority to all looked after children, regardless of faith. In addition, grammar schools must give top priority to looked after children who meet their academic requirements.

Definitions of key terms

Where possible we have taken the definitions in this section from relevant government guidance. This will give you an opportunity to become familiar with some of the key policy documents which influence work in this area.

Designated teacher
A designated teacher is someone with responsibility for looked after children in the school. They are expected to be an advocate for children and young people in public care and ensure that each child/young person has a Personal Education Plan (DfES, 2005a).

Exclusion

Schools can exclude children in limited circumstances, and this should only ever be a last resort. The procedures surrounding exclusions are considerable and must be followed by the school (including timescales for notifications and appeals). The head teacher has the power to exclude children either permanently or temporarily, up to 45 days in any given academic year. The school governors are required to review the decision by the head teacher, and parents can meet with the governing body to discuss the exclusion (make representations). If this does not result in the child being reinstated then in cases of permanent exclusion the parents can then also appeal via the local authority to an independent exclusion panel. If a child is excluded for more than one day then the school should set work for the child and mark it, and in cases of permanent exclusion, all local authorities should provide suitable full-time education for children from day 16 of the exclusion (DfES, 2002).

Independent reviewing officer (IRO)

Independent reviewing officers are registered social workers who are independent of the management of cases of children in care that they review. From September 2004, independent reviewing officers have been required to chair all statutory review meetings for children in care, from which position they can identify any problems in the child's care and any lack of clarity in the care plan.

(DfES, 2006f, p109)

Their duties and responsibilities were further expanded in CYPA 2008, and in March 2010 new statutory guidance was issued on care planning and reviewing arrangements for looked after children.

(DCSF, 2010; see also Chapter 2)

Individual education plan (IEP)

This is a short-term planning document for pupils with special educational needs. It should include three or four short-term targets that match a child's needs; ways of teaching to be used; the help to be put in place; and how the school will decide if the help has been successful.

(DfES, 2005a, p38)

These are different from or additional to those in place for the rest of the class (DfES, 2001a).

Personal education plan (PEP)

Every child and young person in care should have a PEP which sets out academic achievement; identifies developmental and educational needs; and sets out short- and long-term targets and plans. The PEP should be part of the child's care plan and reflect any other education plans such as an IEP, SEN statement, etc.

(DfES, 2005a, p38)

Special educational needs (SEN)

Special educational needs (SEN) refers to those children who have difficulties in learning that affect their progress at school, and who therefore require additional support from their peers to make progress educationally. The legal definition of special educational needs is located in the Education Act 1996, section 312.

Special educational needs arise where a child has difficulties which require additional educational provision to be made. A learning difficulty is defined and arises where:

(a) *he has a significantly greater difficulty in learning than the majority of children of his age,*

(b) *he has a disability which either prevents or hinders him from making use of education facilities of a kind generally provided for children of his age in schools within the area of the local education authority, or*

(c) *he is under compulsory school age and is, or would be if special educational provision were not made for him, likely to fall within paragraphs (a) or (b) when of or over that age.*

(Section 312(2), EA 1996)

There are four levels describing how SEN services are delivered by schools and education authorities.

- School Action: *when a class or subject teacher identify that a pupil has special educational needs they provide interventions that are additional to or different from those provided as part of the school's usual differentiated curriculum. An IEP is usually devised.*

(DfES, 2001b, p206)

- School Action Plus: *when the class or subject teacher and the SENCO are provided with advice or support from outside specialists, so that alternative interventions, additional or different strategies to those provided for the pupil via School Action can be put in place.*

(DfES, 2001b, p206)

- SEN Statement (with educational provision delivered in mainstream schooling) (see below).

- SEN Statement with specialist educational provision delivered in specialist schools (see below).

Special educational needs co-ordinator (SENCO)

Each school must have a SEN Co-ordinator who organises the support for children with special educational needs and liaises with parents and carers over reviews of IEPs and annual reviews of statements.

(DfES, 2005a, p38)

Special school

A school that is just for children with statements of special educational needs.

(DfES, 2001a, p40)

Statutory assessment
A very detailed examination of a child's special educational needs. It may lead to a statement (DfES, 2001a, p40). A parent can request that the local authority undertakes a statutory assessment of their child. If the local authority does not agree to undertake this assessment, they must inform the parent of the reasons. The parent can appeal this decision. If the local authority decides not to make a statement of SEN following the completion of a statutory assessment, then the parent can appeal to the Special Educational Needs and Disability Tribunal.

Statement of special educational needs
A document that sets out a child's needs and all the extra help they should get (DfES, 2001a, p40). This statement is subject to annual review. If specific services are mentioned in the statement then the child must receive them. The school receives additional funding to support additional services a child requires where that child has a statement of SEN. (DfES, 2001b).

Please be aware that the coalition government is planning a major overhaul of SEN services to children. A Green Paper was published in March 2011 (DfE, 2011g), and a draft Bill is expected in 2013. The DfE says it aims to have new arrangements for SEN provision in place for 2014. It is envisaged that the proposed changes will include such measures as personal budgets for special needs provision, and the replacement of the current model of SEN with single plans that will cover education, health and social care services. Such changes will affect around 1.7 million children. Whilst many proposed changes have the potential to simplify the current overly bureaucratic process, and this is to be welcomed, these changes will also significantly reduce the numbers of children who will be eligible for SEN services. Schools are expected to provide targeted support to meet the needs of children who need additional services but who do not meet the requirements of a statutory statement. The level of funding provided for this purpose is still not clear.

What is currently known about looked after children's educational achievement?

Since 2000, information has been collected on the achievements of looked after children within the education system using GCSE and end of key stage results. Comprehensive performance management information is now produced to measure year-on-year improvements in this area. O'Sullivan and Westerman (2007) suggest that the government's use of statistics to drive up standards and performance is an important advance. (See Table 10.1.)

There are two sets of data collected by local authorities through performance management systems. The first is connected to achievements, attendance and permanent exclusions of children and young people who have been looked after for at least one year and the second is concerned with the educational achievements of looked after young people aged 16 or over who have left care. Additionally, information is collected about young people after they have left care at age 19 concerning whether they are involved in further/higher education, training or employment.

Table 10.1a Educational achievement data 2011

	Looked after children		All children	
Key Stage 1	reading	65% (63% in 2010)	reading	85% (85% in 2010)
	writing	57% (56% in 2010)	writing	81% (81% in 2010)
	maths	71% (68% in 2010)	maths	90% (89% in 2010)
Key Stage 2	reading	53 (51% in 2010)	reading	81% (81% in 2010)
	maths	52% (50% in 2010)	maths	80% (81% in 2010)
Key Stage 4: GCSE	At Key Stage 4, 13.2% achieved 5+ A*–C at GCSE or equivalent including English and mathematics compared with 12.0% in 2010		At Key Stage 4, 57.9% achieved 5+ A*–C at GCSE or equivalent including English and mathematics compared with 52.9% in 2010	
Young people moving on	NEET	33% at age 19	NEET	19% at age 19; (21.9% 16-24 year olds are unemployed 2011)
	Further education	30% in 2011, same in 2010.	Further education or employment	40+% in 2011
	Higher education	6% in 2011, compared with 7% in 2010	Higher education	40% in 2010
	Employment	25%	Employment	(see above)

Source: DfE Looked After Statistical Returns 2011a; NCAS summary 2011; ONS labour market statistics 2011.
NEET, not in education, employment or training.

Table 10.1b Percentage of children looked after continuously for 12 months at 31 March and all children, achieving 5 or more GCSEs, 2006 to 2010

	5 or more GCSEs at grade A* to G			5 or more GCSEs at grade A* to C			5 or more GCSEs including English and Maths at grades A* to C		
	Children looked after[1]	All children[2]	Attainment gap	Children looked after[1]	All children[2]	Attainment gap	Children looked after[1]	All children[2]	Attainment gap
2006	41	90	49	12	59	47	6	46	40
2007	41	91	48	14	61	47	7	46	39
2008	46	92	46	17	65	48	9	48	39
2009	50	92	42	21	70	49	10	50	40
2010	51	92	41	26	75	49	12	53	41

Source: DfE, 2011a

[1] Children looked after continuously for 12 months at 31 March each year.

[2] Figures taken from GCSE and equivalent results in England, 2009/10 (Provisional).

Although the percentage of children looked after continuously for 12 months achieving 5 or more GCSEs has increased between 2006 and 2010, the improvement in the attainment of all children means that the attainment gaps which exist between all children and children who have been looked after continuously for 12 months continue to broaden for grades A* to C. For grades A* to G the gap has narrowed in each year since 2006 (DfE, 2011h, p6).

However, in order to contextualise this, education data on length of time children spend in care needs to be understood. There is a great deal of movement within the care population over a year, and those children who spend more than two years in care, or indeed their entire childhoods in care, are a small minority of the overall number of children looked after at any one time.

In 2003 the Social Exclusion Unit published *A better education for children in care*. This document highlighted five 'big issues' affecting the achievement of looked after children (SEU, 2003, pp4–6).

- Instability. Too many children who are looked after have too many placement changes over the period of time they are in care and this inevitably involves changes in school. Children need stability at home and they also need stability of school, where the school meets their educational needs.

- Time out of school. Many children do not attend school because they do not have a school place, or they are excluded, or they do not attend regularly. Other children are not in mainstream school (e.g. a pupil referral unit – PRU) and they may only receive a few hours' schooling per week.

- Help with their education. Many children looked after will require extra support with their education because they may have missed out on large chunks of schooling and/or they may have special needs. This is where initiatives such as designated teachers and personal education plans for every looked after child are important in acknowledging and recording looked after children's needs.

- Support and encouragement. The research literature identifies the importance of the home environment as a key factor affecting success in education (Jackson, 2007). While some looked after children are in placements where their individual learning successes are encouraged, others are not and this inconsistency in support from social workers, foster carers and residential social workers needs addressing.

- Emotional, mental or physical health. Educational outcomes are strongly influenced by a child's emotional, mental and physical health. Schools provide an environment which can improve a child's self-confidence and self-esteem, but frequently children looked after can experience bullying and changes to friendship networks because of placement moves, as well as emotional trauma from abuse and disrupted attachments. Children require ready support for this both within school and within the placement and often this is not forthcoming, although most local authorities now have a range of specialist inter-disciplinary services looking at education, physical health and mental health of looked after children.

RESEARCH SUMMARY

Since 1988, Jackson's work on the education of children in public care (see for example: Jackson 1988; Goddard 2000; Jackson and Sachdev 2001) has led her to believe that state care has not provided and does not provide a suitable environment to enable looked after children to succeed educationally. She argues that it is essential to see education as a key priority for all looked after children. Jackson (2007, pp3–4) highlights a number of 'landmark developments' emerging from the Labour government that have improved the centrality of education for looked after children in their care experience, including: the Quality protects *initiative; the introduction of performance indicators and targets in 2000; the publication of* Education Protects *in 2000 including learning materials for foster carers in their support of looked after children; the transfer of the responsibility of looked after children from the DoH to the then DfES; local joining up of children's social services and education departments; the Children Act 2004 which imposed a statutory obligation on local authorities to promote the education of looked after children; the* Care matters *Green and White papers (2006f; 2007) placing education centrally in the setting out of its vision of state care for future generations of children.*

Jackson also points to the over-reliance of social work on psychoanalytic theories under-pinning work with children, such as attachment and emotional issues. Jackson comments: Although psychoanalysis has long fallen out of favour as the theoretical underpin-ning of social work, its influence lingers on *(2007, p4). She argues that this has been to the detriment of examining educational and sociological literature and research, and integrating these findings into social work policies and procedures. She points out, for example, that this research identifies the influence of the home environment, the educational attainment level of parents and the interest they take in their children's education, as crucial determinants in a child's academic performance. Yet social workers do not link this to expectations of foster carers either at the recruitment stage or in work with children who are placed with them.*

There is another view emerging from social work academics and researchers that is less pessimistic about state care provision per se, and more critical of the basis for the 'evidence' set out above. Stein (2006b) believes that this emphasis on the care system as a catastrophic failure is wrong. He points to problems in analysis in a number of areas including: demographic data of the looked after population in terms of identifying which children within the care system are there for many years and which are highly vulnerable; the importance of pre-care experiences is underplayed as a key determinant of outcomes; and the current outcome measures for looked after children are too crude. Hare and Bullock (2006) and Berridge (2007) concur with this view. Jackson (2007, p4) states:

> As David Berridge has argued in a recent article (2007), there has been little attempt at understanding the more fundamental reasons for the huge and persistent gap in attainment for care leavers and others. I strongly disagree with his conclusion, however, that the answer is to be found in the characteristics of the families from which children in care are drawn and not in the shortcomings of the care system.

So which is correct? There is probably an element of accuracy in both perspectives. It is possible that more could be gained from taking on board the arguments offered from both of these positions than from adopting one perspective in seeking to understand the complexity of educational outcomes for looked after children. As Jackson suggests, there may well be benefits in examining the educational and sociological literature. There may also be benefit in examining the literature from adopting families concerning the educational outcomes of children who have been adopted alongside those children who are looked after (Cooper and Johnson, 2007 – see below). Small-scale studies also show that this group of children continue to have a higher rate of educational support needs than children in the general population. This may indicate that it is not the care system itself that is solely responsible for children's need for increased levels of educational support; rather their pre-care experiences can and do continue to have lasting effects on children's psychological development. Similarly, longitudinal ethnomethodological studies (large population-based studies carried out over time which often can identify rates of prevalence within the population they are studying because the research samples are large) and meta-analyses examining the outcomes for adoption (Van Ijzendoorn and Juffer, 2006), including educational outcomes, also provide information to add to the analysis. Egger and Davey Smith (1997, p137) use Huque's (1988) definition of a meta-analysis: a statistical analysis that combines or integrates the results of several independent clinical trials considered by the analyst to be 'combinable'. *Van Ijzendoorn and Juffer (2006) believe that* adoption can assist in enabling the majority of children to reach their academic potential provided they receive positive, nurturing and warm care*.*

What does all this mean for looked after children?

In any given year, up to 40% of the children who come into care will only do so for a number of weeks or months and will return home within six months. In addition to this, in 2011, 4.7% of children were adopted, with a further 3.7% placed for adoption. Finally, 15% of this number left care aged 16 or older. Of the total number in care at 31 March 2011, 30% (or 20,000 children) had been looked after for at least 2 and a half years, with 69% of this number (or 13,770 children) in the same placement for the preceding two years, or placed for adoption (DfE/ONS, 2011). This is a minority of the overall number of children in care at any one time and it is these 20,000 children who should be regarded as *growing up in care* (Bullock, et al., 2006). Many of these children come into care when they are older, having experienced abuse and neglect prior to entering care. Those children who are older have an increased likelihood of having long-standing physical and mental health issues, including learning disabilities.

For children experiencing this degree of adversity, it follows that their educational achievements will be disrupted, and children will be performing well below the average of their peers. These patterns will already be in place at the point at which a child becomes looked after.

Cooper and Johnson (2007) undertook a study involving 93 adopted children in the Sheffield region. Although this sample is not representative of all adopted children of school age in the UK, it does identify possible trends within this group of children. Of the families sampled 59% of parents said that their child was having difficulties in school. Of this number 39% had SEN, with 23% having SEN statements (see Table 10.2). Nationally 20% of children will have SEN at some point in their educational careers with 2% having statements. Gathering any data on adopted children is difficult because they are not an easily identifiable group in national data sets. This study suggests that problems with educational attainment do not disappear once a child is adopted and is no longer a looked after child. Many of the problems that children enter care with continue to affect their learning abilities.

In addition to the over representation of looked after children in receiving SEN services, looked after children are also over represented in exclusion statistics, with just under 1% of school-age looked after children being permanently excluded from school, compared to 0.1% of all school-aged children (see Table 10.3). Looked after children, traveller children, children with SEN and children of African–Caribbean heritage (mostly boys) are more likely to be excluded than children from any other group (Brammer, 2010, p354). Thirteen percent of looked after children missed at least 25 days of school during the school year (DfES, 2006a).

Table 10.2 Special educational needs data 2006

	Adopted children[1]	Looked after children[2]	All children
Children who have special educational needs	39%		19.2%*
Children who have SEN statements	23%	27.6%	2.9%*

[1] From Cooper and Johnson study (2007) involving 93 adopted children in the Sheffied area.

[2] There were 44,200 children looked after continuously for 12 months at the end of September 2006. Of this number 34,400 were of school age. Data presented refer to those children.

Source: DfES looked after children statistical returns (Sept 2006) (DfES, 2006a)

*DfES SEN statistical returns (Jan 2006) (DfES, 2006c)

Table 10.3 Permanent exclusions 2007–2010

Year	Looked after children %				All children %			
	primary	secondary	special	TOTAL	primary	secondary	special	TOTAL
2007	0.24	0.85	0.22	0.55	0.02	0.23	0.2	0.12
2008	0.23	0.63	0.28	0.44	0.02	0.21	0.19	0.11
2009	0.15	0.58	0.28	0.39	0.02	0.17	0.13	0.09
2010	0.18	0.40	n/k	0.28	0.02	0.15	0.11	0.08

Source: DfE, 2010b

One of the issues frequently mentioned by looked after children is bullying at school. Just as with many problems facing a child or young person within the school arena, sharing any difficulties with members of the school staff team (such as class teacher or designated teacher) can help to bring about a resolution to the concern. Every school will have an anti-bullying policy, and strategies used to stop bullying will vary according to the age and circumstance of the child. The child or young person's views are also important within this decision-making process (DfES, 2005b). See DfEE (2000) for further information.

CASE STUDY

Theresa is 15 and her ethnicity is black Nigerian. She has been accommodated by the local authority since she was ten, along with her older sister (aged 20) and younger brother (aged 14). Theresa lives with a foster carer in a long-term placement where she has been for the past three years. Her mother left the three children five years ago to return to Nigeria and very little has been heard concerning her whereabouts since this time. Initially Theresa's older sister (aged 15 at the time) looked after her two siblings for six weeks until their money ran out and then neighbours contacted social services. Although the children were enabled to continue living together in their home while receiving financial assistance through the local authority, it became very difficult for the older sister to cope with all the demands of caring for her siblings, running a home and also studying in school. Theresa sees her siblings very regularly. She is placed with an older single African–Caribbean woman who expects her do her homework every evening and study hard. While initially Theresa found the rules of the foster home difficult, she has settled and is generally doing well in the placement. You have recently been allocated this case. You attended a parents' evening at Theresa's school last week where you were told that she is doing reasonably well overall academically and will be sitting her GCSEs later in the year. She is struggling with elements of English and would benefit from additional assistance over this year. Also she plays the clarinet in the school orchestra and you note from the last review that the previous social worker said that Theresa's private lessons should continue but Theresa has said to you that her teacher has not been paid for a number of months.

How can you support Theresa?

COMMENT

Within this scenario there are a number of immediate practical tasks requiring attention, (e.g. payment of the music teacher), as well as consideration of longer-term needs that Theresa has. You should explore what is available locally in terms of additional educational support for looked after children through the school or through the local authority (for example, tutorial support, English language support). You will also need to discuss with Theresa what her thoughts and options are for further study and other longer-term ideas and plans she may have in terms of her education. What can you do to help Theresa think about her future education, which examinations to take, as well as ensuring that she has access to the right support while studying? Making sure Theresa has access to good careers counselling (either via school or the leaving care service) and access to external organisations such as Connexions is important. In addition you might also want to think about what support and information the foster carer may need during this time.

Theresa will also be approaching the point where leaving care services will become involved in supporting her, and she may well need your practical and emotional support during this

Continued

period of transition. This is potentially a stressful period for all young people, especially in addition to the pressure they may feel when studying for exams. Bear in mind that when looked after children experience stress, they may express this in different ways.

Also do not forget to celebrate achievements, no matter how small. Some young people may not be able to sit GCSEs but may instead be entered for other vocational courses or examinations.

Recent developments in education for looked after children

In 2010 the Labour government published new statutory guidance for the education of looked after children (DCSF, 2010a), and it remains in force. This guidance is underpinned by the Children Act 1989, Children Act 2004; Children and Young Persons Act 2008 and all associated guidance to these Acts, including the reissued *Volume 2 of the Children Act 1989 Guidance and Regulations: Care Planning, Placements and Case Review Regulations – Statutory Guidance* (DCSF, 2010b).

The duties placed on local authorities to safeguard and promote the welfare of the children they look after are considerable and well documented (see Chapter 2 for further information). In response to the gap in educational attainment between looked after children and all other children, the duties that local authorities have in promoting the educational achievement of the children they look after have been strengthened and these duties apply regardless of whether the children and young people live 'in borough' or 'out of borough'. Local authorities are required to consider the educational implications of every decision taken about a child's care and placement, and this is especially the case for those children sitting GCSE exams. The DfE believes that this emphasis reflects the wider role that a local authority has as a corporate parent: *local authorities must strive to offer all the support that a good parent would give in order to make sure that the children they look after reach their full potential* (DfE, 2012b).

In terms of particular developments that social workers should be aware of that are contained within the statutory guidance and regulations for the education of looked after children, you can find useful information at: www.education.gov.uk/publications/standard/publicationdetail/page1/DCSF-00342-2010). This covers the following areas:

- The statutory role of the designated teacher. (See: www.education.gov.uk/publications/standard/publicationDetail/Page1/DCSF-01046-2009).

- School admissions and exclusions (see earlier in this chapter for further information).

- PEPs (covered earlier)

- Personal Education Allowance (PEA). This is an allowance that is available to a looked after child to assist them with 'catching up' or preventing them falling behind with their education. It should not be used to replace services that the school, local authority or carer should provide or already provides. Many local authorities use this allowance to purchase tutor sessions for children.

- Information about out of authority placements and responsibilities for educational provision.

- The virtual school head role. (See: www.education.gov.uk/childrenandyoungpeople/ families/childrenincare/education/a00208592/virtual-school-head) This role allows the virtual head teacher to act as though she or he was a single head teacher for all the looked after children in one local authority, and to trace the educational progress of all looked after children in that authority attending school, including those children attending schools in other local authorities. A number of pilot studies have commented on the benefits of this role. Information is available on the web link above.

Health

The second area to be covered in this chapter is health. This is another area where official statistics list countless examples of the poor health outcomes looked after children present when compared to their peers not in care. Many government statistical releases state that looked after children have higher rates of substance misuse and teenage pregnancy when compared with children not in care and much higher prevalence of mental health problems (see Chapter 9).

Statistics on regular immunisations, health and dental checks are collected by the DfE in order to produce annual performance indicators on looked after children's physical health. (See Table 10.4.)

Table 10.4 Percentages of looked after children who had health checks

	Annual health check	Annual dental check	Immunisations
2005	80%	82%	77%
2006	83%	85%	80%
2007	84%	86%	80%
2008	87%	87%	82%
2009	85%	86%	84%
2010	84%	81%	77%
2011	84%	82%	79%

Source: SSDA903 data 2005–2011 (DfE, 2011a)

But health is so much more than an annual medical and dental examination. It involves many aspects of daily living to do with not only physical health, but emotional, social, cultural, and spiritual aspects as well. Some pertinent questions relating to the experiences of looked after children include the following:

- Are looked after children able to access leisure and sports activities in the same way that their peers who are not in care are often able to? Who funds this?

- What about educating children about healthy eating, organising for them to have swimming lessons, go to a concert, a football or sports event, an art exhibition or a museum?

- Do looked after children have access to IT facilities at home?

- Are they able to talk about friendship and relationship problems, and receive accurate and timely information about sex education?

- Do they receive the emotional support they need to grow and develop?

The majority of schools will have a range of activities available to children and young people as a part of the National Curriculum. However, although this will ensure that the majority of children will have a range of cultural and sporting experiences as a routine part of their education, this is mostly at an introductory level, and facilitating ongoing access to sporting and cultural opportunities is most often done via home. Children looked after have often come into care from families affected by drugs, domestic violence, alcohol; they may have experience of trauma, abuse, neglect, have special needs or a disability and may also come from highly mobile families (DoH, 2002b). Historically such families may have had very poor access to health and education services (DfES, 2006f; Hunt and Cooke, 2006).

The profile of health for looked after children has changed over the last ten years, helped in part by the previous Labour government's *Quality Protects* initiative, where, as with education, the increase in central government funding and associated monitoring has required social services departments to think about improvement in health outcomes in different ways than had hitherto been the case. Even before this additional funding was available, the problems in looked after children receiving consistent health care were known. In 2002 the DoH published *Promoting the health of looked after children*. This document was suitably critical of the lack of systematic monitoring in this area and also commented on the limited research available, including *small, unrepresentative, uncontrolled samples ... unable to distinguish problems preceding or consequent on the child's care experiences* (DoH, 2002b, p7).

This publication was revised in 2009 (DCSF, 2009), is now statutory guidance and remains in effect and applies to local authorities, Primary Care Trusts (PCTs) and Strategic Health Authorities (and from 2013 their successor bodies). This document outlines responsibilities in the commissioning and provision of services to looked after children, including those children who are placed 'out of borough'. This is an important point, especially in the provision of CAMH services where there is often a shortage of resources, and children placed out of borough are not always seen as a priority for local CAMH services that are stretched. The protocols in the statutory guidance set out arrangements in these circumstances, but this does not remove pressures and tensions.

Although the coalition government has a political interest in increasing opportunities and life chances to looked after children, to date the majority of the government's attention has been levied at adoption services, with further legislation about adoption expected during this government's first term in office (see Chapter 11). At a time when local authorities are facing considerable cuts, there are no increased resources for looked after children. The DfE website points to the National Children's Bureau's 'Healthy Care' programme (www.ncb.org.uk/healthycare).

Hare and Bullock (2006) comment that the current emphasis (referred to as 'the present vogue') within policy and literature for looked after children is on mental health. Please see Chapter 9 in this book for further information on mental health. However, the reason for this current interest in and attention to mental health might be less to do with it being a 'fad' and more to do with it having moved up the political agenda in the past decade. If the unintended outcome of this activity has been that social workers (and others) have an increased awareness and understanding of the critical importance of good mental and emotional health as a protective factor for children, then that is a positive gain. Because the issue of the mental health of all children has moved up the political agenda, this has helped secure additional resources and services for looked after childre with many local authorities now having specialist jointly funded looked after CAMHS services with health (Cocker and Scott, 2006).

The DfE collects annual SDQ scores from the main carer's questionnaire for all looked after children who have been in care for one year or longer. At the time of publication, three years' data was available. See Table 10.5 for the rate of SDQs returned. The range of scores is between 0–40. The scoring of the SDQ enables classification of the results into one of three categories: normal (score is between 0–13); borderline (score is between 14–16); or abnormal (score is between 17–40). The aggregated data provided by the DfE presents an average score that is on the borders of 'normal' and 'borderline'.

Table 10.5 Department for Education annual SDQ scores

	Percentage of eligible children who had an SDQ score submitted	Average score per child
2009	68	13.9
2010	68	14.2
2011	69	13.9

Source: DfE, 2011a

There is some additional descriptive data available about the SDQ scores available in the annual statistical first release data (DfE/ONS, 2011), but it is general. The DCSF has compiled an information leaflet about the SDQ, which contains some interesting answers to Frequently Asked Questions.

Isn't this just more internal administrative burden – collecting data for the sake of it? Evidence clearly suggests that looked after children are nearly 5 times more likely to have a mental health disorder than all children. However, we currently have no national measure to identify the extent of this. The white paper Care Matters: Time for Change highlighted the need to improve the mental health of children and young people in care. The first step in order to make improvements is to identify the scale of the problem and the SDQ is the tool which we will use to obtain this.

While this will inevitably mean that there is a degree of administrative burden in obtaining information for this new indicator, nevertheless the benefits in being able to identify problems for these vulnerable children is an overriding consideration.

So what will local authorities get out of this? Local authorities will be able to build up management information regarding the scale of the emotional/behavioural problems of looked after children in their area which will therefore help inform the appropriate levels of service provision. In the longer term, data from SDQ returns will give an indication on how effective the service provision provided is in meeting the needs of looked after children. Of primary importance to local authorities (given their role as the corporate parents) is that undertaking an SDQ questionnaire early in a child's care history will quickly highlight the likelihood that the child either has, or could develop significant mental health problems. This should then assist in accessing/ commissioning appropriate intervention to support the child.

(DCSF/ONS 2008)

Legal context

Local authorities have general duties under the Children Act 1989 to safeguard and pro-mote the welfare of children, which includes monitoring their developmental progress, and this is routinely undertaken at the beginning of a child becoming looked after and subsequently via the annual medical/dental checks and reviews. This is discussed in Chapter 2. The requirements placed on a local authority in relation to addressing health needs as part of the process of care planning are set out in the Children Act 1989 Volume 2 Guidance and Regulations: Care Planning, Placements and Case Review (DCSF, 2010b) and the Care Planning, Placements and Case Review (England) Regulations (DCSF, 2010c). However, promoting the health of looked after children is not the job of any one person or organisation. As with education, effective multi-agency working between social work-ers, health professionals and carers is essential. In addition to the statutory guidance on care planning, and the government's statutory guidance (DCSF, 2009), the following legal framework applies:

- The Children Act 1989, specifically section 22 (local authority responsibilities toward looked after children) and section 27 (local authorities are entitled to expect other authorities and certain NHS bodies to assist them in discharging their functions to children in need, looked after children and their parents and carers).

- The Children Act 2004: this introduced a new duty (section 10) on local authorities, PCTs and other relevant children's services partners to co-operate at a strategic level. The same partners were also placed under a duty (section 11) to make arrangements to ensure that they take account of the need to safeguard and promote the welfare of children in the discharge of their own functions.

- The Children and Young Persons Act 2008: this amended the Children Act 1989, strengthening the legislative framework underpinning the care system and putting in place the structures to enable children and young people to receive high-quality care and support. Examples of some of the amendments to the Children Act 1989 are: local authorities are required to take steps to ensure that sufficient suitable accommodation is available within their area; and the role of the IRO is strengthened to improve care planning.

- The Care Standards Act 2000: the Care Standards Act 2000 and the Regulations and National Minimum Standards made under it, contain provisions in relation to the welfare, health and illnesses of children who are looked after in establishments regulated by the Act.

- The Mental Health Act 2007: this amended the Mental Health Act 1983. Amongst other provisions it requires hospital managers to ensure that patients aged under 18 admitted to hospital for a mental disorder are accommodated in an environment that is suitable for their needs.

The Children Act (Miscellaneous Amendments) (England) Regulations 2002, amended the Arrangement for Placement of Children (General) Regulations 1991. The main changes include:

7.– (1) …. a responsible authority shall –

(a) before making a placement, or if that is not reasonably practicable, as soon as possible after a placement is made, make arrangements for a registered medical practitioner to conduct an assessment, which may include a physical examination, of the child's state of health;

(b) require the registered medical practitioner who conducts the assessment to prepare a written report of the assessment which addresses the matters listed in schedule 2; and

(c) having regard to the matters listed in schedule 2, …. prepare a plan for the future health care of the child, if one is not already in existence.

(2) A responsible authority shall ensure that each child is provided during the placement with –

(a) health care services, including medical and dental care and treatment; and

(b) advice and guidance on health, personal care and health promotion issues appropriate to his needs.

The responsible local authority should arrange for an annual assessment of the looked after child or young person's health, and this should be conducted by a registered medical practitioner, registered nurse or midwife. This assessment should take place once every six months for a child under five years of age, and annually for all other children. Young people who are looked after can refuse to consent to a medical examination if they are of sufficient age and understanding. The medical officer undertaking the assessment should prepare a written report, which must include a plan of the future health needs of the child or young person in question, see also *Children Act 1989 Volume 2 Guidance and Regulations: Care Planning, Placements and Case Review* (DCSF, 2010b).

In addition, the Children (Leaving Care) Act 2000 stipulates that health issues should be included in the pathway plans made for young people leaving care.

RESEARCH SUMMARY

The SEU (2003) report mentions that educational outcomes are strongly influenced by a child's health and that frequent placement moves (so often mentioned as a problem in terms of the effect that placement moves can have on a child's experience of education – see Sinclair (2005) for further information) can often cause practical problems in ensuring children's health needs are addressed. For some children, problems may not be identified, assessments may not occur and this can add delay to accessing appropriate services. Many children also enter care with health needs (Bebbington and Miles, 1989; DoH, 2002b) and there is considerable discussion as to what effect the care system has on the health and outcomes of looked after children in addition to any issues children may have had prior to their reception into care. Looked after children are the epitome of the inverse care law – their health may not only be jeopardised by abusive and neglectful parenting, but care itself may fail to repair and protect health. Indeed it may even damage and exacerbate abuse (DoH, 2002b, p6).

However, as with education, different views exist on the role of 'care' per se and its effects on children. Scott and Hill (2006) suggest that the general physical health of most (around three-quarters of) looked after and accommodated children in Scotland is good, and this is despite the variety of adverse factors in the backgrounds of these children. They identify two important qualifications to this finding. First, the lifestyles of many young people present major threats to their current and/or future well-being. A number of these issues are discussed below. Secondly, there is a high incidence of mental health problems (including conduct disorders) – this is covered in Chapter 9.

In particular, Scott and Hill (2006) mention a study undertaken by Meltzer and colleagues (2004a) of children looked after in Scotland which showed that children living with foster carers were more likely to be rated as having very good health (70%) compared to children living in other types of placement, particularly residential care (38%).

> An important point made by Meltzer and colleagues (2004) was that the general health of children seemed to improve as placements became more secure. Over two-thirds of children who had been in placement for two years or more were assessed as having very good health, but this reduced to just under half for those who had been in placement for less than two years.

> (Scott and Hill, 2006)

A resource developed by Barnardo's discusses the benefits of creating specific policy about the provision of sexual health and education services for looked after children, including the provision of training and advice for foster carers (Haydon, 2003). Additionally a National Children's Bureau (NCB) project in London has developed and tested a training programme for carers of children in public care. The training materials developed by the programme cover sexual health, relationships, pregnancy and parenthood for vulnerable children and young people in public care (Mackie and Patel-Kanwal, 2003).

Health-related behaviours and lifestyles

Some of the other areas of high risk-taking behaviour indicated in the literature among looked after children include early pregnancy, drug taking and smoking. Scott and Hill (2006) cite a number of Scottish and English studies from which information has been drawn (e.g. Triseliotis, et al., 1995; Saunders and Broad, 1997; Griesbach and Currie, 2001; Scottish Health Feedback, 2003).

In 2006 the DfES began collecting data on rates of substance misuse among looked after children. Five percent of looked after children had a substance misuse problem and 63% of this number received an intervention related to this problem (DfES, 2006b). Meltzer, et al. (2004a) found that looked after and accommodated children in Scotland aged 11 to 17 were twice as likely to smoke, drink or take drugs as their English counterparts (Meltzer, 2004 cited in Scott and Hill, 2006):

44% of looked after and accommodated children in Scotland aged 11 to 17 were smokers and over a quarter of all children who smoked reported that they had started smoking at the age of ten or under. This reflects the responses from young people themselves. Scottish Health Feedback (2003) found that from 96 survey responses of looked after and accommodated young people, 75% were smokers and that more females smoked (79%) than males (73%), in line with national trends....Around a third (31%) had first tried drugs while in care, but just over two-thirds had taken drugs before coming into care.

(Scott and Hill, 2006)

Of the children looked after continuously for 12 months at 31 March 2011, 1,960 children (4.3%) were identified as having a substance misuse problem during the year. Of these, 56.6% received an intervention for the problem and a further 34.9% refused the intervention which was offered. Substance misuse was more common among older children, 1,340 children identified as having a substance misuse problem were in the 16- to 17-year-old age group. This represents 11.9% of all children looked after continuously for 12 months who are in this age group. Of these 1,340 children, 61.6% were boys and 38.4% were girls (DfE, 2011a).

Teenage pregnancies have received national attention in terms of the UK having the highest numbers of teenage pregnancies in western Europe. The Labour government has produced various policy documents outlining strategies to attempt to reduce the numbers of teenagers having children (e.g. SEU, 1999, DfES, 2006a). Chase and Knight (2006) comment that limited research suggests that young people either in or leaving care are even more likely to be mothers/fathers than teenagers within the general population, with two studies (Biehal, et al., 1992, 1995) finding that 25% of care leavers had a child by 16 years of age and that 50% were young mothers within two years of leaving care. However, the numbers of young people included in the sample were small and therefore not indicative of prevalence within the looked after population nationally. Some of the risk factors associated with teenage pregnancy generally include: family relationship disruption; a lack of continuity in care; low self-esteem; not trusting others; feeling rejected; lonely and stigmatised; lack of access to sex and relationships education and difficulties in accessing health services (Chase and Knight, 2006, pp83, 86). Social workers have a role in working with young people (including young men) to ensure they have accurate and relevant information about sex, relationships and contraception advice at a suitable and timely point for the young person (DoH, 2002b; SCIE, 2004b).

Young people who may be lesbian or gay, bisexual or transgender (LGBT) may face a number of additional issues in terms of their education, health and personal security (Freed-Kernis, 2008). In terms of education, the lobbying organisation Stonewall has run a campaign over the last few years that has raised the profile of homophobic bullying in schools. This is a very real problem and something that unfortunately many LGBT young people may experience. Social workers, teachers and carers should be aware of this. Freed-Kernis (2008) suggests that in the experience of the Albert Kennedy Trust (a charity that works with LGBT young people), young people who are lesbian and gay and who are bullied at school will often stop attending, and their academic results will then suffer. We also know that young people in care may well have missed out on chunks of education prior to being in care, which will also affect their academic progress, so this additional school trauma will have much greater negative consequences for looked after young people.

In terms of health, lesbians and gay men have higher rates of mental ill health, than do their heterosexual counterparts (D'Augelli and Hershberger 1993; Warner, et al., 2004); substance misuse rates of alcohol, drugs and tobacco are also higher.

Brown and Cocker comment,

> *One of the major events with which a young lesbian or gay man has to grapple is the 'coming out' process and this marks out lesbian, gay and bisexual young people's experience as different from their heterosexual peers. Often (but not always) this experience can be compounded by a lack of social support available via families, friends and surrounding networks. For lesbian and gay young people who are not living with their birth families, this can create any number of additional tensions, difficulties, pressures and experiences that will affect their development during this time.*

(2011, p143)

The sensitivity that social workers, foster carers and residential workers should demonstrate in such circumstances is well documented (Brown, 1998; Tully, 2000; Freed-Kernis, 2008; Brown and Cocker, 2011). But such sensitivity should be demonstrated in all work with looked after children and young people, not just those who are lesbian and gay. In addition good information about sexual health care and relationships is essential for all looked after children. For further information see Brown and Cocker (2011, pp142–7).

So what does this mean for looked after children?

Looked after children, practitioners and academics have devised a number of practical strategies to assist in improving the health of children in public care. Looked after children should have a core assessment completed about them around the time they enter care, including their health, which should be viewed holistically and not just as a physical examination. This serves as a baseline against which the social worker and other colleagues can measure progress.

The DoH (2002b) identified a number of children with 'special circumstances' within the looked after population who had specific health-related needs. Included within the group were children with disabilities, black and minority ethnic children, asylum-seeking children and refugees, care leavers, and children cared for in secure settings. There are specific chapters in this book which address each of these particular groups of children, except for children in secure accommodation. Chapter 6 discusses asylum-seeking children and refugees; Chapter 7 discusses disabled children; and Chapter 12 looks at issues for young people leaving care. Apart from outlining the legal framework (including responsibilities) for these children in Chapters 2 and 3, we have not examined the specific issues for children who are in secure accommodation (see Pickford and Dugmore 2012 for further information).

In terms of specific health needs for disabled children, where specialist paediatricians and other medical consultants are involved, comprehensive health plans should take into account the child's particular needs as well as any communication issues, support and other practical (equipment) needs. It is also important to involve children in the plans that are made about them and ensure that their wishes and feelings have been considered. In general terms, disabled children have the same developmental needs in terms of social, leisure and recreation as all other children (DoH, 2002b), yet Stewart and Ray (2001) suggest that disabled children and young people are less likely to receive sex and relationship education, whether at home or in school, than other children.

Black and ethnic minority children are identified as *suffer(ing) considerable health disadvantage* (DoH, 2002b) because of the *considerable disparities in health experience between white and black populations as a whole and around childbirth* (Butt, 1998, cited in DoH, 2002b, p39). Further, there are particular hereditary illnesses for specific ethnic and cultural groups that social workers (and others) will need to be familiar with (e.g. sickle cell anaemia). Obtaining accurate health information of family histories is important. This becomes more difficult where children are seeking asylum or are unaccompanied minors, as this information may not be readily available. Additionally, language and cultural barriers may exist and it is essential that those assessing and working with children use interpreters who can communicate clearly with them. There are specialist services available from a number of non-governmental refugee organisations, and specific guidance is available from the King's Fund for medical practitioners assessing refugee children (DoH, 2002b).

For young people leaving care, the pathway plan is an essential tool for social workers working with young people. This plan will identify specific health needs a young person may have and identify resources to meet these identified needs. This should include more than just physical health issues, by covering healthy lifestyle issues and choices previously discussed, as well as friendships and social activities, sports and recreation.

Additionally, social workers should understand the Fraser guidelines:

> *These guidelines state that contraception may be provided for a young person under 16, without parental consent, if the following criteria are fulfilled: the young person understands the advice and is competent to consent to treatment; the young person is encouraged to inform her parents/guardians; it is believed that the young person is likely to commence or continue sexual activity with or without contraception;*

the physical or mental health of the young person will suffer if they do not receive contraceptive advice or supplies; contraceptive advice and treatment is in the best interests of the young person concerned.

(SCIE, 2004b)

Hunt and Cooke (2006) list a number of practical ideas for improving the health outcomes for looked after children, which move beyond the annual physical health assessment of children. These include: good liaison with school health staff; working closely with education colleagues in terms of looked after children benefiting from 'healthy schools' initiatives; health promotion material on the importance of healthy eating, relationships, and physical exercise for all children, being readily available to children within their various placements (foster care, residential care, secure accommodation) as well as material geared towards the specific needs that children may have (e.g. children leaving care, asylum-seeking children and unaccompanied children, ethnic minority children, disabled children); the importance of accurate and up-to-date health records being maintained and shared with birth parents; and the involvement of children and young people in consenting to all health care and treatment, according to their age and understanding.

CASE STUDY

Michael is 15 years old and is of white UK origin. He has been looked after for seven years and is subject to a Care Order made under section 31 of the Children Act 1989 because of experiencing chronic and persistent neglect during his early childhood. During the time he has been in care, he has had ten placements and 12 social workers. He is currently placed with a foster carer and has been in his current placement for two and a half years, which is the longest he has lived anywhere, apart from when he lived with his birth parents. Michael is 4 ft 6 inches tall. He hasn't reached puberty yet. Michael has recently been referred to a consultant because of his delayed puberty and there appears to be some hormonal dysfunction. He has always been rather small for his age in comparison to his peers but this was always attributed to his parents being small – his mother is 5 ft tall, and his father is 5 ft 2 inches tall. Given that Michael moved placements so frequently when he originally came into care, he did not have annual health checks, so his height was not routinely monitored. His early medical records have also gone missing during the transfer of records from GP practice to GP practice. Michael also refused to attend health checks when he was placed in a succession of residential children's homes in three separate county areas. The consultant who saw Michael has recently contacted you to discuss the options open to Michael in terms of further investigations. The consultant has also indicated that she is not happy about the delay in taking Michael to the GP for referral to a specialist.

In your opinion, what do you think has happened?

Outline what action you would take now to ensure that Michael's specific health needs are addressed.

Who would be involved in the decision-making? What would be their role?

What wider health issues might you also consider?

When children have a succession of placement moves, it is often difficult to ensure that there is consistent monitoring of their health during their time in care. Often children in care can miss routine checks for eyes, hearing and teeth (among other things) because of frequent change in schools, GPs and carers. Sometimes other more serious medical conditions fail to be recognised because of the lack of consistent care children experience over time (DoH, 2002b).

For someone like Michael where there is an interplay of various factors which might have contributed to his growth (life experiences in terms of lack of stability during childhood and a background of chronic neglect and failure to thrive; and genetic inheritance) it is important that assumptions are not made about the causes of ill health or development which is outside of the 'normal' trajectory, and that any alternative reasons for situations occurring are also considered.

In terms of who should be involved in making decisions, Michael is of sufficient age and understanding to have a significant role in decisions made about the kind of investigations undertaken. As well as the local authority, Michael's parent(s) also should be consulted.

Although there are specific issues that require follow-up for Michael, there are also routine checks that should be undertaken concerning Michael's hearing, eyesight and teeth. The physical activities that Michael enjoys should be noted, and any specific talents encouraged. Michael should also receive age-appropriate information on personal and intimate relationships. All of these areas should be covered in Michael's looked after child review.

A summary of social work responsibilities for health issues for looked after children:

The statutory guidance for the education of looked after children was published in 2009 (DCSF/DoH, 2009). This built on some of the initiatives contained within the *Care Matters* White Paper. It is essential that social workers understand their responsibilities in this area and, in so doing, have a broad sense of health that goes beyond the annual medical and dental check. The statutory guidance sets out the responsibilities of the local authority:

Local authorities should have arrangements in place, in accordance with relevant regulations, to ensure that every child it looks after, regardless of where that child is placed, has:

- *his/her health needs fully assessed*

- *a health plan which clearly sets out how health needs identified in the assessment will be addressed. This includes intended outcomes, measurable objectives to achieve outcomes, actions needed, who will take them and by when his/her health plan will be reviewed.*

Local authorities should make plans at a strategic level to ensure that local delivery of these arrangements and at an operational level should act as a parent and advocate for each child looked after by them.

Local authorities should make sure that the voices of looked after children are heard as part of the process of informing the commissioning, planning, delivery and evaluation of services.

The child's social worker is responsible for making sure:

- *he or she has a health plan which is drawn up in partnership with the child, his or her carer and (where appropriate) parents, and other agencies and*

- *that (while many actions in the plan may be the responsibility of other agencies) the plan is implemented and reviewed in accordance with the regulations.*

The Independent Reviewing Officer (IRO) should ensure that the child's health plan is reviewed at least every six months in accordance with the regulations.

Social workers should ensure that foster carers are given a written health record for each child in their care. This record should include: the child's state of health and identified health needs and it should be regularly updated and moved with the child.

Local authorities, normally through the social worker, should ensure that foster carers and residential care workers know how to contact designated and lead health professionals for each child in their care and how to access the services the child needs.

Local authorities should provide looked after children with free access to positive activities and related facilities they own, deliver and commission. This includes access for looked after children who are teenage parents with arrangements for necessary childcare.

(DCSF/DoH, 2009, pp2–3)

CHAPTER SUMMARY

Health and education are both areas where children who are looked after underachieve when compared to the outcomes of children who are not in care. The reasons for this have been explored in this chapter.

FURTHER READING

Barnardo's (2006) *Failed by the system.* Ilford: Barnardo's.

This Barnardo's publication gives a robust account of the main issues affecting looked after children and the literature informing the debates in this area.

Connelly, S and Chakrabarti, M (2007) Can Scotland achieve more for looked after children? *Adoption and Fostering,* 31(1), 81–91.

Department for Children, Schools and Families (2010) *Promoting the educational achievement of looked after children: Statutory Guidance for local authorities.* London: HMSO.

Department for Children, Schools and Families and Department of Health (2009) *Statutory guidance on promoting the health and wellbeing of looked after children.* London: HMSO.

Department for Education and Skills (2005) *Who does what: How social workers and carers can support the education of looked after children.* London: TSO.

Horner, N and Krawcczyk, S (2006) *Social work in education and children's service.* Exeter: Learning Matters.

This book gives a more specific account of a social worker's role in education and children's services generally, with some reference to looked after children.

Hunt, R and Cooke, E (2006) *Health and wellbeing: Physical health quality* protects research briefings (No 12) research in practice. Available at: **www.rip.org.uk/publications**

This is one of a number of research briefings published under the Quality Protects series by RiP and DoH, and it is a very handy summary of the main presenting issues, the evidence base and an indication about what might help developments in this area.

Jackson, S (2007) Progress at last? *Adoption and Fostering*, 31(1), 3–5.

Sonia Jackson has written a great deal about education and looked after children. This editorial provides a brief overview of *Adoption and Fostering* journal's special issue on education and looked after children, and also references some of Jackson's earlier work. It is well worth reading for an overview of some of the debates in the area.

Scott, J and Hill, M (2006) *The health of looked after and accommodated children and young people in Scotland – messages from research.* Edinburgh: Scottish Executive. Available online at **www.scotland.gov.uk/Publications/2006/06/07103730/0**

A Scottish perspective on the outcomes for looked after children in Scotland.

Scottish Executive (2007) *Looked after children and young people: We can and must do better.* Edinburgh: Scottish Executive. Available online at **www.scotland.gov.uk/publications/2007/01 /15084446/0**

Social Exclusion Unit (2003) *A better education for children in care.* London: Office for the Deputy Prime Minister.

The Centre for Excellence and Outcomes in Children and Young People's Services: **www.C4eo.org.uk** – click on 'vulnerable children' for a summary of information regarding education (2010) and mental health (2009).

Department for Education: **www.education.gov.uk**

Buttle UK: **www.buttleuk.org**

Who Cares? Trust: **www.thewhocarestrust.org.uk**

Who Cares? Scotland: **www.whocaresscotland.org**

Children in Wales: **www.childreninwales.org.uk/areasofwork/lookedafterchildren/ healthoflookedafterchildren/lahproject/2228.html**

Chapter 11
Adoption and permanence

ACHIEVING A SOCIAL WORK DEGREE

This chapter will help you to develop the following capabilities from the **Professional Capabilities Framework**:

- **Values and ethics**
  Apply social work ethical principles and values to guide professional practice.
- **Diversity**
  Recognise diversity and apply anti-discriminatory and anti-oppressive principles in practice.
- **Justice**
  Advance human rights and promote social justice and economic wellbeing.
- **Judgement**
  Use judgement and authority to intervene with individuals, families and communities to promote independence, provide support and prevent harm, neglect and abuse.
- **Knowledge**
  Apply knowledge of social sciences, law and social work practice theory.
- **Critical reflection and analysis**
  Apply critical reflection and analysis to inform and provide a rationale for professional decision-making.

It will also introduce you to the following standards as set out in the 2008 social work subject benchmark statement
5.1.1 Social work services, service users and carers
5.1.2 The service delivery context
5.1.3 Values and ethics
5.1.5 The nature of social work practice
5.5.3 Analysis and synthesis
5.5.4 Intervention and evaluation

Introduction

Adoption affects many people's lives, including those who have been adopted, adults who have adopted and their immediate and extended families, as well as the birth parents of children who are adopted and their extended families too. This chapter will provide you with an overview of adoption and other routes to permanence for children who are looked after, by outlining a number of historical and current debates in the field. We include: statistical data concerning the numbers of children and trends in adoption in England; a summary of research reviewing the outcomes for children who are adopted; other models of permanence; and give an explanation of some of the terms associated with working in this field, including concurrent planning and permanence.

We outline processes associated with adoption for looked after children and potential adopters. The Adoption and Children Act 2002 underpins work in this area and a summary of the main areas of the Act is included in this chapter. Although adoptions by step-parents make up between one-third and one-half of the numbers of children who are adopted every year, we will not specifically cover these in this chapter. We provide an exercise that examines post-adoption support, but we do not cover adoption issues post-childhood in this chapter.

Historical context

Adoption practice in England and Wales has undergone significant reform since the 1960s when adoption was at its highest point, with over 27,000 adoptions registered in 1968 (Brammer, 2010). Numbers of children available for adoption have consistently fallen since this time. This is because of the enormous social and attitudinal change that has occurred. The stigma once associated with teenage pregnancy and single parenthood no longer applies in the same way (DoH, 1999a; Brayne and Carr, 2010). Additionally, contraception is now widely available, and the legalisation to liberalise abortion means that less babies are available for adoption. The Children Act 1975 and the related Adoption Act 1976 saw adoption as one means by which local authorities could provide permanency for children in public care. Rowe and Lambert's (1973) report was hugely influential in this regard (Brammer, 2010), as it showed that too many looked after children were drifting in care for long periods of time because permanent arrangements for their future had not been made (Triseliotis, et al., 1997).

Current context

The Children Act 1989 was supposed to be the key piece of legislation that covered all law pertaining to children. However, adoption law has always stood outside that piece of legislation (see Brammer, 2010, for further details). After the Adoption Bill 1996 failed to become law, the change in government resulted in a number of key policy initiatives (for example, *Quality protects*) which saw the establishment of performance indicators and targets for local authority services for adoption. Further, a number of independent reports (e.g. Waterhouse Inquiry Report) and research (see Rowe and Lambert, 1973; DoH, 1999a) into looked after children highlighted poor permanency planning, and led to renewed political interest in adoption.

The Prime Minister's review of adoption

In 2000, the White Paper *Adoption: A New Approach* was published, reviewing adoption provision in the UK (PIU, 2000). It identified a number of key gaps in adoption services, including: the need to attract, recruit and support many more adopters and their families; the need to improve the quality and consistency of care planning and local authority performance on adoption; making the court system work better in supporting care planning for looked after children; and changing the law to make it clear and more consistent.

Prime Minister Tony Blair commented in the foreword (PIU, 2000):

> *While there are many options suitable to children's needs, adoption can work well.*
> *There is scope to increase the use of adoption. But there are clear problems with the*
> *way the system of adoption now operates. Poor performance, widespread variations,*
> *unacceptable delays…there is a lack of clarity, of consistency and of fairness…We have*
> *to change this. We have to have a new approach to adoption.*

This White Paper indicated a clear government committment to increasing the use of adoption as a route to permanence for many looked after children. The White Paper suggested raising the target of the numbers of children being adopted via councils by 40% over a four-year period.

However, adoption is only one route to a permanent care arrangement for children when they are unable to return to their birth families. One of the tensions present in the debate around the increased use of adoption as a route for permanence for many children is that for some looked after children, adoption is not an appropriate option. Yet many of the measures introduced since 2000 have focused on increasing adoptions by setting performance targets against which progress is measured (Selwyn and Sturgess, 2002), despite the White Paper identifying a number of other options for permanence. We will revisit this debate later in this chapter.

International comparison

In addition to the White Paper (PIU, 2000) there are a number of different publications that give an overview of how adoption is used in many developed countries (Warman and Roberts, 2001; Adoption Policy Review Group (Scotland), 2005). Essentially all cover similar ground and have concluded that there is a high use of adoption in the UK as a route to permanency for a looked after child, compared to other European countries (see Table 11.1).

Table 11.1 International comparison: percentage of children adopted from care

USA	6.6
England	4
Portugal	1.8
France	1.5
New Zealand	Under 1
Australia	Under 1
Norway	Under 1
Luxembourg	Under 1
Denmark	Under 1
Sweden	0.2

Source: PIU, 2000

The table shows the range in the percentage of children adopted from care from 6.6% in the USA to 0.2% in Sweden, reflecting the different priority given to adoption in each country. The UK, along with the USA, has a considerably higher number of children placed for adoption than other European and Antipodean countries. Elsewhere in Europe, Australia and New Zealand, there is a much greater reluctance to overrule the wishes of parents, and enforce a permanent, legal separation between birth parent and child. In all of the countries included in this comparison, different welfare policies have an effect on the numbers of children in public care; the length of time children are in care; the type of placement they are in; as well as the permanency options available to them.

Adoption: key local authority performance developments

From 1997 to 2010, the Labour government introduced a number of measures to increase the numbers of children adopted from state care.

The *Quality Protects* (QP) initiative was introduced in 1997 to improve performance in children's services. This initiative brought ring-fenced funding to all local authorities for a time-limited period to facilitate improvement in outcomes for children's services. A number of the QP objectives related specifically to adoption, as improvements in the numbers of children being adopted from care was seen as a priority area. Local authorities still have a number of performance indicators (PIs) and Performance Assessment Framework (PAF) indicators in relation to numbers of adoptions achieved per year (see Table 11.2).

The Adoption and Permanence Taskforce was launched in 2000. The aim of the taskforce was to *support local councils in improving their performance on maximizing the use of adoption as an option for meeting the needs of looked after children* (Brammer, 2010, p314).

The National Adoption Standards for England were launched in 2001. The most recent version was published in March 2011 (DfE, 2011b). The National Minimum Standards (NMS), together with the adoption regulations, form the basis of the regulatory framework under the Care Standards Act 2000 for the conduct of adoption agencies and adoption support agencies. These are issued by the Secretary of State under sections 23 and 49 of the Care Standards Act 2000. Successive Governments are clear that 'minimum standards' do not mean standardisation of provision.

> *The standards are designed to be applicable to the variety of different types of adoption agencies and adoption support agencies. They aim to enable, rather than prevent, individual agencies to develop their own particular ethos and approach based on evidence that this is the most appropriate way to meet the child's needs.*

> (DfE, 2011b, p4)

When the standards were launched in 2001 there were 61 – now there are 29, and they provide the framework for the delivery of adoption services to children or young people, birth families, prospective adopters, adopted parents (16 standards) as well as adoption agencies, adoption support agencies and voluntary adoption agencies (13 standards).

Many of the standards are already required either by primary legislation, regulation or statutory guidance (DfE, 2011b).

Further details can be found online at: www.education.gov.uk/publications/standard/Adoptionandforstering/Page1/DFE-00028-2011

Further amendments to the Statutory Guidance on Adoption, published in 2011, were made in 2012. Further details can be found online at: www.education.gov.uk/childrenandyoungpeople/families/adoption/g0072314/guidance.

There is a document that summarises the main changes to the previously issued guidance. This includes changes to the remit of Adoption Panels. Panels will no longer make recommendations on whether a child should be placed for adoption where an application for a Placement Order would be required. This decision will be made by the agency decision maker.

A revised version of the National Care Standards for Adoption Agencies in Scotland was published in 2005 (Scottish Executive 2005), and a revised version of the its national minimum standards for local authority adoption services in Wales was published in 2007 (Welsh Assembly, 2007).

The Adoption Register was launched in 2001. This register was developed after the publication of the PIU report (2000). It provides national information to help link adoptive parents to children who are waiting to be placed in a family. Local authorities are required to register both prospective adopters and children waiting to be matched.

The voluntary-sector organisation Norwood won the contract to monitor and facilitate the register from 2001 to 2004. The British Association of Adoption and Fostering (BAAF) took over responsibility from 1 December 2004. From December 2004 to June 2012, 1,835 children were placed using the register. See: www.adoptionregister.org.uk/ for further information.

Table 11.2 Children looked after, adopted from 2000 to 2012 in England

Year		2000	2001	2002	2003	2004	2005	2006	2007	2008	2009	2010	2011	2012
All		2700	3100	3400	3500	3800	3800	3700	3330	3180	3330	3200	3050	3450
% LAC		5	5	6	6	6	6	6	5.5	5.3	5.4	4.9	4.6	5.1
Sex	M	1400	1600	1700	1900	1900	1900	1900	1670	1640	1680	1640	1560	1740
	F	1300	1500	1700	1700	1900	1800	1800	1660	1540	1640	1560	1500	1710
Age	U1	200	200	200	220	210	210	190	150	110	80	70	60	70
	1–4	1600	1900	2000	2200	2200	2300	2300	2130	2230	2380	2250	2170	2560
	5–9	790	830	990	960	1100	1100	900	880	690	770	780	730	740
	10–15	140	130	180	170	210	170	180	150	120	80	100	90	80
	16+								10	20	10	10	x	10
Average age		4.4	4.3	4.5	4.4	4.5	4.2	4.1	4.2	3.11	3.9	3.11	3.10	3.8

Source: DfE statistics for looked after children in England for the year ending 31 March 2012 (DfE, 2012d)

Table 11.2 shows a continuing year-on-year increase in the numbers of children adopted from 2000 until 2006, when for the first time in six years there was a decrease in the numbers of children adopted. The Labour government's ambitious target of a 50% rise in the numbers of children adopted by 2005–6 from 1999–2000 fell short as the actual increase in children adopted was 34%, but this still represents 900 additional adoptions on 1999–2000 figures. Since 2008, the average age of a child at adoption has dropped below four. During the year ending 31 March 2012, 3,450 looked after children were adopted, which is an increase of 12% from 2011 and this is the first time there has been an increase in adoption figures since 2007. Similarly there has been a decrease in the number of looked after children placed for adoption. This figure has fallen from 2,720 in 2007, to 2,500 in 2010 with a further fall to 2,450 in 2011 (DfE, 2011a). In 2012, 2680 children were placed for adoption, but this is a 1% decrease on percentages from 2011 and a 6% decrease from 2008. There are fewer children being adopted than there were 10 years ago; however, since the Adoption and Children Act 2002 came into force in December 2005, another kind of permanence option has been available for looked after children – Special Guardianship Orders (SGO). Further details of SGOs are given later in the chapter. During the year ending 31 March 2013, 2130 children ceased to be looked after due to SGOs and this marks a 40% increase in these types of Orders on 2010 figures (DfE, 2011a). Numbers of SGOs have increased year on year – see Table 11.3. The majority of SGOs are made to former foster carers; these account for 64% of all SGOs made (DfE, 2011a). Whilst the children who are subject to SGOs may not have been adopted if SGOs did not exist, it is interesting to note the increased use of this type of permanency for looked after children, at a time when it would appear that adoption figures are reducing. Over the same period of time the figures for Residence Orders have remained static. This indicates that SGOs are meeting the permanency needs of some children. The impact of this on the adoption figures may be difficult to discern, as the adoption landscape is changing. We will discuss this later when we identify the new policy initiatives emerging from the coalition government.

Please see www.education.gov.uk/rsgateway/DB/SFR/s001084/index.shtml

Table 11.3 Children who ceased to be looked after by SGO (ACA 2002) and Residence Order (CA 1989)

	2007	2008	2009	2010	2011	2012
All LAC who ceased to be looked after (No. and %)	24,990/100%	24,500/100%	25030/100%	25310/100%	26830/100%	27,350/100%
Adopted (No. and %)	3330/13.3%	3180/12.9%	3330/13.3%	3200/12.6%	3050/11.3%	3450/13%
Residence Order (No. and %)	1,030/4%	910/4%	930/4%	1,010/4%	1,180/4%	1290/5%
Special Guardianship (Foster Carers) (No. and %)	500/2%	770/3%	810/3%	860/3%	1120/4%	1330/5%
Special Guardianship (other) (No. and %)	260/1%	360/1%	430/2%	430/2%	620/2%	800/3%

Source: DfE, 2012e

RESEARCH SUMMARY

There is a significant body of literature available, which gives us some insight into adoption as an appropriate course of action for children. However, there is always more to learn from research in this area.

David Howe's (1998) book Patterns of Adoption *is a particularly useful summary of research undertaken into factors which are significant regarding outcomes of adoptions for children of particular ages.*

The DoH published Adoption Now: Messages from Research *in 1999 (DoH, 1999a). This document summarised the results of a number of research studies commissioned by the DoH during the 1990s. The principal messages about adoption policy and practice arising from these studies were then considered in the adoption reform that followed.*

The government has also funded a significant amount of research into adoption and its effectiveness; see the website www.adoptionresearchinitiative.org.uk for a summary of funded research.

In summary, research in this area states:

- *adoption is an effective option for some looked after children;*

- *early placement is crucial in avoiding disruption;*

- *the most difficult children to place, in terms of finding adopters, are older children, boys, sibling groups and black and ethnic minority children;*

- *older children and those with special needs can successfully be adopted with the right preparation and support;*

- *adoption is not the answer for all looked after children unlikely to return home – some do not wish to be adopted, and some require such intensive support that adoption is never going to be an option.*

(PIU, 2000, p18)

Alternative permanence models practised in the UK and other countries

In many other countries there is a reluctance to permanently extinguish birth parents' rights over their children. A number of other countries use a model where parental responsibilities are shared and ongoing contact with birth families is expected.

The 2000 Adoption White Paper defined permanence as *a secure, stable and loving family to support children through childhood and beyond*. The Adoption and Permanence Taskforce define permanence as *a framework of emotional, physical and legal conditions that gives a child a sense of security, continuity, commitment and identity* (Harnott and Humphreys, 2004, p3). In their comparison of US and UK adoption and permanency legislation, Selwyn and Sturgess (2002) comment that permanency should be viewed as more than a placement category or legal status – it is a complex phenomenon which for some children is best met through a variety of intricate arrangements for maintaining connections and relationships with different people from a child's past and present, including family members, friends, previous carers and other significant adults. They also highlight a number of concerns expressed within the profession about rushing exclusively down the path of adoption as a preferred permanence route. For example, if adoption is now being considered for children who have complex needs, are the post-adoption resources available over the duration of the childhood of these children adequate to support the adoptive placement? There should also be a balance between the need for birth families to have time to address worrying behaviours and difficulties so that children can be safely returned to their families of origin, weighed against the need of the child for a permanent, safe and supportive family environment in which to grow up. There is also a lack of knowledge concerning what distinguishes children who are successfully adopted from those who are not and have to wait a long time for permanency to occur outside of adoption. Table 11.4 presents a comparison of permanence options available in England.

Table 11.4 The legal differences between permanence options (other than adoption) available in England

Permanence options	How long does the order last?	Who has parental responsibility?	Can it be revoked?	Support from local authority?
Special guardianship	Until 18	Birth parent(s) and special guardian(s)	Yes	Yes under ACA 2002
Residence order	Until 16 although can be extended until 18	Birth parent(s) and person with residence order	Yes	Possibly, depending on circumstances
Long-term foster care	Until 18 – pathway planning occurs at age 16 with the local authority having responsibilities toward care leavers until age 24. There are also plans to extend the period of time children can stay with their foster carers post age 18 (see the Green Paper Care Matters for further discussion)	Differences in the legal basis of this provision in the UK (i.e. either section 29 'accommodation'; or section 31 'care order' under the Children Act 1989) means that either the local authority will share PR with the birth parent(s) (section 31) or the local authority will not have PR – only the parent(s) will have this (section 20). Foster carers do not have parental responsibility for children under either of these legal options	N/A	Yes
Residential care	Until 18 – pathway planning occurs at age 16 with the local authority having responsibilities toward care leavers until age 24	Differences in the legal basis of this provision in the UK (i.e. either section 20 'accommodation'; or section 31 Care Order under the Children Act 1989 or Interim Care Order means that the local authority will share PR with the birth parent(s) (section 31) or the local authority will not have PR – only the parent(s) will have this (section 20)	N/A	Yes
Kinship care	Depends on whether the arrangement is formal (arranged through courts) or informal. If kinship carers consider residence order or special guardianship, then this can last until child is 18.	As before	As before	Possibly, depending on circumstances

Some of the alternatives to adoption listed in the literature, including the Scottish Adoption Policy Review Group (2005) publication, include the following.

- Open adoption (widespread in New Zealand).

- Kinship care (widespread in Australia, New Zealand and elsewhere).

- Enduring guardianship (suggested by NZ Law Commission: see www.lawcom.govt.nz/project/adoption/publication/report/2000/adoption-and-its-alternatives-different-approach-and-new-fr for further details).

- Continuum of care options (suggested by NZ Law Commission: see above for further details).

- Special Guardianship (UK; USA; NZ); see below.

- Residence Order (UK). Residence Orders offer a different permanence option to children who cannot remain living with birth parent(s). This is a section 8 Order made under the Children Act 1989, where the holder of the Residence Order obtains parental responsibility for the child. This is shared with others who already have parental responsibility for the child. The child must live with the person named on the order. This order lasts until the child turns 16 (this can now be extended until 18), or until the court rescinds the order. Relatives or significant adults who live with the child can apply for a Residence Order. This order is likely to be used for older children who do not want the legal severing of their relationship with their birth parents. Thoburn (1994) suggests that children in a long-term placement with relatives and friends have a well-developed sense of their own identity and a better sense of permanence than do children in non-relative placements. She suggests that financial support can be an issue for children placed with relatives and that this should not be a reason for preventing an appropriate placement going ahead.

- Residential care.

- Long-term foster care. Children and young people can remain living with a foster carer under a long-term arrangement until the young person turns 18. The White Paper *Care matters* (DfES, 2007) proposes that young people could continue living with their foster carers after turning 18 if this was agreed as part of a care plan with the young person, foster carer and local authority. The foster carers do not have parental responsibility for the child or young person under this option. In terms of the various permanency options available to children and young people, this is often seen as the least 'desirable' because of the legal insecurity of the placement and the higher breakdown rates in long-term placements when compared with adoption (Thoburn, 1994).

The Adoption and Children Act 2002

The introduction of the Adoption and Children Act 2002 updated legislation in this area, bringing adoption legislation in line with the Children Act 1989 and a number of different European legal requirements. Another purpose of this legislation was to set the framework for promoting greater use of adoption for looked after children, including those previously seen as being harder to place (e.g. older children and those with special needs). The Act was fully implemented on 30 December 2005. The paramount consideration in all decisions made about a child by an adoption agency or the court must be the child's welfare throughout her or his life. A number of the key changes to practice include the following.

- The welfare principle is established and a similar welfare checklist to the Children Act 1989 (CA 1989) is included in the Adoption and Children Act 2002.

- The Act improves and extends the regulation of adoption and adoption support services.

- It sets out and modernises the legal basis for the process of adoption.

- It provides for both disclosure of and protection of information about adopted people and their birth relatives.

- It regulates inter-country adoptions.

- It regulates the advertising of children for adoption and payments in connection with adoption.

- It provides the legal underpinning for an Adoption Register.

- It attempts to reduce delay in the adoption process.

   (Brammer, 2010; Brayne and Carr, 2010)

The Act is in three parts.

Part 1 sets out the framework of the law on adoption. This is the most significant section of the Act. It applies whenever the court or the adoption agency is coming to a decision about the adoption of a child. It says that:

- the child's welfare must be the paramount consideration of the court or agency, throughout the child's life;

- the court or agency must at all times bear in mind that, in general, any delay in coming to a decision is likely to prejudice the child's welfare;

- the court or agency must have regard to a list of key matters – the 'welfare checklist'.

   (Brammer, 2010; Brayne and Carr, 2010)

In addition to setting out the legal context in which an adoption can be made, a number of other areas are covered in this section of the Act.

Placement Framework (section 8). A child can only be placed for adoption if the agency has obtained 'authority to place'. This is obtained through placement with consent, under sections 19–20 of the Act, or a placement order, under sections 21–29 of the Act.

Placement with consent (section 19). A child's mother may not give consent for adoption until the baby is six weeks old. The birth mother retains parental responsibility (PR) once consent is given up until a final order is made. The birth mother can ask for the child to be returned to her until the adoption application is made to the court. After the application has been made, the court must agree to the child being removed from the prospective adoptive placement.

Placement Orders (section 21). These can only be applied for by an adoption agency. The adoption agency should have a 'best interests' decision before applying to the court for a Placement Order. In June 2012 the coalition government issued adoption guidance that changed the 'best interest' decision (also known as SBPFA – Should Be Placed For Adoption) from one made by Adoption Panels to one that is made by the agency decision maker. This order authorises the agency to place the child with any prospective adopters chosen by the authority. This order can be made if the local authority does not have a Care Order (section 31 CA 1989) but only if the threshold criteria are met. Where a Care Order already exists, a Placement Order suspends this order. Limited PR is given to the prospective adopters while the child is with them; however, the birth parent retains PR as well as the agency placing the child until the final adoption order is made.

Dispensing with consent (section 52). The six grounds under s16(2) Adoption Act 1976 have been replaced by two grounds. Consent can be dispensed with if the court is satisfied that:

- the parent or guardian cannot be found or is incapable of giving consent; or

- the welfare of the child requires consent to be dispensed with.

Part 2. This makes a series of amendments to the Children Act 1989, such as the updating of the PR of unmarried fathers, and introducing section 14A, creating the new SGO (see below).

This section also includes additional provision for step-parent adoption. Until now, step-parent adoption extinguished the parental responsibility of one birth parent – usually on a *quid pro quo* basis – when parental responsibility was given to the step-parent. The ACA (2002) changes this and it is now not necessary for one birth parent to relinquish their parental responsibility with a step-parent application. The child can take on the step-parent's surname and the birth parent is then released from financial obligations toward the child. Step-parent adoption is now also possible for lesbian and gay partners (Brayne and Carr, 2010; Brammer, 2010).

Special Guardianship (section 115). Section 14A(1) of the CA 1989 creates a SGO, which is an order appointing one or more individuals to be a child's 'special guardian'. A special guardian must be over 18 and not the child's parent. The guardian obtains PR with this order and although this is shared with the birth parent(s), the special guardian can act wholly and solely in exercising this PR. This order discharges any Care Order or section 8 order (including contact and residence orders) which may be in force at the point at which a special guardianship order is made. This order is linked to the PIU (2000) report, which suggested that special guardianship might be appropriate for: *local authority foster parents, relatives, older children who do not wish to be legally separated from their birth family, children cared for on a permanent basis by their wider family, and certain minority ethnic communities with religious and cultural objections to adoption* (cited in Brammer, 2010, p336). A number of individuals can automatically apply for special guardianship, including: any guardian of the child; a holder of a residence order; a local authority foster parent with whom the child has lived for at least one year; and any person with whom the child has lived for at least three years (Brayne and Carr, 2010; Brammer, 2010).

Part 3. This part of the Act contains a series of miscellaneous provisions designed to regulate and improve adoption. This includes regulations about adoption panels.

Adoption panels make recommendations about four main matters. First, whether adoption is in the best interests of the child; secondly, the suitability of prospective applicants to become adopters; thirdly, matching prospective adopters with a suitable child; and finally, the potential adoption support needs of any proposed placement (with attached financial resources). Panels comprise up to ten members, including: chair (independent of the agency); two social workers with three years' relevant post-qualifying experience; an elected member (a local councillor) for local authority panels; a medical adviser; and at least three independent members, including, where possible, two with personal experience of adoption. The adoption agency will also appoint a senior member of staff to be agency adviser to the panel. This person is not a member of the panel. Panel members will be appointed for terms of three years and may serve up to three terms.

Other changes were introduced under the Adoption and Children Act 2002.

- Adopters can be single, co-habitees, lesbian and gay applicants, and married couples.

- Adoption agencies have developed guidelines and policies on maximum ages of adopters, especially in relation to babies (not if the child has special needs). Health issues are also considered by the adoption panel.

- Issues of race and culture operate under the same principles as CA 1989 (welfare checklist and section 22(5)c); however, case law is not consistent on the implementation of this. This is a complex debate and one we will return to below.

(Brammer, 2010; Brayne and Carr, 2010)

Current policy developments

The coalition government has three senior Tory politicians who are interested in adoption. This includes the Prime Minister, David Cameron; the Secretary of State for Education, Michael Gove; and the previous Parliamentary Under-Secretary of State for Children and Young Families, Tim Loughton who was replaced by Edward Timpson in September 2012. This has meant a great deal of activity within the adoption field. Martin Narey's report (Narey, 2011) and subsequent appointment as the coalition government's advisor on adoption has also helped to raise the public profile of adoption. This interest from politicians has led to different kinds of conversations and debates about how adoption is relevant within twenty-first century Britain for looked after children, including the need to review timescales for children for whom adoption is a suitable permanence option, as well as for prospective adopters wishing to adopt children. To give a brief outline of some of the activity: a review of recruitment, training and assessment processes for prospective adopters is under way; the government has published 'adoption scorecards' in a bid to raise standards within adoption agencies, in particular to reduce the timescales for prospective adopter assessments and on the time that children wait for an adoption placement; the government has removed the need for Adoption Panels to make SBPFA decisions, and in so doing, the role of Panels is set to change; and a DfE consultation has begun about placing children in sibling groups for adoption and contact arrangements (DfE, 2012a). Adoption statutory guidance was published in February 2011 (DfE, 2011c), with two revisions published in April 2011 and June 2012 (see: www.education.gov.uk/childrenandyoungpeople/families/adoption/g0072314/guidance). Further legislation is expected in 2013 via a Children and Families Bill (England and Wales). The Coalition government also intend to launch a National Adoption Gateway by the end of 2012, as a first port of call for information for anyone interested in becoming an adopter. The Coalition government is also interested in post-adoption support.

ACTIVITY *11.1*

Read the government's Action Plan on Tackling Delay published on 14 March 2012, at www.education.gov.uk/childrenandyoungpeople/families/adoption/a00205069/action-plan-for-adoption-tackling-delay; and BAAF's response at www.baaf.org.uk/node/4066. Using the material from both documents, write a list of the intended and unintended consequences of these proposed changes.

COMMENT

Change in adoption is coming thick and fast. Some of the ideas around the timeliness of adoptions for children in care are to be applauded. The report from the Family Justice Review into the delays in Care Proceedings and the effects on children is to be welcomed (Ministry of Justice, DfE and Welsh Government, 2011). However, there is also a lot of rhetoric and misinformation around concerning such issues as: the numbers of babies who are available for adoption; the position taken by local authorities concerning transracial placements; and the numbers of children who are supposedly 'languishing in care' because of poor local authority practice. It is difficult to identify and understand all the drivers behind this current reform, because all may not be as it seems. Much emphasis seems to be placed on the prospective adopter's experience of assessment and on matching considerations, specifically about ethnicity (see the section about this later in the chapter; see also Cocker and Anderson, 2011). But what about post adoption support? Despite the emphasis of the ACA 2002 on support plans, this remains patchy at best. With local authorities experiencing significant cuts to their budgets, it is difficult to see where any increased support to adopters who are caring for children with complex histories is going to come from, when it might be needed, as this may be many years after adoption.

Contact

In New Zealand and Australia, the use of open adoption within child-care policy and practice is underpinned by statute. Additionally, within the research literature there is evidence of the benefits to children, birth and adoptive parents (see Ryburn, 1998) of a more open approach to contact with birth families post adoption. Under the ACA 2002 there is no duty to promote contact with the child's family and no presumption for or against contact within this Act. However, the agency must consider contact arrangements where it decides a child should be placed for adoption and when considering a proposed placement. In this regard an adoption panel may advise on contact or a contact order may be applied for by the birth parents under section 26 of the ACA 2002. The court is obliged to consider the contact arrangements that the adoption agency is proposing to make, at the adoption application stage: *before making an adoption order, the court must consider whether there should be arrangements for allowing any person contact with the child; and for that purpose the court must consider any existing or proposed arrangements* (Brammer, 2010, p331). The welfare checklist also applies here, where the adoption agency and the court are required to consider the relationship the child has with relatives, the significance of this and the likelihood of it continuing, and the benefit for the child in it doing so, as well as the wishes and feelings of the child's relatives.

Contact can include the following forms.

- Indirect letterbox contact. This comprises of letters written annually from the adoptive family to the birth parents and vice versa. These letters can also include photos. These letters are sent to the local authority adoption agency to send on to the relevant party.

- Direct contact. This includes direct contact between siblings and/or members of the birth extended family, or with parents.

CASE STUDY

The 'same race placement' debate

You are the social worker for Morgan, who is five years old. He is of mixed parentage – his mother is also mixed parentage (white Scottish and black British) and his father is black African–Caribbean (from Barbados). He has been in care for two years, placed with the same foster family, who are white English. Morgan has not seen his birth father since he was two. His birth mother has a drug addiction problem and has not been able to change this significantly during the two-year period Morgan has been in care in order that Morgan could be safely returned to her. She has had fairly regular contact with Morgan during the time he has been in care. Despite extensive searching in England and Barbados, no suitable extended birth family members have been identified. The adoption agency has also advertised Morgan and a two-female-parent prospective adoptive family has contacted the family-finding social worker. In this family, one parent is Jamaican and the other is white Scottish. They have a nine-year-old son (not adopted) who is of mixed parentage and is the birth child of one of the parents, and has been adopted by the other parent (step-parent adoption). Morgan's foster carers know about this prospective family's interest in adopting Morgan. They ring you and tell you they are also interested in adopting him. How do you go about making your decision as to where Morgan should be placed?

COMMENT

The role of a child's ethnicity and culture and choice of placement

Over the years this debate has stimulated strong opinions with comments about 'loony left' councils, and social workers making 'politically correct' decisions which saw black and ethnic minority children wait longest for placements in order to be placed in culturally appropriate settings. Some practitioners argue that the development of a positive black identity, including learning about the history of different cultural and religious groups, and understanding the experiences of racism and learning how to survive this, is difficult in a family which does not share (at least in some part) the same day-to-day experiences as their child.

Continued

A DoH Circular Adoption: Achieving the right balance (DoH, 1998b) emphasised that all children's needs should be taken into account when planning for adoption, including religion, language, culture and ethnicity, and recognised that a placement with a family of similar ethnic origin is most likely to meet the child's needs. It required local authorities to make efforts to increase the numbers of adopters from ethnic minority and other communities (Frazer and Selwyn, 2005). The same document also comments that children should not be denied the chance of an adoptive placement just because the adopters and child are not from the same cultural background. The importance of this approach has been restated in the National Adoption Standards (DoH, 2001a), where children are expected to be matched and placed with families who can best meet their needs within the given timescales, but children should not be kept waiting for a perfect match (Frazer and Selwyn, 2005). Brammer (2010, pp322) summarises current expected practice:

The emphasis of formal guidance is therefore to find a family of similar ethnic background if possible. If this is not possible the child should not be kept waiting and a family should be found which may not share the same characteristics as the child but is committed to assisting the child to understand his background and culture and be proud of that heritage.

There are still strong arguments to support black children and children of mixed parentage being placed in black families, even though the ethnic origin of the child may not exactly match that of the family. Continued recruitment of ethnic minority families interested in adoption remains a considerable challenge for adoption agencies (see Frazer and Selwyn, 2005). This must be set against other needs that all children have in terms of the need for permanency, and to make positive attachments with caregivers within a family context within realistic timeframes. When decision-making for black or ethnic minority children is reduced solely to the matching of ethnicity between a child and an adoptive family, it is questionable whether this can ever be in anyone's best interests. Ratna Dutt's comment to the Laming inquiry is pertinent here in terms of the identification of basic needs that every child has regardless of their ethnic origin.

There is some evidence to suggest that one of the consequences of an exclusive focus on 'culture' in work with black children and families, is [that] it leaves black and ethnic minority children in potentially dangerous situations, because the assessment has failed to address a child's fundamental care and protection needs.

Comment made by Ratna Dutt, director of the Race Equality Unit in the UK, at the Public Inquiry into the death of Victoria Climbié (Laming 2003)

This issue has recently been raised again by Tim Loughton MP and Michael Gove MP. The government's Action Pan (DfE, 2012a, pp21–22) summarises its current position:

50. The delay faced by black children during this process needs particular attention. They take around a year longer to be adopted after entering care than white and Asian children. One reason for this is that in some parts of the system, the belief persists that ensuring a perfect or near perfect match based on the child's ethnicity is necessarily in the child's best interests, and automatically outweighs other considerations, such as the need to find long-term stability for the child quickly. In Professor Elaine Farmer's study [2010] for the Adoption Research Initiative, attempts to find families of similar ethnicity were a cause of delay for 70% of the black and minority ethnic children who experienced delay. Ethnicity encompasses not only race, but also cultural, religious and linguistic background. A study by Dr Julie Selwyn found that children's profiles often included the specific requirement for the prospective adoptive parents to match the child's ethnicity, with 'same-race' placements dominating the Child Permanence Report over and above other needs. This study also found that some social workers were so pessimistic about finding ethnically matched adopters that there was little family finding activity. Consequently many minority ethnic children had their plan changed away from adoption.

51. In fact, a review of research on transracial adoption by the Evan B. Donaldson Institute [2009] concluded that adoption across ethnic boundaries does not in itself produce psychological or behavioural problems in children. However, where a child is adopted across ethnic boundaries, they and their families can face a range of challenges. The manner in which parents handle these challenges, particularly their sensitivity and approach to racism, facilitates or hinders children's development. The authors conclude that these challenges need to be addressed when matching children with families and in preparing families to meet their children's needs. A recent review of international evidence on matching in adoptions from care has also shown that adoptions across ethnic boundaries are at no greater risk of disruption.

52. That is not to say that ethnicity can never be a consideration. Where there are two sets of suitable parents available then those with a similar ethnicity to the child may be the better match for the child. Sometimes an ethnic match will be in a child's best interests, for example where an older child expresses strong wishes. However, it is not in the best interests of children for social workers to introduce any delay at all into the adoption process in the search for a perfect or even partial ethnic match when parents who are otherwise suitable are available and able to provide a loving and caring home for the child.

53. Similarly, there are approved adopters who are ready and able to offer loving homes but who are too readily disregarded because they are single, or considered too old. These can, of course, be relevant factors, but we know that in most cases delay and the instability associated with it will be the greater potential cause of damage to the child.

54. The government will bring forward primary legislation at the next available opportunity to address these issues. The overriding principle in finding a match for a child will remain what is in the child's best interests throughout their life.

Concurrent planning

Concurrent planning was introduced to England from the USA in the late 1990s to help deal with problems of delay or repeated placements for children prior to adoption. This is not an option that suits all children's circumstances. Efforts to evaluate the outcomes of this have been described as 'promising' against a backdrop of implementation described as 'challenging' (Frame, et al., 2006).

Concurrent planning involves a child following two care plans simultaneously. The child is placed with foster carers who are also prospective adopters, and the birth family have a final chance to work towards rehabilitation. The foster carers help with this plan and if it does not work they then adopt the child. It is a very intensive process and is conducted within strict time limits.

Coram is the only specialist centre for Concurrent Planning practice in the UK and has been involved in some research in this area, examining the social, emotional and educational outcomes for 59 of the children who have reached permanency through the scheme.

> At this early stage, based on preliminary findings, we can be confident that Coram's Concurrent Planning project has succeeded in its aims to increase continuity of placement in infancy, and reduce time to permanency for young children. .. 59 children were placed through the scheme from 2000-2011. Of the 57 children for whom we have data, all have remained with the Coram Concurrent Planning (CCP) carers with whom they were placed. The children are now aged up to 12. None have experienced post placement disruptions, and none have been returned to care.

(Laws, et al., 2012, p2)

Parallel planning or twin-track planning is similar to concurrent planning in that two plans are made for a child and each is followed at the same time. However, in parallel planning, the child may remain with the birth parents or in foster care while a rehabilitation plan with timescales is in place determining work to be done with the birth family. In addition the agency will also have an alternative permanence plan in case of unsuccessful rehabilitation (Harnott and Humphreys, 2004). In this situation, the foster carers will not adopt the child; rather the agency will seek alternative available adopters. This approach to care planning is now relatively common across England.

The adoption processes

Care planning and reviews are essential components of the adoption and permanence process. Statutory child-care reviews must be conducted within specific time schedules once a child comes into care and these time schedules and associated guidance are covered in detail elsewhere in this book. At the second statutory review (held four months after coming into care) a permanence plan must be drawn up. This plan will set out clear objectives, associated timescales, key tasks with an identified person to undertake these tasks, and the criteria by which the plan will be evaluated as successful. This permanence plan will be reviewed at each subsequent review, although it should be continuously monitored as it is not a static document, rather a working tool for those working with the child. The Children Act 1989 requires local authorities to always work toward rehabilitation of a child with parents where this is possible before looking at other permanency options outside of the birth family. Harnott and Humphreys (2004) rightly emphasise the Department of Health (1998b) position on stressing the need to balance attempts at rehabilitation with the birth family with 'child time' – not creating unnecessary delay in achieving permanence for the child.

Mention is made of 'processes' in a plural sense rather than as a single process because adoption is an accumulation of an intricate interplay of developments and courses of action relating to individual children, their birth parents and extended families, prospective adopters and professionals involved in supporting the business of adoption. Cocker and Anderson (2011, pp111 and 115) have produced two flow diagrams which clearly explain the processes involved for all parties listed above. For the purposes of this chapter the process for the child (incorporating the adoption panel and the court), the adopter and the birth parent will be outlined.

The child

A permanence plan should be produced for a child at the second statutory review, which potentially identifies permanency outside of the birth family should attempts at rehabilitation fail. The Child Permanency Record (CPR) will be completed after this review on the child. There are a number of other forms which require completion (obstetric report on mother, neonatal report on child). The completion of these forms may also coincide with the court process, where the local authority will prepare a care plan and submit it to the court.

If parallel planning is agreed, at court or at a statutory review, the social worker then has two months to present this plan to the Adoption Panel.

The case will then go to the agency decision-maker for a recommendation about whether the child should be placed for adoption prior to the final hearing once the outcome of the rehabilitation assessment with the birth parent is known to be negative.

In determining that adoption is in the child's best interest, the social worker will need to show that there has been sufficient exploration of all extended family members and significant others in terms of possible kinship placements. The social worker also needs to give details about the specific placement needs of the child, the wishes and feelings of the child, the proposed contact with siblings (if applicable) if it is not recommended that siblings are to be placed with the child, the relationships that the child has with his or her birth family and proposed contact arrangements.

The final care hearing will occur after this date, with the court receiving information on the plan for family-finding for the child, and associated timescales. The court comments on the care plan submitted by the local authority as a part of the section 31 (Children Act 1989) proceedings, which will include reference to the decision made by the agency decision-maker.

The agency will only be able to place the child for adoption with prospective adopters after either obtaining parental consent for adoption (s19) or obtaining a placement order (s21). This change in practice ensures that this order is obtained earlier in the process in order to avoid delay at the adoption application stage.

Family-finding activity then occurs within the local authority, local consortium or other adoption agencies in order that prospective families can be identified and a suitable match found. Once a match has been identified, papers go back to the Adoption Panel (the child's agency) to recommend the suitability of the prospective adopters matched to the needs of the child concerned. Post-adoption support is also considered. The agency decision-maker must confirm the proposed action.

An introduction planning meeting is convened to arrange the introductory process for the child and new family, with a date set for review of the introductions. This is a complex process and careful, detailed planning is essential to ensure that the arrangements are centred on the needs of the child, and timescales are appropriate to this and the age of the child.

ACTIVITY 11.2

Introductions

Think about how introductions between a child and an adopter would differ if the child was nine months old, and if the child was three years old.

Identify the specific areas you would take into consideration when drawing up a plan for children of different ages.

COMMENT

Introductions usually occur over a two- to three-week period but much younger children can have a more intense introductory process. Prospective adopters will spend time in the foster carer's home getting to know their new child and going over the everyday routines that their child knows and is used to. This will involve learning what the child likes and does not like to eat, preparing meals, bathing the child and getting the child ready for bed, or getting the child up in the morning, as well as playing with the child (does the child have a favourite toy?) to establish the beginnings of a relationship. The foster carer will discuss all aspects of caring for the child, including how they maintain boundaries for the child. Contact will quickly move to the adopters seeing the child every day. The adopters may take the child out of the foster home for short periods of time during this early period. The child will then begin spending time at the prospective adopters' house, with the knowledge from the routines and likes/dislikes of the child transferred to this new environment. The foster carer will also visit the child at the adopters' house to demonstrate continuity for the child during this time of transition. The introductory period may involve an overnight stay in the adoptive placement before the child moves permanently, but this depends on the age of the child, and whether this would be too confusing for the child. It is also important to factor in opportunities for reviewing the progress of the introductions throughout this transition period. The introductions can be slowed down if it is appropriate to do so, if the child is struggling with the transition.

On placement day the social worker must be present to formally place the child with the adoptive parents. The social worker must also visit the child within seven days at their new placement and regularly thereafter. A statutory review will be held after one month, three months and then every six months until an adoption order is made.

After the child has been placed with the prospective adopters for ten weeks the prospective adopters can lodge an adoption application with the court. Under the new ACA 2002 legislation, the issue of consent from birth parents will be dealt with earlier in the court process, so the prospective adopters' application should be dealt with speedily.

The prospective adopters

Following an initial contact with the adoption agency, the prospective adopters may be invited to attend a follow-up interview or information meeting. From this meeting the agency will make a decision about whether or not to continue with an assessment of the prospective adopters.

The assessment, or Prospective Adopters Report (PAR), takes a number of months to complete. Each applicant is seen individually as well as together on a number of occasions; up to five referees are required to be interviewed (including ex-partners and adult children); Criminal Records Bureau check (CRB), adoption medicals and local authority checks are completed on applicants; and applicants also have to complete a number of assessment sessions/workshops with other prospective adopters who are also in the process of being assessed. The assessment undertaken by the social worker is not a static activity – rather it is a process in which the social worker expects the applicants to recount and explore their lives and experiences while the social worker considers the insight and reflective abilities shown by the applicants in the retelling of this story. The social worker is assessing the skills and knowledge that the applicants have about children and parenting and making judgements about the applicants' suitability as a parent for a looked after child who may well have experienced considerable trauma, neglect and rejection prior to their current placement. As a part of this process the applicants will be encouraged to think carefully about the kind of child they envisage joining their family and also to identify situations they might find more difficult to manage.

The PAR is presented to the Adoption Panel by the assessing social worker. The prospective adopters can attend this panel. Following the panel recommendation to the agency decision-maker, the social worker can then begin to identify suitable potential children for matching with the prospective adopters. The prospective adopters might be presented with children's profiles from the assessing agency, from the local consortium (there is usually a fixed period of time when the assessing agency and then the local consortium have priority use of the prospective adopters), before other adoption agencies or the adoption register are used to match the prospective adopters with children. (See Quinton (2012) for an overview of research in this area.)

---

*ACTIVITY **11.3***

Understanding different rationales for decision-making

In identifying and considering the decision-making processes that occur in locating an appropriate adoptive placement for a child, weigh up the different perspectives held by each stakeholder.

- *The social worker.*

- *The prospective adopters.*

- *The birth parents.*

- *The child.*

COMMENT

One of the practice issues to consider is the tensions in decision-making for the social worker and the prospective adopters in this process. The social worker should always make decisions they believe are in the best interests of the child in question. However, the agency has responsibilities to many other children requiring permanency – how are these different responsibilities weighed up? The child needs a placement which is matched to his or her needs and can provide love, security and stability throughout childhood and beyond. The prospective adopters make decisions according to what they judge is right for their family, as the consequence of their decision is very long-term.

ACTIVITY 11.4

Sharing information about children during the adoption process

Download the following newspaper article (Dyer, 2002) from the Guardian Unlimited website: www.guardian.co.uk/society/2002/oct/17/adoptionandfostering.adoption

Briefly summarise the position argued by the adopters.

Think about the issues for you when 'matching' children with prospective adopters. How much information should you share?

COMMENT

The prospective adopter can expect the agency responsible for the child to give them full information about the child's background, health, development, and any other needs the child may have. The prospective adopters will be given opportunities to discuss any concerns or queries they might have with suitably qualified people (for example, paediatrician, child's therapist, foster carers, and any other specialist working with the child).

The birth parents

The local authority should make available a separate support worker for the birth parents of a child from the time that a plan of adoption is proposed by the local authority. This will enable the birth parents to receive support (not just legal support) in order that they can give an account of their view of events and comment on what is said about them.

Adoption support

The Adoption Support Services (Local Authorities) (England) Regulations 2003 came into effect ahead of the ACA 2002. These regulations outline the duty of the local authority to assess the adoption support needs of the adopted child and the adopters when considering an adoptive placement. Once this assessment has been made, the local authority then has to decide whether to provide any services. If this is the case an adoption support plan will be completed and kept under review. The placing local authority is responsible for post-adoption support for the first three years after the making of an Adoption Order.

As well as a range of mainstream services available to adopters and adopted children, there are a number of adoption support services that local authorities are required to provide under the 2003 regulations. These include: counselling; financial support; support groups for adopted families; assistance with contact arrangements; therapeutic services for adopted children; services to ensure the continuance of adoptive relationships (Harnott and Humphreys, 2004).

Financial support may be payable (but there is no automatic entitlement) when it is necessary to ensure adopters can care for the child; the child has special needs; it facilitates the placement of the child with her or his sibling, or because of the child's age or ethnic origin, it is necessary to support contact; legal costs, introductions or remuneration for foster carers who adopt a child whom they have previously cared for (Brayne and Carr, 2010).

ACTIVITY **11.5**

Post-adoption support

Look at the following websites:

www.pac.org.uk

www.familyfutures.co.uk/home.html

www.afteradoption.org.uk

Compare and contrast the different services offered by these organisations.

What information would you give to adopters about post-adoption services within your authority and independent of your authority?

Lesbian and gay adopters

The Adoption and Children Act 2002 brought a change to the ability of lesbian and gay applicants to jointly apply to adopt. Previously only one partner within a lesbian or gay couple could apply to adopt as a single person. Although the actual assessment would include both partners, only one partner could adopt the child and the other partner could apply for a joint residence order in order to obtain parental responsibility.

This is an area which has received considerable public attention and debate. The political context to this development is considerable and beyond the scope of this book – see the work of Brown and Cocker (2011) and Hicks (2012) for further information. In summary, the positive developments within the Adoption and Children Act 2002 must be viewed against wider political and legal changes within public life over the last ten years, including: the lowering of the age of consent to 16 for gay men; the Civil Partnership Act 2003; the Sexual Orientation Regulations 2007; and the Equality Act 2010 which have provided a secure legal basis for lesbians and gay men to be equal participants in as many aspects of public and private life as are their heterosexual counterparts. However, there are a number of points to make in order to place these developments in context in relation to adoption. First, all decision-making in relation to adoption must have the child as its central focus. Although lesbians and gay men can now be jointly assessed, lesbians and gay men are required to demonstrate suitability as adopters alongside all candidates putting themselves forward for assessment. Secondly, there is a developing evidence base from longitudinal research studies conducted in the US and the UK (see the work of Susan Golombok (2000) and Fiona Tasker (2005) (UK); and Charlotte Patterson (2005) (USA)) on outcomes for children raised in (predominantly) lesbian families, which concludes that children raised in lesbian families show very little difference in terms of their social adjustment from children raised in heterosexual families. Thirdly, there is a shortage of suitable prospective adopters coming forward to be assessed. Widening the pool of potential adopters through this legal change may mean that children will not have to wait longer than is absolutely necessary to be matched to a stable and secure permanent family. See Brown and Cocker (2008); Cocker and Brown (2010); Cocker (2011); and Cocker and Anderson (2011) for more information.

CHAPTER SUMMARY

The effects of adoption are far-reaching and permanent. An adoption order terminates the parental responsibility of anybody else, as the adopters become the 'legal' parents of the child named in the order. Once made, an adoption order cannot be revoked.

Adoptions can only be made for children under the age of 18. Adoptions by step-parents make up between one-third and one-half of the numbers of children who are adopted every year. The children who are adopted from public care represent a small number of children where permanency outside birth families is the planned outcome. The Adoption and Children Act 2002 introduced a 'Special Guardianship Order' as an alternative to adoption, where the level of legal protection to the carer and security to the child is high but the severing of legal links to the birth parent does not occur with the making of this order.

FURTHER READING

Douglas, A and Philpot, T (2003) (eds) *Adoption: Changing families, changing times.* Abingdon: Routledge.

This is an edited text which looks at contemporary adoption practice in the UK.

Howe, D (1998) *Patterns of adoption.* Oxford: Blackwell.

This book gives a comprehensive overview of the trends and patterns of adoption, and uses research to inform knowledge and understanding of practice in this area. Case studies are used to illustrate and apply the material presented to practice contexts.

Lord, J (2008) *The adoption process in England. A guide for children's social workers.* London: BAAF.

This book outlines the adoption process in more detail than this chapter allows, and is used by social workers.

Rushton, A and Monck, E (2009) *Enhancing adoptive parenting: A test of effectiveness.* London: BAAF.

The literature review in this book is particularly good.

Schofield, G and Simmonds, J (eds) (2008) *The child placement handbook: Research, policy and practice*. London: BAAF.

This is an edited text that covers a variety of areas concerning the placement experiences of looked after children. The various chapters are authored by an impressive array of well-known academics and researchers.

Triseliotis, J, Shireman, J and Hundlebury, M (1997) *Adoption: Theory, policy and practice.* London: Cassell.

This book presents an analysis of policies, practice and theoretical issues concerning adoption.

Voluntary-sector organisations specifically involved in providing information about adoption or post adoption support are:

British Agency for Adoption and Fostering: **www.baaf.org.uk**

Post Adoption Centre: **www.pac.org.uk**

After Adoption: **www.afteradoption.org.uk**

Family Futures: **www.familyfutures.co.uk**

Adoption UK: **www.adoptionuk.org.uk**

Other online resources:

Adoption Research Initiative: **www.adoptionresearchinitiative.org.uk**

New Family Social: **www.newfamilysocial.co.uk**

Chapter 12
Leaving care

Introduction

This chapter focuses on social work practice with young people who are leaving care and those who are receiving aftercare support. The chapter starts by exploring the development of policy and legislation in relation to young people leaving care, with a focus on the processes of change leading up to the implementation of the Children (Leaving) Care Act 2000 and the new framework, *Volume 3: Planning Transition to Adulthood for Care Leavers (including guidance on The Care Leavers (England) Regulations 2010*. This was published by the DfE in October 2010 and came into force in April 2011. We will then consider some of the key challenges faced by young care leavers, and the specific issues faced by young people who are disabled, those who are unaccompanied asylum-seeking young people, and those who become young parents. This will involve reviewing research and findings about what interventions and support are linked to improving outcomes and future life chances for young people leaving care (Tyrer, et al., 2005; Knight, et al., Wade and Dixon, 2006; Barn and Mantovani, 2007; Cameron, 2007; Jackson and Ajayi, 2007).

You will remember from previous chapters how children enter care primarily because they have suffered abuse or neglect. Young care leavers are therefore likely to have specific vulnerabilities, which may be intensified as they face adolescence and the key transitions which are involved in this developmental stage in terms of friendships, sexuality and intimacy, education and employment and managing a home (Crawford and Walker, 2007). In working with and understanding young people leaving care we agree with Biehal, et al., (1995), who suggest that it is important to understand identity development and its dynamic nature as this influences how young people cope with the challenges of transitions.

> *The way that individuals cope with changes in their lives will be influenced by two main aspects of identity; their sense of who they are (self-concept) and their sense of self-esteem.* (p107)

We will also explore the role of leaving care teams and other services in supporting young people. Finally, we will consider the theoretical knowledge that can help you to understand the needs of young people leaving care, with a focus on attachment theory.

As well as looking at key issues of policy, practice and theory we will also ask you to reflect on your own experiences of leaving home. We want you to think about this because young people who are care leavers generally leave home much earlier and with far less support than other young people, who may spend many years moving backwards and forwards from their family home until they feel finally ready to leave home. Young care leavers often have a rapid acceleration to living independently with little time to adjust to a range of new responsibilities (Biehal, et al., 1995; Stein, 2004). This is also discussed by Briggs (2008) who refers to the risks associated between those young people who take the 'fast track' to adulthood and those who remain on the 'slow track'. Studies show that the fast-track route to adulthood is one that is more likely to lead to poverty and social exclusion (Stein, 2005; Barn, et al., 2005). Care leavers are more likely to be on a 'fast-track' trajectory to adulthood although government policies have tried to mitigate against this through implementing supports and safeguards including educational opportunities and greater practical and emotional support for care leavers.

ACTIVITY 12.1

To start with, we would like you to think about when you left home for the first time. Did you have a choice about when you left home? Did you receive ongoing financial support? Who helped you through your education and who helped and advised you in getting a job? Could you have returned to live at home if things were not going well? Could you go home to visit your family if you were feeling lonely and upset?

You may have had considerable support in the process of leaving home and you may have returned to live with your parents at different stages. Your experiences may have differed fundamentally from those of looked after children or you may share similarities with looked after children.

Policy and legislation

Concerns about the challenges faced by young people leaving care started to gain momentum in the mid-1970s, following the documentation of care leavers' experiences through projects like the Who Cares? Project (Page and Clark, 1977), the National Association of Young People in Care (NAYPIC), and through a magazine for young people in care called *Who cares news*. Alongside this, studies of young people's experiences showed key themes in relation to their feelings of powerlessness while in care. These included exclusion from their review meetings; lack of control over their finances; and limited experience in terms of independent living skills, including shopping and budgeting (Godek, 1976; Stein and Ellis, 1983; Stein and Carey, 1986). Stein and Carey (1986) carried out their study in 1982 with young people leaving care over a period of two and a half years. A summary of issues from that study showed the precariousness of life for young care leavers, with budgeting a major anxiety, frequent changes of accommodation after leaving care, unemployment and poverty plus uncertain personal relationships and minimal support from social work services. Many of the recommendations from Stein and Carey's (1986) study and from others are now accepted as good practice and enshrined in legislation. These include the need for specialist leaving care services, leaving care plans, involving young people, the promotion of educational opportunities and rights to accommodation.

The legislation governing practice from the 1970s, until the introduction of the Child Care Act 1980, was the Children and Young Persons Act 1969 (implemented in 1971). Stein (2004) describes how its introduction coincided with social workers moving away from specialist children's services to working within generic teams where young care leavers were not deemed to be a priority. Stein (2004) goes on to link these developments with the significant ideological tensions found in the emerging theoretical underpinnings in social work practice at this time. This featured a rise in radical theory, influenced by Marxism, and a rejection by many of psychological theories, which were critiqued as being oppressive (Bower, 2005). The rise of radical social work, although strong on advocacy, is critiqued as being unhelpful in meeting the needs of vulnerable young people (Stein, 2004, p14). He goes on to makes links between the *philosophical and theoretical void* (Stein, 2004, p15) affecting policy and practice developments in relation to residential care and leaving care services and how the lack of a coherent policy framework surrounding residential care had a negative impact on care leavers. This policy-free zone thus *operated in a climate of denial and welfare planning blight* (Stein, 2004, p15), leaving young people unprepared for leaving care and living alone.

Broad (1998) goes on to highlight how the introduction of the Child Care Act 1980 contained a duty to advise and befriend young people between 16 and 18 years old who were in care at age 16. However, it was the discretionary nature of the powers within the 1980 Act that so disadvantaged the young people in Stein and Carey's 1986 study in terms of lack of financial, practical and emotional support. Biehal, et al. (1995) outline how the combination of the voices of young people being heard through publicity and campaigning, coupled with the gathering of research evidence, strengthened the case for legal reform. With the introduction of the Children Act 1989 there was some increase in the duties required of local authorities with respect to care leavers but this is described as minimal by Broad (1998). His research in fact showed that since the implementation of the Children Act 1989 *in nine areas of social policy there had been a significant deterioration* (Broad, 1994, cited in Broad, 1998, p50) in relation to financial support for daily living costs, accommodation options and in education and training.

Children (Leaving Care) Act 2000

Ongoing demands for change and improvement resulted in the Children (Leaving Care) Act 2000, which was introduced in 2001. Key developments influencing the legislation were the *Review of the safeguards for children living away from home* (Utting, 1997) and the Quality protects initiative (DoH, 1998d). The importance of QP was twofold in that there was significant funding attached, with links made to key objectives with measurable outcomes. Objective 5 was aimed at services for young people leaving care and stated that local authorities were required to *ensure that young people leaving care, as they enter adulthood, are not isolated and participate socially and economically as citizens* (DoH, 1998d). There were specific performance measures related to education and employment, services remaining in contact until young people were 19 years old and a focus on securing suitable accommodation (DoH, 1998d).

In terms of the main aims of the Children (Leaving Care) Act 2000, Brayne and Carr (2010, pp278–80) outline how the Act sought to redress the failings of local authorities as corporate parents in respect of their duties to both prepare young people for leaving home and to provide ongoing support, both tasks which research had shown they had failed to do satisfactorily. Stein (2004) summarises the main features of the Act as:

- delaying young people leaving care until they are prepared and ready;

- strengthening the assessment, preparation and planning for leaving care;

- providing improved personal support after young people have left care;

- improving financial arrangements (p19).

The mechanisms by which these aims are achieved are linked to the legislation which specifies the entitlement of specific groups of young people in accordance with their circumstances. These can be found in sections 23B, 23C, 23D and 23E of the Act. 'Eligible children' are 16- and 17-year-olds who have been looked after for a given period. 'Relevant children' are 16- and 17-year-olds who have left care but meet the criteria of 'eligible children', as they have been looked after for a given period. 'Former relevant children' are over 18 years but were prior to this either 'eligible' or 'relevant'. The local authority is required to assess the needs of each 'eligible' child and the local authority is defined as the one that last looked after a child who is under the criteria of 'relevant' or 'eligible' (Brayne and Carr, 2010, p279). Section 24 of the Act requires local authorities to stay in touch with young people if at college or university and if necessary provide vacation accommodation. However, all young people who are 'eligible', 'relevant' or 'former relevant' should have a personal adviser and a pathway plan (see Care Leavers (England) Regulations 2010). The pathway plan should be completed with the young person and be used to assess and plan how to meet the young person's individual needs with a review every six months or more often if circumstances change (Johns, 2011). The personal adviser's role is to act as a co-ordinator of services, offer advice and support to the young person in all areas including education, keep records and stay in contact until the young person is 24 years old if they are in further or higher education.

As previously stated, a new framework, *Volume 3: Planning Transition to Adulthood for Care Leavers (including guidance on The Care Leavers (England) Regulations 2010)*, was published by the DfE in October 2010 and came into force in April 2011. The guidance gives information about the *Care Leavers (England) Regulations 2010* which replaces some of the previous guidance and regulations associated with the Children (Leaving Care) Act 2000. In addition, the Children and Young Person Act 2008 became law on 13 November 2008, and has within it a number of provisions from the White Paper, *Care Matters: Time for change* (DfES 2007). There is a focus on the needs of adolescents who are looked after and young people who are making the transition from care into independence, with key changes in relation to accommodation and moving placement. It is stated that looked after children must not move from a regulated placement (for example a foster placement or a children's home) to an unregulated placement or accommodation without a formal review. The review meeting should be chaired by an IRO who has to be able to confirm that the young person is ready for the transition and that the new accommodation will meet their needs.

In the new framework, *Planning Transition to Adulthood for Care Leavers* (DfE, 2010), provision is made regarding the advice, assistance and support local authorities give to children and young people aged 16 years and over who are no longer 'looked after'. The framework aims to ensure care leavers are given the same level of care and support that their peers would expect from a responsible parent and that they are provided with the opportunities and chances needed to help them move successfully to adulthood.

ACTIVITY 12.2

Andrew is 19 years old and was defined as an 'eligible child' when younger. He is studying at university some distance away from his responsible local authority. On entering his second year at university, he has told you, his social worker, over the telephone that he is struggling with some aspects of the course, in particular statistics and maths, which he must pass in order to progress in his computer science degree. He has not been managing his weekly budgeting very well and says he has been skipping meals to save money.

ACTIVITY 12.2 *continued*

1. *Is Andrew an 'eligible', 'relevant' or 'former relevant' young person?*

2. *What support is he entitled to and what information would you review to help you plan your intervention?*

3. *What action would you take to support Andrew?*

COMMENT

1. *Andrew is a 'former relevant' young person as at 16 and 17 years he met the criteria due to having been in care for a prescribed period.*

2. *Andrew is entitled to support as a care leaver in higher education and may need additional funds to cover expenses at this point. You should read again his pathway plan and establish what support you and Andrew initially identified when it was drawn up, as it may need to be reviewed.*

3. *As the representative of the responsible local authority it may be that you need to fund additional tuition for Andrew to help him with his maths and statistics. In the interim, it may help Andrew to meet with one of his tutors to get advice on this area. It would be important to arrange a meeting with Andrew to discuss budgeting and how he is managing this and the ongoing pressures of his studies. Given the significant achievement Andrew has made in reaching university, it is important that every support is offered to him in order for him to progress.*

Key challenges facing young care leavers
Education

Young people leaving care face many disadvantages in terms of opportunities to progress educationally, due to their adverse experiences prior to and sometimes during being looked after (Cheung and Heath, 1994; Biehal, et al., 1995; Broad, 1998). We are reminded that *educational disadvantage casts a long shadow. Care leavers are more likely to be unemployed than other young people aged 16–19* (Stein, 2004, p33). The recent Social Exclusion Unit report (2003) *A Better Education for Children in Care* highlights concerns about educational attainment for all looked after children. The government responded to this by introducing a number of measures, including strengthening the secondary transfers system, and making looked after children a priority for secondary school places. They also introduced section 52 of the Children Act 2004, where there is a specific requirement to promote the educational achievement of looked after children. In addition, the Children and Young Persons Act 2008 extends the duty of local authorities to appoint a personal adviser, to undertake an assessment and develop a pathway plan towards former relevant children who are over 21 years but under 25 years even if they have completed or not finished their original education programme (Brayne and Carr 2010; Johns, 2011). Although education attainment levels are lower for young people leaving care than for the general population, not all young care leavers have difficulties achieving education-ally. This can be seen, for example, in the overall increase in young care leavers accessing further and higher education: *from 17.5 per cent in 1998 to 31 per cent in 2003* (Stein, 2004, p20). More recent data show an increase over five years of young people age 19 years accessing further education, with 15% in 2002 increasing to 26% in 2007 (CSF, 2007a). The factors associated with higher levels of educational achievement for young people leaving care are summarised as being linked with stable placements, lengthy or delayed process of leaving care, plus caring and supportive relationships with adults who are encouraging and interested in education (Stein, 2006a). In a follow-up study of 106 young people by Wade and Dixon (2006), the most significant factor in relation to a posi-tive career outcome was young people leaving care at 18 years or over. The introduction of local authorities as corporate parents (see Chapter 1) aims to strengthen educational opportunities for young people before and after care. However, a recent study shows that many young people are often self-reliant. It is suggested that practice needs to catch up with how young people themselves are navigating pathways through further and higher education so that the support they need is readily available (Cameron, 2007).

Housing

Homelessness and insecure housing have historically been a feature of life for young care leavers. Other problems highlighted by Biehal, et al. (1995) show how planning processes sometimes became dominant and young people were often swept along with timeta-bles for moving into independent accommodation because they were available and could not be held for more time although often the young people themselves were not ready. The study recommended that a more individual approach be taken in terms of meeting the needs of young people for housing, taking into account their diverse needs. Other findings show high levels of mobility for young care leavers. The research study by Hai and Williams (2004) (cited in Stein, 2004) following the introduction of the Children (Leaving Care) Act 2000 showed that accommodation options had improved with almost 90% of the young people who were interviewed reporting to be happy with their accom-modation (Hai and Williams, 2004, cited in Stein, 2004, p30). This study also showed improvements in other areas, including increased staffing, additional resources and the implementation of pathway plans.

Challenges in relation to housing have been trying to ensure that the most vulnerable young people, who may have emotional and behavioural difficulties, a history of offend-ing behaviour or have had multiple and disruptive placements in care, have access to supported housing. This can act as a stepping stone before moving on to more independ-ent accommodation (Hutson, 1997).

Health and well-being

You will remember from Chapter 9 the particular vulnerabilities looked after children experience in relation to mental health. Young care leavers may need additional support to help them manage and make sense of the painful experiences of loss and rejection they have suffered earlier in their lives. They may have been fortunate and had strong supportive carers with whom they had an opportunity to feel they belonged and feel cared for or they may have had less positive care experiences and suffered a great deal of stress and sorrow, with resulting low self-esteem. This might result in them forming relationships with others who are exploitative and unreliable. Young people are likely to need support around their general health, advice about sexual health and some young people may require additional support from adult mental heath services. Some research has shown that young people in care have higher levels of illicit drug use compared to the general population (Newburn, et al., 2002). Furthermore, it is stated that *evidence suggests that children in care are four times more likely than their peers to smoke, use alcohol and misuse drugs* (DfES, 2007, p90). It is important therefore that your assessments are non-judgemental but informed in relation to drug and alcohol misuse. You may have to refer the young person for specialist advice or give them details of services which give accurate information to young people about the impact of drug and alcohol misuse.

Other research has shown that young women who have been looked after are over-represented in those who are involved in selling sex (Pearce, et al., 2003; Coy, 2008). A *kaleidoscope of push factors* is identified by Coy (2008, p3), including previous abuse, family breakdown, substance abuse, placement breakdowns and disruptions, running away and homelessness. Many of these factors exist in the lives of young women leaving care who you will work with and they will require sensitive care and support. They are likely to have a fragile sense of self, and may have had very little experience of care and support from adults. Coy (2008) suggests that the young women in her study who were selling sex saw themselves as 'survivors', as they did not get the support they needed when leaving care. It is suggested that:

> *practical measures such as safe accommodation, regular and sufficient income and opportunities to access employment, training and leisure activities can alleviate the socio-economic barriers that young women seek to overcome by selling sex.*

> (Coy, 2008, p14)

CASE STUDY

Donna is an 18-year-old care leaver and has just moved into her new flat. She has informed you that she has been to see her GP, who has confirmed that she is ten weeks pregnant. She says that both she and her boyfriend Pete are excited about having a baby. Donna talks about how having a baby will give her life meaning as she will have someone of her own to love and look after. She has little contact with her own family but says her boyfriend's mother has offered to help her. What issues do you think there will be for Donna and Pete in looking after their baby? What support and intervention might be helpful?

Donna and Pete are becoming parents at a young age with limited support systems in place, which may put a strain on their relationship. We know that the challenges of parenting can be difficult to manage for those who have experienced abusive and conflictive relationships in their own families, as Donna has. You may have started to think about the need for extra support for Donna and her boyfriend, perhaps involving a meeting with Pete's mother. It will be important that Donna accesses health care advice and support and thinks about finances and what her entitlement is to financial support after the baby is born. You could encourage Donna to discuss her options with her college, where she is attending a course, so that she is able to plan her studies. You may also wish to discuss with Donna the support that local baby groups could offer in that they help to prepare mothers for having a baby and encourage women to make friends in their local neighbourhoods.

Working with specific groups of young people leaving care and how services can support them

Disabled young people

There is limited research in this area of practice, with most of the discussions focused on transition planning between children's and adult social services for young people with severe and complex disabilities who are leaving care. Young disabled people, who do not meet the threshold for services from adult social services, are required to access leaving care provision in children's services. Overall, research shows that young disabled care leavers have limited choices, and those young disabled people who are eligible for services under the Community Care legislation have minimal contact with leaving care teams (Stein, 2004). Research involving a small sample of young disabled care leavers showed that, due to overprotection, the young people had not had the opportunity to familiarise themselves with the experiences many young adults have in preparing for adulthood. This was felt to be a disadvantage for them in preparing for leaving care, and it was suggested that these young people have comprehensive assessments regarding their skills in order to establish realistic goals (Biehal, et al., 1995). Housing, education and subsequent employment have been identified as forming the bedrock for helping young people to make a successful transition to independent living (Wade and Dixon, 2006). Housing emerges in particular as an area *in which positive post-care interventions could (and should) make a substantial difference to...early housing careers and to their overall sense of well-being* (Wade and Dixon, 2006, p203). Given that we know that young disabled care leavers are likely to need more support than some other young people, it was of concern in Wade and Dixon's study that they found young disabled care leavers did not have access to more supported leaving-care accommodation. As a result, some of these young people had subsequent difficulties in managing aspects of independent living. As the social worker for a young disabled person leaving care, it will be important that you spend time getting to know that young person, their needs and areas of vulnerabilities and that you fully involve them in your discussions and plans. The new guidance, *Volume 3: Planning Transition to*

Adulthood for Care Leavers (including guidance on The Care Leavers (England) Regulations 2010 (DfE, 2010), strengthens support for young people and as previously stated creates a slower track to adulthood with more intensive support for young people with specific needs.

Unaccompanied asylum-seeking young people and young people leaving care from black and minority ethnic communities

Young people of dual heritage were the largest group of black people in the study by Biehal, et al. (1995). Educational achievement and progress for the black young people in the study showed slightly higher levels than those achieved for young people from white ethnicities although employment levels were similar. Biehal, et al., (1995) emphasises the importance of black young people having access to and information about positive role models. It is also suggested that young people of dual heritage should have the opportunity to explore all aspects of their identity, both their white and black cultural heritage. A more recent study examining the experiences of 261 young people leaving care, where 44% were from minority ethnic groups, found that white young people were more disadvantaged while in care and in leaving care and had the poorest outcomes of all groups of young people. Caribbean young people had higher rates of participation in further and higher education. African, Asian and Caribbean young people had experienced a more stable placement history, with fewer placement moves than white and dual-heritage young people (Barn, et al., 2005).

In terms of unaccompanied asylum-seeking young people, Stein (2004) refers to government statistics showing that approximately 7% of all care leavers are asylum-seeking young people. More recent data shows that 2,100 unaccompanied asylum-seeking young people over 16 years old are looked after (DCSF, 2007a). However, there has been a reduction in the numbers of unaccompanied asylum seeking young people who are looked after. Data from the DfE (2011a) shows that for the year ending March 2011 there was a decrease of 22% from 2010. This will invariably lead to a reduction in young people who will access leaving care services. As outlined in Chapter 6, these young people leaving care face many challenges in addition to those faced by all young people as their immigration status is often uncertain, resulting in them having to engage with legal processes in trying to remain in the UK. In addition, there has been a great deal of caution and ambivalence from government in relation to supporting asylum-seeking young people leaving care and fierce arguments about funding between central and local government. These young people often face challenges in accessing suitable accommodation and may be isolated from their communities. You will remember from Chapter 6 how many of the young people choose to remain silent about their past lives and this is something you will have to work with as there are likely to be very strong reasons about their enduring silence linked to fear, trust and uncertainty about what might happen if they break their silence (Kohli, 2007, p105).

Young parents

Statistics show that the UK has high rates of teenage pregnancy (SEU, 1999; UNICEF, 2001), which the government has attempted to address through the Teenage Pregnancy

Strategy (Teenage Pregnancy Unit, 2005). Studies have shown that young people who have experienced multiple disadvantages in childhood are more likely to become young parents and their children are also more likely to be disadvantaged economically and in terms of their education attainment (SEU, 1999; Barn and Mantovani, 2007). Research has identified that young people who are care leavers are one of the groups who are vulnerable to teenage pregnancy and early parenthood (Biehal, et al., 1995). Looked after young people are likely to have experienced disruptive family relationships, and a study by Barn and Mantovani (2007) found that the majority of the young women who were care leavers had a high number of placement changes and moved between five and ten times.

Stein (2004) asserts that early parenthood should be seen in a context of young people not having access to care and support, good advice about sexual health, being vulnerable and sometimes lonely, which may result in them becoming parents earlier than they planned.

Despite much of the concern, other studies show that young care leavers were positive about becoming parents (Biehal, et al., 1995; Chase, et al., 2003). Biehal, et al. (1995) found that many young people were excited and optimistic about having a baby and the study reported that many of the young women were managing reasonably well. Young fathers are reported as being positive about fatherhood although the group of 16 young fathers who were leaving care and interviewed as part of a research study reported feeling excluded from advice from professionals and planning about the baby (Tyrer, et al., 2005). When working with young parents or young people who are pregnant it is important that you support them at an early stage in accessing health advice. In addition, it is recommended that young parents leaving care should have access to a range of accommodation options, support in alleviating poverty and in returning to education plus advice about local informal support (Biehal, et al., 1995).

Role of the leaving care team and support services

Leaving care services were created in the mid-1980s in response to the concerns raised from young people themselves, and from research studies showing that the needs of young care leavers were being squeezed out in mainstream social work services (Stein and Carey, 1986; Biehal, et al., 1995; Stein, 2004). There are now discrete teams within local authorities that work in partnership with a range of other agencies to offer ongoing support to young people leaving care in the areas of housing, education, employment, independent living skills, as well as offering emotional support. Social workers have a central role which includes assessing needs, plus agreeing the pathway plan and co-ordinating its implementation and review. The guidance from Volume 3 (DfE, 2010) emphasises that the role should be carried out in line with the guiding principles of delivering a quality service, giving young people second chances where this is needed and tailoring plans to meet individual needs. Young people leaving care should have an allocated worker and a pathway plan. Although positive changes have been reported following the introduction of the Children (Leaving Care) Act 2000 (Stein, 2006a), some young people have reported feeling *swept along by the fast pace of change required of them after the age of 16 and many young people reported finding their pathway plans disappointing* (Barn, et al., 2005, p3). Again this highlights the importance of trying to proceed at the pace of the young person, taking time to check out with them whether they feel they are managing and slowing things down if they feel overwhelmed by the pace of change.

How can theory help?

Attachment theory offers a theoretical framework which will help you to understand the perspectives and experiences of many of the young people you will work with, who are leaving care. They are likely to have experienced disrupted relationships, insecure attachments, loss and separation. Young people leaving care may therefore find it difficult to trust the adults around them, as they have not had a secure base, and had limited experience of loving, caring relationships (Howe, 1995; Stein, 2004; Crawford and Walker, 2007). See also Chapter 8 of this book.

A helpful way of considering the centrality of attachment theory in understanding young people's experiences of leaving care is to hear the voices of young people themselves. Schofield (2003) examines the experiences of young people aged between 18 and 30 who were formally in long-term foster care, in order to discover how foster care can meet the needs of looked after children. She reports that continuing relationships with the foster carers offered *part of an elaborate structure of ties that provided its own kind of scaffolding for adulthood* (Schofield, 2003, p229). In addition, the individual journeys and reflections of the young adults highlighted how:

> the secure base found in foster families appeared to be closely connected for many fostered children with the idea of the foster families as a 'real family'.

> (Schofield, 2003, p229)

For the young adults interviewed, belonging was described as having five linked features: *family solidarity, family identity, family rituals, family relationships and family culture* (Schofield, 2003, p229). Some long-term foster families were described as *offering not just emotional healing but a place in society* (p232).

In hearing the voices of young adults you will see how the care history and pathways of children and young people looked after have a significant impact on their long-term well-being. Schofield (2003) discusses the centrality of placement stability and how this can offer hope for the future and sustain young people through challenges and adversity. Schofield (2003) makes links to a psycho-social model created from the key themes of the study entitled 'Lessons for Life' and suggests that young people are more likely to be able to cope with the challenges of adulthood if they have had the opportunity to experience the following:

- love for others and feeling lovable;

- being effective, learning and exploring;

- being able to make sense of the past and the present;

- having an ability to plan for the future, to think and adapt;

- feeling a sense of family and kinship.

    (adapted from Schofield, 2003, p210)

In working with young people leaving care it may be helpful to think about some of these key areas and how losses in some areas can be bolstered and compensated through direct work and sensitive and reliable support.

CHAPTER SUMMARY

Leaving care may represent the final journey for young people who have experienced care but it is also the start of a new journey for young people into adulthood. Research and the voices of young people themselves have shown how important this key transition stage is, where young people need help to navigate the major challenges of adulthood. They need help not only in practical terms, but also in terms of emotional support and life skills, perhaps in maintaining contact with foster carers or in managing relationships with their birth families. The chapter began by introducing some of the key issues in leaving care and went on to explore some of the challenges faced by young people who are leaving care. The exploration of theory and how it can help social workers to understand the position of young care leavers is central. We invited you to reflect on your own experiences of leaving home, as being reflective will help you to work with vulnerable young people in an open and non-judgemental way. In this chapter links are made back to discussions about the importance of placement stability and the core skill of assessment and planning involving young people and their families. On this final stage of a young person's pathway through care, young people need social work support as much as they did at previous stages of their journey. They may return to you to help them understand mistakes they have made, for advice and to help them make difficult choices. In this chapter we have shown how individual young people have a range of needs and that working in partnership with them and others will help you to meet those needs.

FURTHER READING

Shaw, C (1998) *Remember my messages: The experiences and views of 2000 children in public care in the UK*. London: Who Cares? Trust.

This report gives clear information from a questionnaire answered by looked after children and young people aged between eight and 20 years old. Questions focus on aspects of their lives in relation to the looked after system and recommendations are made about how practice and services for looked after children could be improved.

Wheal, A (ed.) (2002) *The companion to leaving care*. Lyme Regis: Russell House.

This book charts key issues in terms of policy and practice with young people leaving care and includes comments and observations from young care leavers themselves.

Conclusion

In many ways the needs of looked after children are the same as those of every other child. However, they do have additional needs which relate specifically to their experiences of harm, abuse or separation from their families. Unfortunately, often both their basic and additional needs can get forgotten or go unacknowledged, as they are not 'held in mind' by individuals and the various systems they work within, which are complex and bureaucratic. One of the things that strongly emerges from the literature is the importance of placement stability with adults who provide consistent care, nurture, support and who are interested in these children growing and developing as best as they are able. It is not often that you will read the word 'love' in terms of attributes and skills required for caring for looked after children – see Alan Johnson's foreword to *Care matters: Time for change* (DfES, 2007). However, there is something important about warm and nurturing parenting which has to transcend institutional care when caring for other people's children in order to demonstrate compassion and which recognises the uniqueness of every child.

In this book we have explored and examined how adverse pre-care experiences have contributed to children's difficulties in forming and maintaining relationships with adults and with their peers. Although there are many ways in which the care system could improve, this book is not offering a comprehensive critique of the care system *per se*. We wish to add our voice to the ever-increasing criticism of the way in which outcomes for children are determined by a system which measures 'outputs'. This approach often fails to recognise the complexity of the care system in terms of knowing which children do best in care, and the effect that children's pre-care experiences can and do have on their health, education and all other areas of development while in care.

Our original motivation in writing this book was to create a text that contained key contemporary issues in social work practice for looked after children, although as with many endeavours it has grown into so much more. During the writing of this book we have thought about the stories of many of the looked after children we have worked with over the years and our roles in those children's lives. We have also read accounts of other looked after children's experiences, including what they said was important for their lives, what made them sad, frightened, angry, as well as hopeful, happy and feeling loved. There are many important messages to be heard and acted on by the professional networks working with looked after children in terms of what children and young people value about their experiences in care, and what is difficult too.

From a policy perspective there have been a number of significant changes since the first edition of this book was published in 2008. The Labour government introduced a number of improvements in relation to services to looked after children, which included additional investment in the looked after children's system. A recent All Party Parliamentary Group has welcomed such investment and improvement but also commented that more work still needs to be done (House of Commons (Education Committee), 2011). The new policy journey led by the coalition government has been discussed in this new edition. Time will tell whether the coalition government's suggested changes will produce the required improvements hoped for in the everyday lives and experiences of looked after children.

There is a real wish by politicians, policy-makers, social work academics, researchers and social workers to involve looked after children themselves in planning how care can positively affect their lives. We think that the government's emphasis on improving education is important. However, changes to current practice should show awareness of why educational achievement is such a problem for looked after children. The problem of low achievement does not begin when a child becomes accommodated and it is simplistic to suggest that this measure is a solid test of the efficacy of the entire looked after system. Pre-care experiences should be understood in terms of how they can impact on children's ability to learn. Thus the solution to this does not rest solely with social workers but also in the education community.

We think that mental health and emotional well-being are a lynchpin which should be at the forefront of all professional's practice in terms of understanding attachment, loss, separation, trauma and how this affects the everyday life of a looked after child. Knowledge of child development and attachment, and understanding how and why children display challenging behaviours are important. Children need to be offered understanding and therapeutic support where necessary. In addition, appropriate support should be given to carers of these children. If we have not got that bit of the service right for looked after children then the rest will not follow. Maintaining appropriate levels of resourcing in front-line services remains a challenge in this area.

Making a difference to the lives of looked after children involves recognising and responding to the uniqueness of each child. In doing this, it is important to balance the organisational and procedural demands of practice alongside the everyday needs of the child in order to achieve quality care and create worthwhile possibilities and clearer understandings about their futures. This will always be a demanding task but one we hope will be rewarding for you and the looked after children you work with.

Appendix 1 Professional capabilities framework

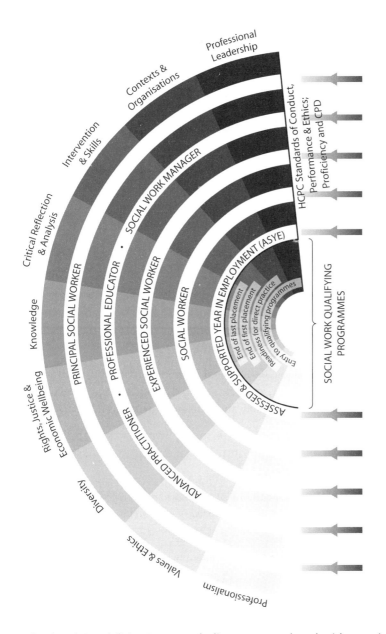

Professional Capabilities Framework diagram reproduced with permission of The College of Social Work

See page x for the full list of standards.

Appendix 2 Subject benchmark for social work

Subject benchmark for social work

5 Subject knowledge, understanding and skills

Subject knowledge and understanding

5.1 During their degree studies in social work, honours graduates should acquire, critically evaluate, apply and integrate knowledge and understanding in the following five core areas of study.

5.1.1

Social work services, service users and carers, which include:

- the social processes (associated with, for example, poverty, migration, unemployment, poor health, disablement, lack of education and other sources of disadvantage) that lead to marginalisation, isolation and exclusion, and their impact on the demand for social work services

- explanations of the links between definitional processes contributing to social differences (for example, social class, gender, ethnic differences, age, sexuality and religious belief) to the problems of inequality and differential need faced by service users

- the nature of social work services in a diverse society (with particular reference to concepts such as prejudice, interpersonal, institutional and structural discrimination, empowerment and anti-discriminatory practices)

- the nature and validity of different definitions of, and explanations for, the characteristics and circumstances of service users and the services required by them, drawing on knowledge from research, practice experience, and from service users and carers

- the focus on outcomes, such as promoting the well-being of young people and their families, and promoting dignity, choice and independence for adults receiving services

- the relationship between agency policies, legal requirements and professional boundaries in shaping the nature of services provided in interdisciplinary contexts and the issues associated with working across professional boundaries and within different disciplinary groups.

5.1.2

The service delivery context, which includes:

- the location of contemporary social work within historical, comparative and global perspectives, including European and international contexts

- the changing demography and cultures of communities in which social workers will be practising

- the complex relationships between public, social and political philosophies, policies and priorities and the organisation and practice of social work, including the contested nature of these

- the issues and trends in modern public and social policy and their relationship to contemporary practice and service delivery in social work

- the significance of legislative and legal frameworks and service delivery standards (including the nature of legal authority, the application of legislation in practice, statutory accountability and tensions between statute, policy and practice)

- the current range and appropriateness of statutory, voluntary and private agencies providing community-based, day-care, residential and other services and the organisational systems inherent within these

- the significance of interrelationships with other related services, including housing, health, income maintenance and criminal justice (where not an integral social service)

- the contribution of different approaches to management, leadership and quality in public and independent human services

- the development of personalised services, individual budgets and direct payments

- the implications of modern information and communications technology (ICT) for both the provision and receipt of services.

5.1.3

Values and ethics, which include:

- the nature, historical evolution and application of social work values

- the moral concepts of rights, responsibility, freedom, authority and power inherent in the practice of social workers as moral and statutory agents

- the complex relationships between justice, care and control in social welfare and the practical and ethical implications of these, including roles as statutory agents and in upholding the law in respect of discrimination

- aspects of philosophical ethics relevant to the understanding and resolution of value dilemmas and conflicts in both interpersonal and professional contexts

- the conceptual links between codes defining ethical practice, the regulation of professional conduct and the management of potential conflicts generated by the codes held by different professional groups.

5.1.4

Social work theory, which includes:

- research-based concepts and critical explanations from social work theory and other disciplines that contribute to the knowledge base of social work, including their distinctive epistemological status and application to practice

- the relevance of sociological perspectives to understanding societal and structural influences on human behaviour at individual, group and community levels

- the relevance of psychological, physical and physiological perspectives to understanding personal and social development and functioning

- social science theories explaining group and organisational behaviour, adaptation and change

- models and methods of assessment, including factors underpinning the selection and testing of relevant information, the nature of professional judgement and the processes of risk assessment and decision-making

- approaches and methods of intervention in a range of settings, including factors guiding the choice and evaluation of these

- user-led perspectives

- knowledge and critical appraisal of relevant social research and evaluation methodologies, and the evidence base for social work.

5.1.5

The nature of social work practice, which includes:

- the characteristics of practice in a range of community-based and organisational settings within statutory, voluntary and private sectors, and the factors influencing changes and developments in practice within these contexts

- the nature and characteristics of skills associated with effective practice, both direct and indirect, with a range of service-users and in a variety of settings

- the processes that facilitate and support service user choice and independence

- the factors and processes that facilitate effective interdisciplinary, interprofessional and interagency collaboration and partnership

- the place of theoretical perspectives and evidence from international research in assessment and decision-making processes in social work practice

- the integration of theoretical perspectives and evidence from international research into the design and implementation of effective social work intervention, with a wide range of service users, carers and others

- the processes of reflection and evaluation, including familiarity with the range of approaches for evaluating service and welfare outcomes, and their significance for the development of practice and the practitioner.

Subject-specific skills and other skills

5.2 As an applied subject at honours degree level, social work necessarily involves the development of skills that may be of value in many situations (for example, analytical thinking, building relationships, working as a member of an organisation, intervention, evaluation and reflection). Some of these skills are specific to social work but many are also widely transferable. What helps to define the specific nature of these skills in a social work context are:

- the context in which they are applied and assessed (eg, communication skills in practice with people with sensory impairments or assessment skills in an interprofessional setting)

- the relative weighting given to such skills within social work practice (eg, the central importance of problem-solving skills within complex human situations)

- the specific purpose of skill development (eg, the acquisition of research skills in order to build a repertoire of research-based practice)

- a requirement to integrate a range of skills (ie, not simply to demonstrate these in an isolated and incremental manner).

5.3 All social work honours graduates should show the ability to reflect on and learn from the exercise of their skills. They should understand the significance of the concepts of continuing professional development and lifelong learning, and accept responsibility for their own continuing development.

5.4 Social work honours graduates should acquire and integrate skills in the following five core areas.

Problem-solving skills

5.5 These are sub-divided into four areas.

5.5.1

Managing problem-solving activities: honours graduates in social work should be able to plan problem-solving activities, ie to:

- think logically, systematically, critically and reflectively

- apply ethical principles and practices critically in planning problem-solving activities

- plan a sequence of actions to achieve specified objectives, making use of research, theory and other forms of evidence

- manage processes of change, drawing on research, theory and other forms of evidence.

5.5.2

Gathering information: honours graduates in social work should be able to:

- gather information from a wide range of sources and by a variety of methods, for a range of purposes. These methods should include electronic searches, reviews of relevant literature, policy and procedures, face-to-face interviews, written and telephone contact with individuals and groups

- take into account differences of viewpoint in gathering information and critically assess the reliability and relevance of the information gathered

- assimilate and disseminate relevant information in reports and case records.

5.5.3

Analysis and synthesis: honours graduates in social work should be able to analyse and synthesise knowledge gathered for problem-solving purposes, ie to:

- assess human situations, taking into account a variety of factors (including the views of participants, theoretical concepts, research evidence, legislation and organisational policies and procedures)

- analyse information gathered, weighing competing evidence and modifying their viewpoint in light of new information, then relate this information to a particular task, situation or problem

- consider specific factors relevant to social work practice (such as risk, rights, cultural differences and linguistic sensitivities, responsibilities to protect vulnerable individuals and legal obligations)

- assess the merits of contrasting theories, explanations, research, policies and procedures

- synthesise knowledge and sustain reasoned argument

- employ a critical understanding of human agency at the macro (societal), mezzo (organisational and community) and micro (inter and intrapersonal) levels

- critically analyse and take account of the impact of inequality and discrimination in work with people in particular contexts and problem situations.

5.5.4

Intervention and evaluation: honours graduates in social work should be able to use their knowledge of a range of interventions and evaluation processes selectively to:

- build and sustain purposeful relationships with people and organisations in community-based, and interprofessional contexts

- make decisions, set goals and construct specific plans to achieve these, taking into account relevant factors including ethical guidelines

- negotiate goals and plans with others, analysing and addressing in a creative manner human, organisational and structural impediments to change

- implement plans through a variety of systematic processes that include working in partnership

- undertake practice in a manner that promotes the well-being and protects the safety of all parties

- engage effectively in conflict resolution

- support service users to take decisions and access services, with the social worker as navigator, advocate and supporter

- manage the complex dynamics of dependency and, in some settings, provide direct care and personal support in everyday living situations

- meet deadlines and comply with external definitions of a task

- plan, implement and critically review processes and outcomes

- bring work to an effective conclusion, taking into account the implications for all involved

- monitor situations, review processes and evaluate outcomes

- use and evaluate methods of intervention critically and reflectively.

Communication skills

5.6 Honours graduates in social work should be able to communicate clearly, accurately and precisely (in an appropriate medium) with individuals and groups in a range of formal and informal situations, ie to:

- make effective contact with individuals and organisations for a range of objectives, by verbal, paper-based and electronic means

- clarify and negotiate the purpose of such contacts and the boundaries of their involvement

- listen actively to others, engage appropriately with the life experiences of service users, understand accurately their viewpoint and overcome personal prejudices to respond appropriately to a range of complex personal and interpersonal situations

- use both verbal and non-verbal cues to guide interpretation

- identify and use opportunities for purposeful and supportive communication with service users within their everyday living situations

- follow and develop an argument and evaluate the viewpoints of, and evidence presented by, others

- write accurately and clearly in styles adapted to the audience, purpose and context of the communication

- use advocacy skills to promote others' rights, interests and needs

- present conclusions verbally and on paper, in a structured form, appropriate to the audience for which these have been prepared

- make effective preparation for, and lead meetings in a productive way

- communicate effectively across potential barriers resulting from differences (for example, in culture, language and age).

Skills in working with others

5.7 Honours graduates in social work should be able to work effectively with others, ie to:

- involve users of social work services in ways that increase their resources, capacity and power to influence factors affecting their lives

- consult actively with others, including service users and carers, who hold relevant information or expertise

- act cooperatively with others, liaising and negotiating across differences such as organisational and professional boundaries and differences of identity or language

- develop effective helping relationships and partnerships with other individuals, groups and organisations that facilitate change

- act with others to increase social justice by identifying and responding to prejudice, institutional discrimination and structural inequality

- act within a framework of multiple accountability (for example, to agencies, the public, service users, carers and others)

- challenge others when necessary, in ways that are most likely to produce positive outcomes.

Skills in personal and professional development

5.8 Honours graduates in social work should be able to:

- advance their own learning and understanding with a degree of independence

- reflect on and modify their behaviour in the light of experience

- identify and keep under review their own personal and professional boundaries

- manage uncertainty, change and stress in work situations

- handle inter and intrapersonal conflict constructively

- understand and manage changing situations and respond in a flexible manner

- challenge unacceptable practices in a responsible manner

- take responsibility for their own further and continuing acquisition and use of knowledge and skills

- use research critically and effectively to sustain and develop their practice.

ICT and numerical skills

5.9 Honours graduates in social work should be able to use ICT methods and techniques to support their learning and their practice. In particular, they should demonstrate the ability to:

- use ICT effectively for professional communication, data storage and retrieval and information searching

- use ICT in working with people who use services

- demonstrate sufficient familiarity with statistical techniques to enable effective use of research in practice

- integrate appropriate use of ICT to enhance skills in problem-solving in the four areas set out in paragraph 6.2

- apply numerical skills to financial and budgetary responsibilities

- have a critical understanding of the social impact of ICT, including an awareness of the impact of the 'digital divide'.

References

Abbott, D, Morris, J and Ward, L (2001) *The best place to be? Policy, practice and the experiences of residential school placements for disabled children*. York: Joseph Rowntree Foundation

Adoption Policy Review Group (Scotland) (2005) *Adoption: Better choices for our children*. Edinburgh: Scottish Executive

Ahmed, S, Cheetham, J and Small, J (eds) (1986) *Social work with black children and their families*. London: Batsford

Ainsworth, M, Blehar, M, Waters, E and Wall, S (1978) *Patterns of attachment: A psychological study of the strange situation*. Hillside, NJ: Erlbaum

Allain, L (2007) An investigation of how a group of social workers respond to the cultural needs of black, minority ethnic looked after children. *Practice* 19(2), 127–41

American Psychiatric Association (1994) *Diagnostic and statistical manual of mental disorders* (4th edition). Washington, DC: American Psychiatric Association

Archer, C (1999a) *First steps in parenting the child who hurts: Tiddlers and toddlers*. London: Jessica Kingsley

Archer, C (1999b) *Next steps in parenting the child who hurts: Tykes and teens*. London: Jessica Kingsley

Archer, C (2003) Weft and warp: Developmental impact of trauma and implications for healing. In Archer, C and Burnell, A (eds) *Trauma, attachment and family permanence: Fear can stop you loving*. London: Jessica Kingsley

Aries, P (1962) *Centuries of childhood*. London: Jonathan Cape

Asthana, A and Hinsliff, G (2004) Equality chief branded as 'right wing'. *Observer*, Sunday 4 April

Atwool, N (2006) Attachment and resilience: Implications for children in care. *Child Care in Practice* 12(4), 315–30

Audit Commission (1999) *Children in mind: Child and adolescent mental health services*. Oxford: Audit Commission Publications

Baker, C (2006) Disabled foster children and contacts with their birth families. *Adoption and Fostering* 30(2), 18–28

Baldwin, T and Rozenberg, G (2004) Britain 'must scrap multiculturalism'. *Times*, Saturday 3 April

Barn, R (1993) *Black children in the public care system*. London: Batsford

Barn, R (ed.) (1999) *Working with black children and adolescents in need*. London: BAAF

Barn, R, Andrew, L and Mantovani, N (2005) *Life after care: The experiences of young people from different ethnic groups*. York: Joseph Rowntree Foundation

Barn, R and Mantovani, N (2007) Young mothers and the care system: Contextualising risk and vulnerability. *British Journal of Social Work* 37(2), 225–43

Barn, R, Sinclair, R and Ferdinand, D (1997) *Acting on principle: An examination of race and ethnicity in social services provision for children and families*. London: BAAF

Bebbington, A and Miles, J (1989) The background of children who enter local authority care. *British Journal of Social Work* 19(5), 349–68

Bee, H (2000) *The developing child* (9th edition). Boston: Allyn and Bacon

Berk, L (2003) *Child development* (6th Edition). Boston: Allyn and Bacon

Berridge, D (2007) Theory and explanation in child welfare: Education and looked after children. *Child and Family Social Work* 12(1), 1–10

Berridge, D (2012) Reflections on child welfare research and the policy process: Virtual school heads and the education of looked after children. *British Journal of Social Work* 42, 26–41

Bhatti-Sinclair, K (2011) *Anti-racist practice in social work*. Basingstoke: Palgrave

Bhavnani, R, Mirza, H and Meetoo, V (2005) *Tackling the roots of racism*. Bristol: Policy Press

Biehal, N, Clayden, J, Stein, M and Wade, J (1992) *Prepared for living? A survey of young people leaving the care of three local authorities*. London: National Children's Bureau

Biehal, N, Clayden, J, Stein, M and Wade, J (1992) *Moving on: Young people and leaving care schemes*. London: HMSO

Biehal, N, Ellison, S and Sinclair, I (2011) Intensive fostering: an independent evaluation of MTFC in an English setting. *Children and Youth Services Review* 33, 2043–9

BMA (1999) *Growing up in Britain: Ensuring a healthy future for all our children. A study of 0–5 year olds.* London: BMA

Bower, M (ed.) (2005) *Psychoanalytic theory for social work practice: Thinking under fire*. Abingdon: Routledge

Bowlby, J (1969) *Attachment and loss: Vol 1. Attachment*. New York: Penguin

Boylan, J and Ray, M (2012) *Curriculum guide: Human growth and development*. London: College of Social Work, SWAP/Higher Education Academy

Brammer, A (2010) *Social work law* (3rd edition). Harlow: Pearson Education

Brayne, H and Carr, H (2010) *Law for social workers* (10th edition). Oxford: Oxford University Press

Bridge Child Care Development Service, Southampton Area Child Protection Committee (2000) *Jason: An independent review of the circumstances surrounding his death*. Newbury: Bridge Publishing House

Briggs, S (2008) *Working with adolescents and young adults* (2nd edition). Basingstoke: Palgrave

Broad, B (1998) *Young people leaving care: Life after the Children Act 1989*. London: Jessica Kingsley

Broad, B (ed.) (2001) *Kinship care: The placement choice for children and young people*. Lyme Regis: Russell House

Bronfenbrenner, U (1986) Ecology of the family as a context for human development: Research perspectives. *Developmental Psychology* 22, 723–42

Brophy, J (2006) *Research review: Child care proceedings under the Children Act 1989*. London: Department for Constitutional Affairs

Brown, G (2007) We need a United Kingdom. *Telegraph*, Saturday 13 January

Brown, HC (1998) *Social work and sexuality: Working with lesbians and gay men*. Basingstoke: BASW/Macmillan

Brown, HC and Cocker, C (2008) Lesbian and gay fostering and adoption: Out of the closet into the mainstream? *Adoption and Fostering* 32(4), 19–30

Brown, HC and Cocker, C (2011) *Social work with lesbians and gay men*. London: Sage

Brown, HC, Fry, E and Howard J (eds) (2005) *Support care: How family placement can keep children and families together*. Lyme Regis: Russell House

Brown, K and Rutter, L (2006) *Critical thinking for social work*. Exeter: Learning Matters

Brown, L (2003) Mainstream or margin? The current use of family group conferences in child welfare practice in the UK. *Child and Family Social Work* 8(4), 331–40

Bullock, R, Courtney, M, Parker, R, Sinclair, I and Thoburn, J (2006) Can the corporate state parent? *Children and Youth Services Review* 28, 1344–58

Butler, G (2007) Reflecting on emotion in social work. In Knott, C and Scragg, T (eds) *Reflective practice in social work*. Exeter: Learning Matters

Butt, J and Mirza, K (1996) *Social care and black communities: A review of recent research studies*. London: HMSO

Cafcass (2011) The baby Peter effect and the increase in s31 care order applications. London: Cafcass

Cameron, C (2007) Education and self-reliance among care leavers. *Adoption and Fostering* 31(1), 39–49

Carr, A (1999) *The handbook of child and adolescent clinical psychology: A contextual approach*. Abingdon: Brunner Routledge

Cavet, J and Sloper, P (2004) The participation of children and young people in decisions about UK service development. *Child Care, Health and Development* 30(6), 613–21

Chase, E and Knight, A (2006) Is early parenthood such a bad thing? In Chase, E, Simon, A and Jackson, S (eds) *In care and after: A positive perspective*. Abingdon: Routledge

Chase, E, Knight, A, Warwick, I and Aggleton, P (2003) *Teenage pregnancy and young people in and leaving local authority care: Determinants and support. report for the Department of Health*. London: Thomas Coram Research Unit

Cheung, S and Heath, A (1994) After care: the education and occupation of adults who have been in care. *Oxford Review of Education* 20(3), 361–74

Children and Young People's Unit (CYPU) (2001) *Learning to listen: Core principles for involvement of children and young people*. London: Children and Young People's Unit

Cleaver, H (2000) *Fostering family contact: A study of children, parents and foster carers*. London: TSO

Clifford, D and Burke, B (2004) Moral and professional dilemmas in long-term assessment of children and families. *Journal of Social Work* 4(3), 305–21

Clough, R, Bullock, R and Ward, A (2006) *What works in residential child care. A review of research evidence and the practical considerations*. London: National Centre for Excellence in Residential Child Care. National Children's Bureau

Cocker, C (2011) Sexuality before ability? The assessment of lesbians as adopters. In Hafford-Letchfield, T and Dunk, P (eds) *Sexual identities and sexuality in social work*. London: Ashgate

Cocker, C and Anderson, J (2011) Adoption, in C Cocker and L Allain (eds), *Advanced social work in practice with children and families*. Exeter: Learning Matters

Cocker, C and Brown, H C (2010) Sex, sexuality and relationships. *Adoption and Fostering* 34(1), 20–32

Cocker, C and Scott, S (2006) Improving the mental and emotional well-being of looked after children: Connecting research, policy and practice. *Journal of the Royal Society for the Promotion of Health* 126(1), 18–23

Colton, M, Sanders, R and Williams, M (2001) *An introduction to working with children: A guide for social workers*. Basingstoke: Palgrave

Cooper, A (2000) Looked after children. In Richardson, J and Joughin, C (eds) *The mental health needs of looked after children*. London: Gaskell/Royal College of Psychiatrists

Cooper, A (2005) Surface and depth in the Victoria Climbié inquiry report. *Child and Family Social Work* 10(1), 1–9

Cooper, M, Hooper C and Thompson, M (2005) *Child and adolescent mental health: Theory and practice*. London: Edward Arnold

Cooper, P and Johnson, S (200) Education: The views of adoptive parents. *Adoption and Fostering* 31(1), 21–7

Coulshed, V and Orme, J (2006) *Social work practice* (4th edition). Basingstoke: Palgrave

Coy, M (2008) Young women, local authority care and selling sex: Findings from research. *British Journal of Social Work* 38(7), 1408–24

Crawford, K and Walker, J (2007) *Social work and human development* (2nd edition). Exeter: Learning Matters

Curtis, K, Roberts, H, Copperman, J, Downie, A and Liabo, K (2004) 'How come I don't get asked no questions?' Researching 'hard to reach' children and teenagers. *Child and Family Social Work* 9(2), 167–75

Daniel, B and Wassell, S (2002a) *The early years: Assessing and promoting resilience in vulnerable children 1*. London: Jessica Kingsley

Daniel, B and Wassell, S (2002b) *The school years: Assessing and promoting resilience in vulnerable children 2*. London: Jessica Kingsley

Daniel, B and Wassell, S (2002c) *Adolescence: Assessing and promoting resilience in vulnerable children 3*. London: Jessica Kingsley

Daniel, B, Wassell, S and Gilligan, R (1999) *Child development for care and protection workers*. London: Jessica Kingsley

Daniel, B, Wassell, S and Gilligan, R (2010) *Child development for child care and protection workers* (2nd edition). London: Jessica Kingsley

D'Augelli, R R and Hershberger, S L (1993) Lesbian, gay and bisexual youth in community settings: Personal challenges and mental health problems. *American Journal of Community Psychology* 211, 421–48

Department for Children, Schools and Families (2007a) National statistics: Children looked after in England (including adoption and care leavers) year ending 31 March 2007. London: HMSO

Department for Children, Schools and Families (2007b) Multidimensional treatment foster care. London: HMSO

Department for Children, Schools and Families (2007c) *The children's plan: Building brighter futures*. London: The Stationery Office

Department for Children, Schools and Families (2010a) *Promoting the educational achievement of looked after children: Statutory guidance for local authorities*. London: HMSO

Department for Children, Schools and Families (2010b) *Children Act 1989 volume 2 guidance and regulations: Care planning, placements and case review*. London: HMSO

Department for Children, Schools and Families (2010c) *Care planning, placements and case review (England) regulations*. London: HMSO

Department for Children, Schools and Families (2010d) *IRO handbook: Statutory guidance for Independent Reviewing Officers and local authorities on their functions in relation to case management and review for looked after children*. London: HMSO

Department for Children, Schools and Families (2010e) Short breaks: Statutory guidance on how to safeguard and promote the welfare of disabled children using short breaks. Nottingham: DCSF Publications

Department for Children, Schools and Families/Office of National Statistics (2008) *Guidance on data collection on the emotional health of looked after children.* (Accessed on 26.7.12 at www.education.gov.uk/ childrenandyoungpeople/families/childrenincare/a0065777/promoting-health-and-wellbeing)

Department for Children, Schools and Families and Department of Health (2009) *Statutory guidance on promoting the health and wellbeing of looked after children.* London: HMSO

Department for Constitutional Affairs (2004) *Involving children and young people: Action plan 2004–5.* London: Youth Parliament and National Children's Bureau

Department for Education (2010) *The Children Act 1989: Guidance and regulations, volume 3: Planning transition to adulthood for care leavers.* London: TSO

Department for Education (2010b) *Statistical first release: Outcomes for children looked after by local authorities in England, as at 31 March 2010.* London: DfE

Department for Education (2011a) *Statistical first release: Children looked after in England (including adoption and care leavers) year ending 31 March 2011.* London: HMSO. (Accessed on 8.5.2012 at www.education.gov.uk/rsgateway/ DB/SFR/s001026/index.shtml)

Department for Education (2011b) *Adoption: National minimum standards.* London: HMSO

Department for Education (2011c) *Adoption and Children Act 2002: Adoption statutory guidance.* London: HMSO

Department for Education (2011d) *The Children Act 1989 guidance and regulations, volume 4: Fostering services.* London: DfE

Department for Education (2011e) Delivering intensive interventions for looked after children and those on the edge of the edge of care or custody and their families. (Accessed on 1.8.12 at www.education.gov.uk/publications/standard/ publicationDetail/Page1/DFE-00034-2011#downloadableparts)

Department for Education (2011f) *Fostering services: National minimum standards.* London: DfE

Department for Education (2011g) *Support and aspiration: A new approach to special educational needs and disability: A consultation.* London: DfE

Department for Education (2011h) *The Children Act 1989 guidance and regulations, volume 5: Children's Homes.* London: DfE

Department for Education (2012a) *An action plan for adoption: Tackling delay.* London: HMSO

Department for Education (2012b) *The role of local authorities in the education of looked after children* (Accessed on 25.7.12 at www.education.gov.uk/childrenandyoungpeople/families/childrenincare/education/a00208589/role-of-local-authorities)

Department for Education (2012c) *Working together to safeguard children: Draft guidance, June 2012.* (Accessed on 1.8.12 at www.education.gov.uk/aboutdfe/departmentalinformation/consultations/a00211065/revised-safeguard-ing-guidance)

Department for Education (2012d) *Statistical first release: Children looked after in England* (including adoption and care leavers) *year ending 31 March 2012.* London: HMSO. Available online at www.education.gov.uk

Department for Education (2012e) *Statistical first release: Outcomes for children looked after by local authorities in England as at 31 March 2012.* London: DfE

Department for Education and Employment (2000) *Don't suffer in silence*. London: TSO

Department for Education and Employment/Department of Health (2000) Guidance on the education of children and young people in public care. London: DfEE/DoH

Department for Education and Skills (2001a) *Special educational needs: A guide for parents and carers*. London: TSO

Department for Education and Skills (2001b) *Special educational needs: Code of practice*. London: TSO

Department for Education and Skills (2002) *Improving behaviour and attendance: Guidance on exclusion from schools and pupil referral units*. London: TSO

Department for Education and Skills (2003) *Every child matters*. London: TSO

Department for Education and Skills (2004) *Every child matters: Change for children*. London: TSO

Department for Education and Skills (2005a) *Who does what: How social workers and carers can support the education of looked after children*. London: TSO

Department for Education and Skills (2005b) *Choice protects (LAC)*. London: HMSO

Department for Education and Skills (2006a) *Statistical first release: Outcome indicators for looked after children: Twelve months to 30 September 2006 – England*. London: TSO

Department for Education and Skills (2006b) *National statistics SFR 44/2006 children looked after in England (including adoptions and care leavers (2005–6)*. London: TSO

Department for Education and Skills (2006c) *Statistical first release: Special educational needs in England: January 2006*. London: TSO

Department for Education and Skills (2006d) *Teenage pregnancy next steps: Guidance for local authorities and primary care trusts on effective delivery of local strategies*. London: TSO

Department for Education and Skills (2006e) *Teenage pregnancy: Accelerating the strategy to 2010*. London: TSO

Department for Education and Skills (2006f) *Care matters: Transforming the lives of children and young people in care*. London: TSO

Department for Education and Skills (2007) *Care matters: Time for change*. London: TSO

Department for Education and Skills and Department of Health (2003) *Together from the start – practical guidance for professionals working with disabled children (birth to third birthday) and their families*. London: TSO

Department for Education and Skills and Department of Health (2004a) *National service framework for children, young people and maternity services: The mental health and psychological well-being of children and young people*. London: TSO

Department for Education and Skills and Department of Health (2004b) *Disabled children in residential placements*. London: TSO

Department for Education and Skills and Department of Health (2004c) *National service framework for children, young people and maternity services: Standard 8 – disabled children and young people and those with complex health needs*. London: TSO

Department For Education/Office of National Statistics (2011) *Children looked after by local authorities in England (including adoption and care leavers) – year ending 31 March 2011*. London, HMSO (Accessed on 2/4/12 at: www.education.gov.uk/researchandstatistics/statistics/a00196857/children-looked-after-by-local-authorities-in-engl)

Department of Health (1989) *An introduction to the Children Act 1989*. London: HMSO

Department of Health (1995) *Looking after children: Good parenting, good outcomes, training guide.* London: HMSO

Department of Health (1998a) *Caring for children away from home: Messages from research.* Chichester: Wiley

Department of Health (1998b) *Adoption: Achieving the right balance. Circular LAC (98)20.* London: Department of Health

Department of Health (1998c) *Modernising social services: Promoting independence, improving protection, raising standards.* London: HMSO

Department of Health (1998d) *Quality protects.* London: Department of Health, TSO

Department of Health (1999a) *Adoption now: Messages from research.* Chichester: Wiley

Department of Health (1999b) *'Me, survive, out there?' – New arrangements for young people living in and leaving care.* London: Department of Health

Department of Health (1999c) *The government's objectives for children's social services, quality protects.* London: Department of Health

Department of Health (2000a) *Framework for assessment of children in need and their families.* London: HMSO

Department of Health (2000b) *Assessing children in need and their families: Practice guidance.* London: The Stationery Office

Department of Health (2001a) *National adoption standards for England.* London: Department of Health

Department of Health (2001b) *Valuing people: A new strategy for learning disability in the 21st century.* London: The Stationery Office

Department of Health (2001c) *Education protects: Guidance on the education of children and young people in public care – summary for foster carers.* London: DoH

Department of Health (2002a) *Requirements for social work training.* London: Department of Health

Department of Health (2002b) *Promoting the health of looked after children.* London: TSO

Department of Health, Home Office, Department for Education and Employment (1999) *Working together to safeguard children: A guide to inter-agency working to safeguard and promote the welfare of children.* London: TSO

Dickens, J (2006) Care, control and change in child care proceedings: dilemmas for social workers, managers and lawyers. *Child and Family Social Work* 11(1), 23–32

Dickens, J, Howell, D, Thoburn, J and Schofield, G (2007) Children starting to be looked after by local authorities in England: An analysis of inter-authority variation and case centred decision making. *British Journal of Social Work* 37(4), 597–618

Dimigen, G, Del Priore, C, Butler, S, Evans, S, Ferguson, L and Swan, M (1999) Psychiatric disorder among children at time of entering local authority care: Questionnaire survey. *British Medical Journal* 319, 675

Dixon, J and Wade, J (2007) 'Leaving care'? Transition planning and support for unaccompanied young people. In Kohli, R and Mitchell, F (eds) *Working with Unaccompanied Asylum-Seeking Children: Issues for Policy and Practice.* Basingstoke: Palgrave Macmillan

Dogra, N (2005) Cultural diversity in the medical undergraduate curriculum. *Diversity in Health and Social Care.* 2, 233–45.

Donaldson, T (2006) Pathways to permanence: Accommodation, compulsion, and permanence under the Children (NI) Order (1995). In Iwaniec, D (ed.) *The Child's Journey Through Care: Placement Stability, Care Planning and Achieving Permanency.* Chichester: John Wiley

Dyer, C (2002) Couple sue over adopted 'wild child'. *Guardian*, 17 October

Egger, M and Davey Smith, G (1997) Meta-analysis: Potentials and promise *BMJ* 7119(315) 1371–4

Evan B Donaldson Institute (2009) *Finding families for African American children*. New York: Eran B Donaldson Institute (Accessed 27/09/12 from www.adoptionistitute.org/research/2008_5_mepa.php)

Fahlberg, V (1994) *A child's journey through placement (UK Edition)*. London: BAAF

Farmer, E, Dance, C, Beecham, J, Bonin, E and Ouwejan, D (2010) An investigation of family finding and matching in adoption – briefing paper. DfE-RBX-10-05 London: Department of Education

Flynn, R (2001) *Short breaks: Providing better access and more choice for black, disabled children and their parents*. Bristol: Policy Press

Fonagy, P, Steele, M, Steele, H, Higgit, A and Target, M (1994) The theory and practice of resilience. *Journal of Child Psychology and Psychiatry* 35(2), 231–57

Frame, L, Berrick, J and Coakley, J (2006) Essential elements of implementing a system of concurrent planning. *Child and Family Social Work* 11, 357–67

Franklin, A and Sloper, P (2006) Participation of disabled children and young people in decision-making within social services departments: A survey of current and recent activities in England. *British Journal of Social Work* 36(5), 723–41

Frazer, L and Selwyn, J (2005) Why are we waiting? The demography of adoption for children of black, Asian and black mixed parentage in England. *Child and Family Social Work* 10, 135–47

Freed-Kernis, A (2008) We're all human beings, aren't we? Working with lesbian, gay, bisexual and transgender young people in care. In Luckock, B and Lefevre, M (eds) *Direct work: Social work with children and young people in care*. London: BAAF

Frost, N and Parton, N (2009) *Understanding children's social care: Politics, policy and practice*. London: Sage

Garrett, P (2003) *Remaking social work with children and families: A critical discussion on the 'modernisation' of social care*. Abingdon: Routledge

Garrett, P M (2009) The case of 'Baby P': Opening up spaces for debate on the 'transformation' of children's services? *Critical Social Policy* 29, 535–47

Giddens, A (1993) *Sociology* (2nd edition). Oxford: Polity Press

Gill, O and Jackson, B (1983) *Adoption and race: Black, Asian and mixed race children in white families*. London: BAAF

Gilligan, R (1997) Beyond permanence? The importance of resilience in child placement practice and planning. *Adoption and Fostering* 21(1), 12–20

Gilligan, R (2000) The key role of social workers in promoting the well-being of children in state care-a neglected dimension of reforming policies. *Children and Society* 14(4), 267–76

Gilligan, R (2001) *Promoting resilience: A resource guide on working with children in the care system*. London: BAAF

Godek, S (1976) *Leaving care*. Ilford: Barnardo's

Golombok, S (2000) *Parenting: What really counts?* Abingdon: Routledge

Greco, V, Sloper, P, Webb, R and Beecham, J (2006) Key worker services for disabled children: The views of staff. *Health and Social Care in the Community* 14(6), 445–52

Griesbach, D and Currie, C (2001) Health behaviours of Scottish schoolchildren: Report 7. Control of adolescent smoking in Scotland. St Andrews: Child and Adolescent Health Research Unit (CAHRU)

Hafford-Letchfield, T (2007) *Practicing quality assurance in social care*. Exeter: Learning Matters

Hare, A and Bullock, R (2006) Dispelling misconceptions about looked after children. *Adoption and Fostering* 30(4), 26–35

Harker, M, Dobel-Ober, D, Berridge, D and Sinclair, I (2004) *Taking care of education*. London: National Children's Bureau

Harnott, C and Humphreys, H (eds) (2004) *Permanence planning: Notes for practitioners – adoption and permanence taskforce*. London: Social Care Institute for Excellence

Haydon, D (2003) *Teenage pregnancy and looked after children/care leavers. Resource for Teenage Pregnancy Co-ordinators*. Ilford: Barnardos

Heaphy, G, Ehntholt, K and Sclare, I (2007) Groupwork with unaccompanied young women. In Kohli, R and Mitchell, F (eds) *Working with unaccompanied asylum-seeking children: Issues for policy and practice*. Basingstoke: Palgrave

Hendrick, H (1994) *Child Welfare: England, 1872–1989*. Abingdon: Routledge

HM Courts and Tribunal Services (2010) *Practice direction public law proceedings guide to case management: April 2010*. London: HMSO. (Accessed 27.09.12 at www.justice.gov.uk/downloads/protecting-the-vulnerable/care-proceeding-reform/public_outline.pdf)

HM Treasury and Department for Education and Skills (2007) *Aiming high for disabled children: Better support for families*. London: TSO

Hicks, S (2012) *Lesbian, gay and queer parenting: Families, intimacies, genealogies*. Basingstoke: Palgrave

Hingley-Jones, H (2011) An exploration of the use of infant observation methods to research the identities of severely learning disabled adolescents and to enhance relationship-based practice for professional social work. *Infant Observation* 14(3), 317–33

Hodges, J, Steele, M, Hillman, S, Henderson, K and Kaniuk, J (2003) Changes in attachment representations over the first year of adoptive placement. *Psychiatry and Psychology* 8(3), 351–67

Holland, S, Faulkner, A and Perez-del-Aguila, R (2005) Promoting stability and continuity of care for looked after children: A survey and critical review. *Child and Family Social Work* 10, 29–41

Hollows, A and Nelson, P (2006) Equity and pragmatism in judgement-making about the placement of sibling groups. *Child and Family Social Work* 11(4), 307–15

Holmes, J (1993) *John Bowlby and attachment theory (makers of modern psychotherapy series)* Abingdon: Routledge

Holmes, L, Westlake, D and Ward, H (2008) *Calculating and comparing the costs of Multidimensional Treatment Foster Care, England (MTFCE): Report to the Department for Children, Schools and Families*. Loughborough: Centre for Child and Family Research, Loughborough University

Home Office (2008) *Better outcomes: the way forward – improving the care of unaccompanied asylum seeking children*. London: Border and Immigration Communications Directorate

Home Office (UK Border Agency) and Department for Children, Schools and Families (2009) *Every child matters, change for children: Statutory guidance to the UK Border Agency on making arrangements to safeguard and promote the welfare of children*. London: Office of the Children's Champion

Hopper, H (2007) *Counselling and psychotherapy with children and adolescents*. Basingstoke: Palgrave

Horner, N and Krawczyk, S (2006) *Social work in education and children's services*. Exeter: Learning Matters

Hothersall, S (2008) *Social work with children, young people and their families in Scotland* (2nd edition). Exeter: Learning Matters

House of Commons (2010–12) The child protection system in England, written evidence submitted by the NSPCC. (Accessed on 6.8.2012 at: www.publications.parliament.uk/pa/cm201213/cmselect/cmeduc/writev/1514/cp54.htm)

House of Commons (2011) *5th Special report of session 2010–11, Education Committee: Looked after children: Further government response to the third report from the Children, Schools and Families Committee, 2008–9*. London: TSO

Howard, J (2005) Partnership with parents: Making it happen. In Brown, HC, Fry, E and Howard J (eds) *Support Care: How family placement can keep children and families together*. Lyme Regis: Russell House

Howe, D (1995) *Attachment theory for social work practice*. Basingstoke: Macmillan

Howe, D (1996) *Attachment and loss in child and family social work*. Aldershot: Avebury.

Howe, D (1998) *Patterns of adoption*. Oxford: Blackwell

Howe, D, Brandon, M, Hinings, D, Schofield, G and Brandon, M (1999) *Attachment theory, child maltreatment and family support*. Basingstoke: Palgrave

Howe, D and Fearnley, S (1999) Disorders of attachment and attachment therapy. *Adoption and Fostering* 23(2), 19–30

Howe, D (2005) *Child abuse and neglect: Attachment, development and intervention*. Basingstoke: Palgrave

Howe, D (2006) Disabled children, parent–child interaction and attachment. *Child and Family Social Work*, 11(2), 95–106

Hughes, L and Pengelly, P (1997) *Staff supervision in a turbulent environment*. London: Jessica Kingsley

Hunt, R and Cooke, E (2006) Health and well-being: Physical health. *Quality Protects Research Briefings (No. 12)* DFES, Research in Practice, Making Research Count. London: DfES

Hunter, M (2001) *Psychotherapy with young people in care: Lost and found*. Abingdon: Brunner Routledge

Hutchinson, J and Smith, A (eds) (1996) *Ethnicity*. Oxford: Oxford University Press

Hutson, S (1997) *Supported housing: The experience of young care leavers*. Ilford: Barnardo's

Ivaldi, G (1998) *Children adopted from care: An examination of agency adoptions in England, 1996*. London: BAAF

Jackson, S (1988) Education and children in care. *Adoption and Fostering* 12(4), 6–11

Jackson, S (2007) Progress at last? *Adoption and Fostering* 31(1), 3–5

Jackson, S and Ajayi, S (2007) Foster care and higher education. *Adoption and Fostering* 31(1), 62–72

Jackson, S and Morris, K (1999) Family group conferences: user empowerment or family self-reliance? A development from Lupton. *British Journal of Social Work* 29(4), 621–30.

Jackson, S and Sachdev, D (2001) *Better education, better futures: Research, practice and the view of young people in public care*. Ilford: Barnardo's

Jasper, L (2005) Trevor Phillips is in danger of giving succour to racists. *Guardian*, Wednesday 12 October

Jeyarajah Dent, R and Cocker, C (2005) Serious case reviews – lessons for practice in cases of child neglect. In Daniel, B and Taylor, J (eds) (2005) *Neglect: Issues For Health And Social Care*. London: Jessica Kingsley

Johns, R (2011) *Using the law in social work* (5th edition). Exeter: Learning Matters

Jones, D (2003) *Communicating with vulnerable children: A guide for practitioners*. London: Gaskell

Kirby, P, Lanyon, C, Cronin, K and Sinclair, R (2003) *Building a culture of participation*. Nottingham: Department for Education and Skills

Knight, A (1998) *Valued or forgotten? Disabled children and independent visitors.* London: National Children's Bureau in association with the Joseph Rowntree Foundation

Knight, A, Chase, E and Aggleton, P (2006) Teenage pregnancy among young people in and leaving care: Messages and implications for foster care. *Adoption and Fostering* 30(1), 58–69

Knott, C and Scragg, T (eds) (2007) *Reflective practice in social work.* Exeter: Learning Matters

Kohli, R (2006) The comfort of strangers: social work practice with unaccompanied asylum-seeking children and young people in the UK. *Child and Family Social Work* 11(1), 1–10

Kohli, R (2007) *Social work with unaccompanied asylum-seeking children.* Basingstoke: Palgrave

Kohli, R and Mitchell, F (eds) (2007) *Working with unaccompanied asylum-seeking children: Issues for policy and practice.* Basingstoke: Palgrave Macmillan

Koprowska, J (2010) *Communication and interpersonal skills in social work* (3rd edition). Exeter: Learning Matters

Koprowska, J and Stein, M (2000) The mental health of looked-after young people. In Aggleton, P, Hurry, J and Warwick, I (eds) *Young people and mental health.* Chichester: John Wiley

Korbin, J (2002) Culture and child maltreatment: cultural competence and beyond. *Child Abuse and Neglect* 26, 637–44

Laming, H (2003) *The Victoria Climbié Inquiry Report. Cm5730.* London: The Stationery Office.

Laws, S, Wilson, R and Rabindrakumar, S (2012) *Coram concurrent planning study: Interim report, July 2012.* London: Coram

Lefevre, M (2010) *Communicating with children and young people: Making a difference.* Bristol: Policy Press

Leverett, S (2008) Children's participation. In Foley, P and Leverett, S (eds) *Connecting with children, developing working relationships.* Bristol: Policy Press

Levy, A and Kahan, B (1991) The Bindown experience and the protection of children: The report of the Staffordshire Child Care Enquiry. Stafford: Staffordshire County Council

Littlechild, B (2007) Editorial. *British Journal of Social Work* 37(4), 593–6

Luckock, B and Lefevre, M (eds) (2008) *Direct work: Social work with children and young people in care.* London: BAAF

Luckock, B, Lefevre, M, Orr, D, Jones, M, Marchant, R and Tanner, K (2006) *Teaching, learning and assessing communication skills with children and young people in social work education (SCIE Knowledge Review).* London: Social Care Institute for Excellence

Luckock, B, Lefevre, M and Tanner, K (2007) Teaching and learning communication with children and young people: Developing the qualifying social work curriculum in a changing policy context. *Child and Family Social Work* 12(2), 192–201

Lupton, C (1998) User empowerment or family self-reliance? The family group conference model. *British Journal of Social Work* 28(1), 107–128

Macdonald, G and Turner, W (2005) An experiment in helping foster-carers manage challenging behaviour, *British Journal of Social Work* 35(8), 1265–82

Malik, S (2012) Adoption process will be made fairer and faster, says David Cameron. *The Guardian*, 9 March 2012.

Mason, D (2000) *Race and ethnicity in modern Britain* (2nd edition). Oxford: Oxford University Press

Masson, J, Pearce, J, Bader, K, Joyner, O, Marsden, J, and Westlake, D (2008) *Care profiling study*. Ministry of Justice Research Series, 4/08. London: Ministry of Justice

Mackie, S and Patel-Kanwal, H (2003) *Let's make it happen: Training on sex, relationships, pregnancy and parenthood for those working with looked after children and young people*. London: National Children's Bureau

McCann, J, James, A, Wilson, S and Dunn, G (1996) Prevalence of psychiatric disorders in young people in the care system. *British Medical Journal* 313, 1529–30

McConkey, R and Adams, L (2000) Do short breaks services for children with learning disabilities match family needs and preferences? *Child: Care, Health and Development* 26, 429–44

McConkey, R, Truesdale, M and Conliffe, C (2004) The features of short-break residential services valued by families who have children with multiple disabilities. *Journal of Social Work* 4(1), 61–75

McGill, P, Tennyson, A and Cooper, V (2006) Parents whose children with learning disabilities and challenging behaviour attend 52-week residential schools: Their perceptions of services received and expectations of the future. *British Journal of Social Work* 36(4), 597–616

McNeish, D (1999) Promoting participation for children and young people: Some key questions for health and social welfare organisations. *Journal of Social Work Practice* 13(2), 191–203

McSherry, D, Larkin, E and Iwaniec, D (2006) Care proceedings: Exploring the relationship between case duration and achieving permanency for the child. *British Journal of Social Work* 36(6), 901–19

Meltzer, H, Gatward, R, Corbin, T, Goodman, R and Ford, T (2003) *The mental health of young people looked after by local authorities in England*. London: ONS–TSO

Meltzer, H, Gatward, R, Goodman, R and Ford, T (2000) *The mental health of children and adolescents in Great Britain*. London: Office of National Statistics – The Stationery Office

Meltzer, H, Lader, D, Corbin, T, Goodman, R and Ford, T (2004a) *The mental health of young people looked after by local authorities in Scotland*. Edinburgh: The Stationery Office

Meltzer, H, Lader, D, Corbin, T, Goodman, R and Ford, T (2004b) *The mental health of young people looked after by local authorities in Wales*. Norwich: TSO

Mental Health Foundation (1999) Bright futures: Promoting children and young people's mental health. London: The Mental Health Foundation

Middleton, L (1996) *Making a difference: Social work with disabled children*. Birmingham: Venture Press

Miller, D (2003) Disabled children and abuse. In *Report of the National Working Group on Child Protection and Disability, 'It doesn't happen to disabled children': Child protection and disabled children*. London: NSPCC

Miller, L (2006) *Counselling skills for social work*. London: Sage

Milner, J, and O'Byrne, P (2002) *Assessment in social work* (2nd edition). Basingstoke: Palgrave

Ministry of Justice and Department for Education (2012) *The government response to the Family Justice Review: A system with children and families at its heart*. London: TSO

Minnis, H and Del Priore, C (2001) Mental health services for looked after children: Implications from two studies. *Adoption and Fostering* 25(4), 27–37

Minnis, H and Devine, C (2001) The effect of foster carer training on the emotional and behavioural functioning of looked after children. *Adoption and Fostering* 25(1), 44–54

Minnis, H, Rabe-Hesketh, S and Wolkind, S (2002) Development of a brief, clinically relevant, scale for measuring attachment disorders. *International Journal of Methods in Psychiatric Research*, 11(2), 90–8

Morris, J (1995) *Gone missing? A research and policy review of disabled children living away from their families.* London: Who Cares? Trust

Morris, J (2002) *A Lot to Say: A guide for social workers, personal advisors and others working with disabled children and young people with communication impairments.* London: Scope

Morris, K and Burford, G (2007) Working with children's existing networks – building better opportunities? *Social Policy and Society* 6(2), 209–17

Mullender, A (ed.) (1999) *We are family: Sibling relationships in placement and beyond.* London: BAAF

Munro, E (2001) Empowering looked after children. *Child and Family Social Work* 6(2), 129–37

Munro, E (2010a) *The Munro review of child protection. Part one: A systems analysis.* London: London School of Economics

Munro, E (2010b) *The Munro review of child protection. Interim report: The child's journey.* London: London School of Economics

Munro, E (2011) *The Munro review of child protection: Final report. A child-centred system.* London: HMSO

NACRO (2004) *Youth crime briefing: Remand fostering.* London: NACRO

Narey, M (2011) *The Narey report on adoption: Our blueprint for Britain's lost children* London: The Times Newspaper

National Care Advisory Service (2011) *Statistical briefing: Looked after children and care leavers 2011.* London: NCAS

Newburn, T, Ward, J and Pearson, G (2002) *Drug use among young people in care, Research Briefing 7.* Swindon: Economic and Social Research Briefing

Newman, T (2004) *What works in building resilience?* Ilford: Barnardo's

NHS Health Advisory Service (1995) *Child and adolescent mental health services: Together we stand.* London: HMSO

Office for National Statistics Census (2001). London: ONS (Accessed 27.09.12 at **www.statistics.gov.uk**)

Office for National Statistics (2011) *Labour market statistics.* London: ONS

O'Hagan, K (2001) *Cultural competence in the caring professions.* London: Jessica Kingsley

Oliver, M and Sapey, B (2006) *Social work with disabled people* (3rd edition). Basingstoke: Palgrave

O'Sullivan, A and Westerman, R (2007) Closing the gap: Investigating the barriers to educational achievement for looked after children. *Adoption and Fostering* 31(1), 13–20

Page, R and Clark, G (eds) (1977) *Who cares? Young people in care speak out.* London: National Children's Bureau

Pallett, C, Blackeby, K, Yule, W, Weissman, R and Scott, S (2005) *Fostering changes: How to improve relationships and manage difficult behaviour. A training programme for foster carers.* London: BAAF

Papadopoulos, I (2003) The Papadopoulos, Tilki and Taylor model for the development of cultural competence in nursing. *Journal of Health, Social and Environmental Issues* 4(1), 5–7

Papadopoulos, I, Tilki, M and Lees, S (2004) Promoting cultural competence in healthcare through a research-based intervention in the UK. *Diversity in Health and Social Care* 1, 107–15

Parekh, B (2000) *The future of multi-ethnic Britain.* London: Profile Books

Parker, J and Bradley, G (2003) *Social work practice: Assessment, planning, intervention and review.* Exeter: Learning Matters

Parton, N (2006) *Safeguarding childhood: Early intervention and surveillance in a late modern society*. Basingstoke: Palgrave Macmillan

Pascall, G and Hendey, N (2004) Disability and transition to adulthood: The politics of parenting. *Critical Social Policy* 24(2), 165–86

Patterson, CJ (2005) *Lesbian and gay parenting*. Washington, DC: American Psychological Association

Pearce, J, Galvin, C, Williams, M (2003) *It's someone taking part of you: A study of young women and sexual exploitation*. London: National Children's Bureau

Performance and Innovation Unit (PIU) (2000) *The Prime Minister's review of adoption*. London: HMSO

Pickford, J and Dugmore, P (2012) *Youth justice and social work* (2nd edition). London: Sage/Learning Matters

Pinney, A (2005) *Disabled children in residential placements*. Available at: www.everychildmatters.gov.uk/resources-and-practice

Prevatt-Goldstein, B (1999) Black, with a white parent, a positive and achievable identity. *British Journal of Social Work* 29(2), 285–301

Prevatt-Goldstein, B (2002) Black children with a white parent, social work education. *Social Work Education* 21(5), 551–63.

Prewett, B (1999) *Short-term break, long-term benefit: Family-based short-term care for disabled children and adults*. Sheffield: Joint Unit for Social Services Research, Sheffield University and Community Care

Priestley, M (2003) *Disability: A life course approach*. Cambridge: Polity Press

Prime Minister's Strategy Unit (2005) *Improving the life chances of disabled people*. London: TSO

Quinney, A. (2006) *Collaborative social work practice*. Exeter: Learning Matters

Quinton, D (2012) *Matching in adoptions from care: A conceptual and research review*. London: BAAF

Ramesh, R (2012) Poor families, poor research: Eric Pickles' flawed recasting of society. *The Guardian*, 11 June

Reder, P and Duncan, S (1999) *Lost innocents: A follow-up study of fatal child abuse*. Abingdon: Routledge

Richardson, J and Joughin, C (2000) *The mental health needs of looked after children*. London: Royal College of Psychiatrists

Roberts, H (2000) *What works in reducing inequalities in child health?* Ilford: Barnardo's

Roberts, R (2007) A new approach to meeting the needs of looked after children experiencing difficulties: The Multidimensional Treatment Foster Care in England Project. ACAMH Occasional Papers No. 26, *Fostering, Adoption and Alternative Care*. (Available 27.09.12 at www.mtfce.org.uk/library/ACAMH_MTFCE_2007.pdf)

Roberts, R, Jones, H and Scott, S (2005) Treatment foster care in England. In *The RHP Companion to Foster Care* (2nd edition). Lyme Regis: Russell House Publishing

Robinson, L (1995) *Psychology for social workers: Black perspectives*. Abingdon: Routledge

Robinson, L (2007) *Cross-cultural child development for social workers: An introduction*. Basingstoke: Palgrave

Romaine, M, with Turley, T and Tuckey, N (2007) *Preparing children for permanence: A guide to undertaking direct work for social workers, foster carers and adoptive parents*. London: BAAF

Rowe, J and Lambert, L (1973) *Children who wait: A study of children needing substitute families*. London, ABBA

Rushton, A and Dance, C (2002) *Adoption support services for families in difficulty: A literature review and UK survey*. London: BAAF

Rushton, A and Minnis, H (2002) Residential and foster family care. In Rutter, M and Taylor, E (eds) *Child and Adolescent Psychiatry* (4th edition) Oxford: Blackwell

Rushton, A and Monck, E (2009) *Enhancing adoptive parenting: A test of effectiveness*. London: BAAF

Rutter, M (1985) Resilience in the face of adversity: Protective factors and resistance to psychiatric disorder. *British Journal of Psychiatry* 147, 598–611

Ryan, T and Walker, R (1993) *Life story work*. London: BAAF

Ryburn, M (1998) In whose interests? – Post adoption contact with the birth family. *Child and Family Law Quarterly* 10(1), 53

Saunders, L and Broad, B (1997) The health needs of young people leaving care. Leicester: De Montfort University

Save the Children (2003) *Policy on children's participation*. London: Save the Children

Schofield, G (2001) Resilience and family placement: A lifespan perspective. *Adoption and Fostering* 25(3), 6–19

Schofield, G (2003) *Part of the family: Pathways though foster care*. London: BAAF

Schofield, G and Beek, M (2006) *Attachment handbook for foster care and adoption*. London: BAAF

Schofield, G and Simmonds, J (eds) (2008) *The Child Placement Handbook*. London: BAAF

Schofield, G, Beek, M, Sargent, K, with Thoburn, J (2000) *Growing up in foster care*. London: BAAF

Schofield, G, Thoburn, J, Howell, D and Dickens, J (2007) The search for stability and permanence: Modelling the pathways of long-stay looked after children. *British Journal of Social Work* 37(4), 619–42

Scott, J and Hill, M (2006) *The health of looked after and accommodated children and young people in Scotland – messages from research*. Edinburgh: Scottish Executive

Scott, S (2003) Integrating attachment theory with other approaches to developmental psychopathology. Attachment and Human Development 5(3), 307–12

Scott, S (2004) Reviewing the research on the mental health of looked after children: Some issues for the development of more evidence informed practice. *International Journal of Child and Family Welfare* 2004(2–3), 86–97

Scott, S and Lindsey, C (2003) Therapeutic approaches in adoption. In H, Argent (ed.) *Models of adoption support: What works and what doesn't*. London: BAAF

Scottish Executive (2005) *National care standards for adoption agencies*. Edinburgh: Scottish Executive

Scottish Health Feedback (2003) The health needs and issues of young people from Glasgow living in foster care settings. Glasgow: The Big Step

Scottish Institute for Residential Child Care (2006) *The contemporary role and future direction of residential care for children and young people in Scotland*. Glasgow: SIRCC

Sellick, C and Howell, D (2003) *Innovative, tried and tested: A review of good practice*. London: Social Care Institute

Sellick, C, Thoburn, J and Philpot, T (2004) *What works in adoption and foster care?* (2nd edition). Ilford: Barnardo's

Selwyn, J and Sturgess, W (2002) Achieving permanency through adoption: Following in US footsteps? *Adoption and Fostering* 26(3), 40–9

Selwyn, J, Frazer, L, and Quinton, D (2006) Paved with good intentions: The pathway to adoption and the costs of delay. *British Journal of Social Work* 36(4), 561–76

Selwyn, J, Quinton, D, Harris, P, Wijedasa, D, Nawaz, S and Wood, M (2010) *Pathways to permanence for black, Asian and mixed ethnicity children*. London: BAAF

Shemmings, D (2004) Researching relationships from an attachment perspective: the use of behavioural, interview, self-report and projective methods. *Journal of Social Work Practice* 18(3), 299–314

Simon, A and Owen, C (2006) Outcomes for children in care: What do we know? In Chase, E, Simon, and Jackson, S (eds) *In Care and After: A Positive Perspective*. Abingdon: Routledge

Sinclair, I (2005) *Fostering now: Messages from research*. London: Jessica Kingsley

Sinclair, I, Gibbs, I and Wilson, K (2004a) *Foster carers: Why they stay and why they leave*. London: Jessica Kingsley

Sinclair, I, Gibbs, I and Wilson, K (2004b) *Foster placements: Why they succeed and why they fail*. London: Jessica Kingsley

Smale, G, Tuson, G, Biehal, N and Marsh, P (1993) Empowerment, assessment, care management and the skilled worker. *National Institute for Social Work Practice and Development Exchange*. London: HMSO

Smith, M (2009) *Rethinking residential child care: Positive perspectives*. Bristol: Policy Press

Social Care Institute for Excellence (2004a) *SCIE Research briefing 5: Short breaks (respite care) for children with learning disabilities*. London: SCIE.

Social Care Institute for Excellence (2004b) *Research briefing 9: Preventing teenage pregnancy in looked after children*. London: SCIE

Social Exclusion Unit (1999) *Teenage pregnancy*. London: Office of the Deputy Prime Minister

Social Exclusion Unit (2003) *A better education for children in care*. London: Office of the Deputy Prime Minister

Solomos, J (2003) *Race and racism in Britain* (3rd edition). London: Palgrave

Sroufe, L, Egeland, B, Carlson, E and Collins, W (2005) *The development of the person: The Minnesota study of risk and adaptation from birth to adulthood*. New York: The Guilford Press

Stalker, K and Connors, C (2003) Communicating with disabled children. *Adoption and Fostering*, 27(1), 26–35

Steele, H (2003) Holding therapy is not attachment therapy: Editor's introduction to the Special Issue. *Attachment and Human Development* 5(3), 219

Stein, M (1983) Protest in care. In Jordan, B and Parton, N (eds) *The Political Dimensions of Social Work* Oxford: Blackwell

Stein, M (1997) *What works in leaving care*. Ilford: Barnardo's

Stein, M (2004) *What works for young people leaving care?* Ilford: Barnardo's

Stein, M (2005) *Resilience and young people leaving care: overcoming the odds*. York: Joseph Rowntree Foundation

Stein, M (2006a) Research review: Young people leaving care. *Child and Family Social Work* 11(3), 273–9

Stein, M (2006b) Wrong turn. *Guardian*, 6 December 2006

Stein, M (2006c) Missing years of abuse in children's homes. *Child and Family Social Work* 11(1), 11–21

Stein, M and Carey, K (1986) *Leaving care*. Oxford: Blackwell

Stein, M and Ellis, S (1983) *Gizza say. Reviews and young people in care*. London: NAYPIC

Stewart, D and Ray, C (2001) *Ensuring entitlement: Sex and relationships education for disabled children*. London: Sex Education Forum, National Children's Bureau/Council for Disabled Children

Sugarman, L (1986) *Life-span development: Theories, concepts and interventions*. London: Methuen

Talbot, R (2002) *Young minds: Looking after the mental health of looked after children – a training resource pack for professionals caring for and working with children and young people in public care*. Brighton: Pavilion Publishing

Tasker, F (2005) Lesbian mothers, gay fathers and their children: A review. *Journal of Developmental and Behavioral Pediatrics* 26, 224–40

Taylor, C (2004) Underpinning knowledge for child care practice: Reconsidering child development theory. *Child and Family Social Work* 9(3), 225–36

Teenage Pregnancy Unit (2005) *Teenage pregnancy: An overview of the research evidence.* London: TPU

Thoburn, J (1994) *Child placement: Principles and practice* (2nd edition). Aldershot: Ashgate

Thoburn, J, Chand, A and Proctor, J (2005) *Child welfare services for minority ethnic families – the research reviewed.* London: Jessica Kingsley

Thomas, N (2005) *Social work with young people in care: Looking after children in theory and practice.* Basingstoke: Palgrave Macmillan

Travis, A (2012) UK Migrants to face 'patriotic' citizenship test. *The Guardian*, 1 July. (Available 27.09.12 at: www.guardian.co.uk/uk/2012/jul/01/uk-migrants-patriotic-citizenship-test)

Trevithick, P (2005) Social work skills: A practice handbook (2nd edition). Maidenhead: Open University Press

Trinder, L (1996) Social work research: the state of the art (or science). *Child and Family Social Work* 1(4), 233–42

Triseliotis, J, Borland, M, Hill, M and Lambert, L (1995) Teenagers and the social work services. London: HMSO

Triseliotis, J, Shireman, J and Hundlebury, M (1997) *Adoption: Theory, policy and practice.* London: Cassell

Tully, C T (2000) *Lesbians, gays and the empowerment perspective.* New York: Columbia Press

Tyrer, P, Chase, E, Warwick, I and Aggleton, P (2006) 'Dealing with it': Experiences of young fathers in and leaving care. *British Journal of Social Work* 35(7), 1107–21

United Nations Children's Fund (UNICEF) (2001) *A league table of teenage births in rich nations, Innocenti Report Card No. 3.* Florence: UNICEF

Utting, W (1991) *Children in the public care: A review of residential care.* London: HMSO

Utting, W (1997) *People like us: The report of the safeguards for children living away from home.* London: Department of Health

Van Ijzendoorn, M and Juffer, F (2006) The Emanuel Miller Memorial Lecture 2006: Adoption as intervention. Meta-analytic evidence for massive catch-up and plasticity in physical, socio-emotional, and cognitive development. *Journal of Child Psychology and Psychiatry* 47(12), 1228–45

Van Ijzendoorn, M and Kroonenberg, P (1988) Cross cultural patterns of attachment: A meta-analysis of the strange situation. *Child Development* 59, 147–56

Waddell, M (2002) *Inside lives: Psychoanalysis and the growth of the personality.* London: Karnac

Wade, J and Dixon, J (2006) Making a home, finding a job: investigating early housing and employment outcomes for young people leaving care. *Child and Family Social Work* 11(3), 199–208

Walker, S (2005) *Culturally competent therapy: Working with children and young people.* Basingstoke: Palgrave

Ward, A (2006) Models of 'ordinary' and 'special' daily living: matching residential care to the mental-health needs of looked after children *Child and Family Social Work* 11(4), 336–46

Ward, H and Skuse, T (2001) Performance targets and stability of placements for children looked after away from home. *Children and Society* 15, 333–46

Ward, L, Mallett, R, Heslop, P and Simons, K (2003) Transition planning: how well does it work for young people with learning disabilities and their families? *British Journal of Special Education* 30(3), 132–7

Warman, A and Roberts, C (2001) *Adoption and looked after children: international comparisons Family Policy Briefing 1*. Oxford: Department of Social Policy and Social Work

Warner, J, McKeown, E, Griffin, M, Johnson, K, Ramsay, A, Cort, C and King, M (2004) Rates and predictors of mental illness in gay men, lesbians and bisexual men and women: Results from a survey based in England and Wales, *Journal of British Psychiatry* 185 (December), 479–85

Warner, N (1992) *Choosing with care: The report of the committee of inquiry into the selection, development and management of staff in children's homes*. London: HMSO

Waterhouse, S and Brocklesby, E (1999) Placement choices for children – giving more priority to kinship placements? In Greef, R (ed) *Fostering Kinship*. Aldershot: Ashgate

Waterhouse, R (2000) *Lost in care: Report of the tribunal of inquiry into the abuse of children in care in the former County Council areas of Gwynedd and Clwyd since 1974*. London: The Stationery Office

Watson, N, Shakespeare, T, Cunningham-Burley, S and Barnes, C (1999) *Life as a disabled child: A qualitative study of young people's experiences and perspectives*. (Accessed on 12.12.07 at www.leeds.ac.uk/ disability-studies/ projects/children.htm)

Watson, D, Abbott, D, Townsley, R (2006) Listen to me, too! Lessons from involving children with complex healthcare needs in research about multi-agency services. *Child: care, health and development* 33(1), 90–5

Webb, S (2001) Some considerations on the validity of evidence-based practice in social work. *British Journal of Social Work* 31(1), 57–79

Welsh Assembly Government (2007) *National minimum standards for local authority adoption services for Wales*. Cardiff: Welsh Assembly

Werner, E (2001) Protective factors and individual resilience. In Shonkoff, J and Meisels, S (eds) *Handbook of Early Childhood Intervention* (2nd edition). Cambridge: Cambridge University Press

Wheatley, H (2006) *Pathways to success: Good practice guide for children's services in the development of services for disabled children*. London: Council for Disabled Children

Wilson, K, Ruch, G, Lymbery, M, and Cooper, A (2011) *Social work: An introduction to contemporary practice* (2nd edition). London: Pearson Longman

World Health Organization (1993) *The ICD-10 classification of mental and behavioural disorders: Diagnostic criteria for research*. Geneva: World Health Organization

Yeo, S (2003) Bonding and attachment of Australian Aboriginal children. *Child Abuse Review* 12, 292–304

Index